ESSENTIAL BREAKTHROUGHS

Conversations about Men, Mothers, and Mothering

EDITED BY

Fiona Joy Green and Gary Lee Pelletier

DEMETER PRESS

The publisher gratefully acknowledges the the financial assistance of the Government of Canada through the Canada Book Fund.

Canada

Demeter Press
140 Holland Street West
P. O. Box 13022
Bradford, ON L3Z 2Y5
Tel: (905) 775-9089
Email: info@demeterpress.org
Website: www.demeterpress.org

Demeter Press logo based on the sculpture "Demeter" by Maria-Luise Bodirsky <www.keramik-atelier.bodirsky.de>

Front cover artwork and design: David A. King

Printed and Bound in Canada

Library and Archives Canada Cataloguing in Publication

        Essential breakthroughs: conversations about men, mothers, and mothering / edited by Fiona Joy Green and Gary Lee Pelletier.

Includes bibliographical references.
ISBN 978-1-926452-16-6 (paperback)

Cataloguing data available from Library and Archives Canada.

For Mariette and Guy,
whose beautiful care taught me how to,
this book is a curiosity ignited by your love.
Gary

For Barry,
the father of our son,
who models and inspires love and caring.
Fiona

Table of Contents

Chapter 10
Mommie Dearest:
Undoing a Gay Identity through Pregnancy
Jack Hixson-Vulpe

Chapter 11
The Ties that Bind Are Broken:
Trans* Breastfeeding Practices, Ungendering Body Parts,
and Unsexing Parenting Roles
A.J. Lowik

Chapter 12
Becoming Mother's Nature:
A Queer Son's Perspective on Mothering
in an Era of Ecological Decline
Michael Young

Contributor Biographies

Acknowledgements

The breakthroughs staged throughout these pages are indebted to a variety of caring souls whose scholarship, energy, and time have proved essential—and we're not ones to use this term lightly—to their fruition. First and foremost, our gratitude begins with maternal studies and feminist trailblazer Andrea O'Reilly, who, along with the Motherhood Initiative for Research and Community Involvement and Demeter Press, relentlessly continues to fight the good small-publisher fight. Her efforts to procure both the space and support for us to explore this brave project are greatly appreciated.

We also note our deep gratitude to Andrea Doucet, who valued *Essential Breakthroughs* from its inception and generously offered to write the foreword. Her prolific research on gender and care, in tandem with Sara Ruddick's foundational maternal and feminist corpus, set the stage for the collection. Thank you also to our peer reviewers for their careful attention to each chapter and to our overall aims.

We owe love to the thoughtful and visionary David King, who brilliantly translated and transported our vision for and message of the collection into the beautiful illustration on the cover.

We are proud of all the feminists, queers, and men who love their mothers and resist the maternal allergy that plagues queer, feminist, and mainstream cultures alike through their unabashed theorizing at the intersection of care and the maternal. We respect our contributors' courageous research regarding the complexities of intersectionality and gendered caring, and we honour the personal experiences and attachments that add immensely to their work.

Foreword

ANDREA DOUCET

Feminist philosopher Nancy Hartsock, who passed away in 2015, wrote in the introduction to her seminal text *The Feminist Standpoint Revisited and Other Essays* that all of her writing "responded to questions that arose from the social contexts in which I found myself.... They are autobiographical in that they respond to issues I found urgent at different times" (1). I thought about these lines as I read *Essential Breakthroughs: Conversations about Men, Mothers, and Mothering* and reflected on how, about a quarter century ago, the "Do men mother?" question found its way into my thinking. Indeed, my journey with that question was autobiographical, temporal, and urgent. It was autobiographical in that it was seeded from my own biography as a mother parenting with a man who was judged harshly when he tried, in 1991, to join a local moms and tots group in England. It was and continues to be temporal, as concepts—including that of a maternal lens—are "words in their sites" (Hacking 68); they "lack natures or essences" but instead "have histories, networks, and narratives" (Somers, *Genealogies of Citizenship* 267). And it was an urgent question as I joined a chorus of feminist scholars who argued that women's socioeconomic equality with men was dependent on men's participation in shared parenting or mothering. Questions about men and mothering remain urgent, although the shape of this urgency, as *Essential Breakthroughs* reveals, also shifts across time.

Perhaps the strongest connection with questions of men, mothering, and maternal lenses began, for me, with Sara Ruddick. As scholars, we read hundreds, perhaps thousands, of books and academic journal articles, but there are only a few that stay with us. In a sense, we fall in love with these authors, their ideas, their words (Allan). They keep us awake at night; we take them to bed; we sneak them into our suitcases while on holidays. Ruddick is one of those authors for me and *Maternal Thinking* (1995) is one of those books. When I read her bold statements that "men are mothers" and that "men can and do mother" (40), I felt what Bronwyn Davies describes as "a tickle in the brain" (83).

That "tickle" stayed with me when, between 2000 and 2004, I interviewed 101 fathers about their experiences of primary care-giving for *Do Men Mother?* These fathers were single or married, living with men or women, parenting alone or with others, and while most were white and middle class, there were also low-income fathers, and indigenous, multi-racial, and new immigrant fathers. I was interested in their stories, but I was also epistemologically interested in how and why particular stories are told and how identities are made and remade within particular conditions of possibility that are "temporal, relational, and cultural, as well as institutional, material, and macro-structural" (Somers, "The Narrative" 607). Those were early days in the slow process of socially recognizing primary-caregiving fathers. Ten years ago, men spoke to me about feeling surveilled and judged as they moved through the social landscapes of parenting, through what one father called "estrogen-filled worlds" (Doucet 139). Fathers who sat outside what Judith Butler called the "heterosexual matrix" (*Gender Trouble* 206) and fathers who spent their days caring and not working for pay outside the home were, as Barrie Thorne put it, entrenched in social judgments that view them as a "failed males" (qtd. in Doucet 161). Their stories, which varied among brave, humorous, practical, lamenting, and heroic in their own eyes or in the eyes of others, were told from social worlds where men were viewed as incompetent or secondary caregivers. I listened and retold (through my own lenses) these stories, calling attention to the need to expand our understandings of caregiving. And I also argued for a widening of a maternal lens that focused on entanglements of holding on and letting go, and dependence /independence /inter-dependence. I argued that fathers' stories enriched how we think about mothering and caregiving.

Since that time, the social worlds of parenting, public perceptions of men and care, and "the possibilities for a livable life" (Butler, *Undoing Gender* 8) have all widened. When my book, *Do Men Mother?*, was published ten years ago, it addressed a small corner of the question in a particular place and time. As *Essential Breakthroughs* shows so well, there is still much at stake and, therefore, much to discuss. As Pelletier and Green write in their introduction, "There is potential to improve our systems of childcare within the negotiations of our gendered, sexed, classed, raced, and otherwise (de)constructed selves." Each contributor attempts such a negotiation with compassion and an eye for transformative justice.

Reading the wonderfully provocative essays in this collection, I was reminded of Donna Haraway's metaphor of the two-person string game, cat's cradle, as dialogue and as world-making. She writes:

> Cat's cradle invites a sense of collective work, of one person not being able to make all the patterns alone. One does not "win" at cat's cradle; the goal is more interesting and more open-ended than that. It is not always possible to repeat interesting patterns, and figuring out what happened to result in intriguing patterns is an embodied analytic skill.... Cat's cradle is both local and global, distributed and knotted together. (268)

This exciting new collection of essays brings rich, colourful, and textured debate to the cat's cradle that has been woven around men and mothering. *Essential Breakthroughs: Conversations about Men, Mothers, and Mothering* weaves historical narratives together as it connects back twenty years to *Maternal Thinking*, back ten years to *Do Men Mother?*, and across decades of excellent publishing by Demeter Press on the outstanding diversity of mothering experiences and identities. In this book there is a dialogic tapestry with creative tensions, knots, frayed threads, and places where new strings of thought jostle and pull at the others. The editors and contributors carefully think though what might still "be gained from the use of a maternal lens with respect to fathering and masculinities, and to sons, men, mothers, and mothering more generally" (*Essential Breakthroughs*, Introduction). In doing so, *Essential Breakthroughs* continues to weave the threads of men and mothering questions, forging new dialogue and remaking caregiving possibilities and social worlds.

—Andrea Doucet
St Catharines, Ontario
May, 2015

WORKS CITED

Allan, Jonathan A. "Falling in Love with Eve Kosofsky Sedgwick." *Mosaic: A Journal for the Interdisciplinary Study of Literature* 48.1 (2015): 1–15. Print.

Butler, Judith. *Gender Trouble: Feminism and the Subversion of Identity*. New York: Routledge, 1990. Print.

Butler, Judith. *Undoing Gender*. New York: Routledge, 2004. Print.

Davies, Bronwyn. "Identity, Abjection and Otherness: Creating the Self, Creating Difference." *The RoutledgeFalmer Reader in Gender and Education*. Ed. Madeleine Arnot and Mairtin Mac An Ghaill. London: Routledge, 2006. 72–90. Print.

Doucet, Andrea. *Do Men Mother? Fathering, Care, and Domestic Responsibility*. Toronto: University of Toronto Press, 2006. Print.

Hacking, Ian. *Historical Ontology*. Cambridge: Harvard University Presss, 2002. Print.

Haraway, Donna. *Modest-Witness@Second-Millennium Female-man-Meets-Oncomouse: Feminism and Technoscience*. New York: Routledge, 1997. Print.

Hartsock, Nancy C. M. *The Feminist Standpoint Revisited and Other Essays*. Boulder: Westview Press, 1998. Print.

Ruddick, Sara. *Maternal Thinking: Towards a Politics of Peace*. 2nd ed. Boston: Beacon Press, 1995. Print.

Somers, Margaret. *Genealogies of Citizenship: Markets, State-lessness, and the Right to Have Rights*. New York: Cambridge University Press, 2008. Print.

Somers, Margaret. "The Narrative Constitution of Identity: A Relational and Network Approach." *Theory and Society* 23.5 (1994): 605–49. Print.

Introduction

GARY LEE PELLETIER AND FIONA JOY GREEN

I N CONVERSATIONS ABOUT CHILDCARE, it is easy to get lost in a quagmire of semantics. *Mother*, *father*, *parent*, *guardian*, *child*, and *care* are all open to interpretation. What might exist in one context (legal, social, medical, theoretical, hypothetical) may cease to be in another. In addition to the friction that such discursive distinctions may cause—in the courtroom, the playground, or the anthology—these identifications have real socioeconomic and political consequences for childcare providers and those in their care. However, a fundamental problem remains once the dust has settled on any chosen nomenclature: neither what one identifies as care nor what one chooses to call those who provide it ensures or fosters care in the first place. From custody battles to theoretical debates, the shapes and styles of childcare, as well as the identifications of those who perform it, are not as agreed upon as the underlying need.

There is potential to improve our systems of childcare within the negotiations of our gendered, sexed, classed, raced, and otherwise (de)constructed selves. We, both as mothers and as children—and also as co-editors of this collection—honour the necessity of childcare, an "essential." We are okay with its naming but refute the stubborn gender essentialisms that plague the experiences of both paid and unpaid childcare providers, excluding them from or tethering them to some identity, practice, or theory. This is not to say we are staunch supporters of identity neutralizing terms and practices. It's not that simple. Although *parent*, for example, is commonly suggested as a "gender neutral" substitute for *mother* and *father*, the discursive move to *parent* (and, consequentially, the departure from something else) is never apolitical. *Essential Breakthroughs*, therefore, charts a course somewhere between defying and affirming essentialism—gender essentialism in particular—in childcare practices and provider identities by learning from the historically essentialized relations between gender and care. To foster a greater societal ethic of care, specifically a feminist one, we concur that gender-essentialized norms should be contested, and we consider the maternal lens of motherhood studies a helpful feminist tool with which to do so.

THE CONVERSATIONS

The notion that men are "caring deficient," as enforced by hegemonic masculinities and femininities, is directly contested by our contributors. Through explorations of care work and familial life via male and masculine perspectives, *Essential Breakthroughs* has two major objectives: 1) to examine male mothering, and/or male caring more generally, through a feminist maternal lens and 2) to demonstrate how maternal thinking is needed to disrupt the gender essentialism presupposed by certain discourses of mothering and fathering. Our project asserts that once it has been established that men can and do care, it should be accordingly disproven that women have some natural affinity for care work. As Andrea O'Reilly sees it, "The work of mothering [must be] rendered separate from the identity of mother—so that care is divested of biology" ("Outlaw(ing)" 377). The move from "a politic of maternalism to what Judith Stadtman Tucker perceptively defines as a 'feminist ethic of care' framework," ("Outlaw(ing)" 377) is a worthy goal, and male caring perspectives in conjunction with maternal thinking provide insight for getting there.

Our solution to break through the essentialist care discourse is in philosophical sync with recent efforts to queer motherhood (Gibson; Park), although *Essential Breakthroughs* already assumes a queered motherhood. We follow in Sara Ruddick's footsteps, who, arguably, queered motherhood over three decades ago when she first began to theorize the gender flexibility of maternal practice, which she and many maternal theorists purport is not limited to biological mothers or women but is open to any individual who "takes upon the work of mothering as a central part of her or his life" (*Maternal Thinking* 40). Therefore, while Shelley M. Park uses the vehicle of queer sexuality to critique motherhood, illuminating the resistance of monomaternalism in adoptive, lesbian, blended, and polygamous families, we look to perspectives of men and masculinities to facilitate the disruption of gender-essentialist care norms.

The seahorse, genus Hippocampus, inspires our thinking. We are not marine biologists but we find seahorses both interesting and queer, particularly for their "illegitimate natures" within their reproductive sex and gender roles: seahorses are the only non-human creatures on earth known to experience male pregnancy (Mortimer-Sandilands and Erickson 32). Males provide the sperm, females the eggs, but it is the female seahorse who deposits her eggs into the male seahorse's brood pouch (located on his stomach) via her ovipositor (an egg-laying appendage) and it is the male who gives birth to upwards of two thousand little seahorses via muscle contractions. The females' eggs come pre-packaged with nutrient filled casings, while the males' brood pouches "protect, aerate, osmoregulate, and nourish the developing embryos for several weeks before releasing them as independent young" (Vincent).

Transgender support and social organizations like Seahorse Victoria in Australia have taken up the seahorse as a type of queer mascot. Although we are not the first to tug at the seahorse's perceived queer/trans-ecological threads (Wallace), we are wary of the potential to essentially transgress here, which comes with the territory of idolizing a particular animal on one's book cover. We resist the urge to simplistically anthropomorphize the seahorse by looking to *Queer Ecologies: Sex, Nature, Politics, Desire* (2010) as an effective template for how to "balance between legitimizing queer behavior (it is, after all, a profound part of life all over the planet) and delegitimizing the binary constructions of sexuality and animality that have informed scientific and cultural discussions of sex" (Mortimer-Sandilands and Erickson 32), to which we add for our own purposes, gender.

It is not exactly known why seahorse reproductive capabilities have evolved this way, but it is speculated that male pregnancy allows the species to reproduce more quickly (Harris). Since female seahorses do not have to expend energy giving birth, they can focus on recuperating and creating more eggs with which to impregnate the male seahorse, which is capable of giving birth and becoming pregnant again in the same day (Harris). Once seahorses are born, they receive no care from their parents, and so raising up seahorses as an example of "good fathers" is absurd, although not uncommon ("Seahorse"; Hood). Nevertheless, considering male pregnancy amongst seahorses reminds us of the adaptability of bodies, the flexibility of the "natural," and the distance between reproductive capabilities and nurturing care.

The conflation of "good fathering" and "good mothering" with birthing capabilities is common in popular reproductive and cultural discourses, and part of *Essential Breakthroughs'* agenda is to explore and disrupt this often-automatic impulse. While we do not deem specific reproductive capabilities essential to maternal or parental identifications, we do understand the theoretical, physiological, and psychic nuances that pregnancy, birth, and lactation can contribute to care-taking identities. We support projects to "unsex" parenting (Rosenblum 78) and "ungender" body parts (Spade), including a delinking of mothering from the "biological realities of pregnancy and lactation" (Rosenblum 78). Yet, we also acknowledge the importance of theories of mothering that take into account such biological realities, such as Adrienne Rich's seminal text *Of Woman Born: Motherhood as Experience and Institution* (1986).

Seahorses, therefore, are a wedge into what often appears to be a tightly sealed-up essentialist reproductive reality. Considering this creature's radical reproductive capabilities helps us enter into discussions of nature, reproduction, sex, gender, and care. Fundamentally, *Essential Breakthroughs* queries gender as a means to queer care and its contributors are unified in their efforts to find the right balance between combating gender essentialism and honouring the differences that define our lives. Considering the centuries that women and mothers have endured being written about by out-of-touch male "experts" regarding anything from periods to orgasms to wrinkles (and everything in between), a collection filled with male perspectives honing a variety of feminist and maternal lenses is a breakthrough in and of itself.

We deem maternal theory essential for what, arguably, qualifies it as essentialist: its attachment to the "mother." We are aware that this position requires a strong defense. The premise of the essentialist critique of motherhood studies is that "mother" risks perpetuating the very gender norms the discipline is attempting to combat. It is argued that maternal theory's "mother" predisposition works to demarcate mothers as the primary care-providers in children's lives, a trend of thinking which, despite (man)y inroads into childcare, is socially rampant. Andrea Doucet, feminist scholar of gender and care, argues "studying fathers' caregiving through the lens of men and mothering ultimately limits our understandings of fathers' caring" ("Taking Off" 177). Accordingly, a "pervasive feminist discomfort with all things maternal" is easily detectable within both queer studies and women's and gender studies (O'Reilly "Aint I" 6). As Park observes, "In seeking to find a scholarly home within queer theory, I frequently have to bracket my interest in mothering. Insofar as mothers are 'breeders' and breeders are the presumed antithesis of queer, the notion of queer mothering is rendered oxymoronic" (1).

Regardless of substantial critiques of the universalizing female maternalisms of the late nineteenth and early twentieth centuries, maternal theory continues to raise some scholarly eyebrows. This unease is obvious in contemporary rebukes of heteronormative futurities, such as critiques of repro-narrativity (Warner), reproductive futurism (Edelman), and the "norms, forms, and crimes" of intimacy (Berlant 288). Gender essentialism causes feminists and queers alike to cringe; therefore "motherhood becomes highly problematic," as O'Reilly further explains:

> Motherhood, more than anything else, is what marks our essential gender difference; only biological females can biologically become mothers. And because gender difference is seen as structuring and maintaining male dominance, many feminists seek to downplay and disavow anything that marked this difference; the main one being of course motherhood. Thus for many feminists, to talk of mother-

hood, to acknowledge women's specific gendered subjectivity as mothers, to develop a mother-centered feminism, is to play into patriarchy; acknowledge and affirm that is which is seen as marking and maintaining gender difference and hence the oppression of women. ("Ain't I" 8)

This scholarly distaste for motherhood studies is exacerbated by what Julie Stephens terms "postmaternal thinking," a pervasive "process where the ideals intimately bound up with the practices of mothering are disavowed in the public sphere, and conflicted in the private" (ix). Rather than scapegoat second-wave feminists though, Stephens wags her finger at neoliberalism. We hate neoliberalism too.

Regardless of its exact origins, a social, political, and intellectual maternal aversion colours the present. And so, in our feminist and queer rebukes of the hollow significations that gender essentialism promote, we must be cautious to not "disavow motherhood to facilitate [a] destabilizing of gender" (O'Reilly, "Ain't I" 9), thereby further contributing to the exiling of the maternal. Attentive and nurturing care, despite its essentialized femininity, is essential to a child's livelihood. For better or for worse, many women and/or feminized individuals have learned how to care. *Essential Breakthroughs* operates from the belief that this knowledge should be respected. Such respect is a feminist action that acknowledges the childcare timecards women have historically punched within the patriarchal institutions of motherhood and the home. Although, as Doucet suggests, "fathers are reconfiguring fathering and masculinities and what it means to be a man in the twenty-first century" in their own nuanced ways, *Essential Breakthroughs* affirms there is substantial insight to be gained from the use of a maternal lens with respect to fathering and masculinities, as well as to sons, men, mothers, and mothering more generally ("Taking Off" 177).

THE BREAKTHROUGHS

Each essay uniquely affirms O'Reilly's assertion that it's possible to "simultaneously argue that gender is constructed and that motherhood matters [and] . . . that maternity is integral to mother women's sense of self and her experience of the world" ("Ain't I" 9). Just as queer theorists do not wish to reduce themselves solely to sexed identities, or critical race theorists to racialized beings, so too "maternal scholars do not reduce women's sense of self to motherhood" ("Ain't I" 9). Furthermore, the contributors do not waste their time dividing the academic from the anecdotal and the theoretical from the guttural. Their work blends feelings, ideas, experiences, and hunches. We contend that these refreshing voices are better equipped to describe the realities of care—from the blissful to the unbearable—than most of the stodgy and pretentious "scholarship" that abounds today. We and our authors pride ourselves on the disciplines we hail from and the identities we hold, in large part, because of their propensities to breakthrough such boring, washed out, and often patriarchal thinking.

The first two chapters speak to the importance of, as well as utilize, a maternal feminist lens in their theoretical analyses of male care. In her chapter "Parental Thinking: What Does Gender Have to Do with It?," Joanne S. Frye goes further than cursory debates around language by identifying the theoretical "sticking points" of purporting and practicing "parental thinking" as opposed to "maternal thinking": the reproductive body, the feminine and primary caregiving mother, and defensive masculinity. Frye acknowledges the importance of affirming what Ruddick refers to as "an ethics of sexual difference" ("Maternal Thinking" 362) and ultimately agrees with Doucet that claiming "men engage in 'maternal thinking' doesn't work; it is too fraught with a re-emphasis on the femininity of parental commitments: men do not mother" (Frye). Instead, Frye advocates for a "transformed parental thinking," whose definition she carves out of Ruddick's envisioning of maternal thinking, and deems it a "significant step toward nourishing all children as it encourages in both men and women the full range of human capacities that we can develop through caring for children." Although Frye does not discover a particularly harmonious relationship between male care and maternal thinking, her conclusions are arrived at through "an approach grounded in [her] experiences as a mother and [her] ongoing commitment to feminist change." Gary Lee Pelletier's analysis of paid male childcare providers in Chapter 2, "Does The Manny Mother?," passionately responds to Frye's and to Doucet's recommendations. His analysis of the cultural obsession of male nannies in popular discourses has led him to cherish the "mother" of motherhood studies and maternal theory. Rather than trade her in for a shiny, newly re-imagined "parent," he proposes the feminist function of developing the maternal lens and questions "whether the maternal lens is something that can be uninstalled," likening it to a "commitment to a historical feminist consciousness."

The following four chapters address the dialectics of mother/son relationships. In "'Is he the son of no one?': A Son's Relational Narrative on his Mother" and "Why Isn't Everyone Celebrating Me?... My Mom, Bankruptcy, and my Ego," Nick Mulé and Justin Butler, respectively, reflect on their relationships with their mothers. Both authors share the standpoint of "therapist." The psychodynamic elements of their analyses not only provide a rich contribution to their perspectives but also function to prevent either author from identifying their mother as the "sole culprit in [their] development" (Butler). In addition to their shared but unique feminist analyses, each author incorporates significant aspects of their own identities into their projects: Mulé reflects on his queerness, while Butler responds to his "grandiose sense of self." Alys Einion and Ruth Trinidad Galván take up mother-son relationships from the purview of maternal identity and agency. In "Lesbian Families, Sons, and Mothering: Parenting outside the Boundaries," Einion explores the feminist implications of lesbian mothering of sons alongside lesbian separatist politics and gay assimilationist expectations in the United Kingdom. Her own maternal experience couples with her theoretical engagements to gesture towards a "radical re-visioning of family," and she ponders whether "lesbian feminists and lesbian mothers of sons, and maybe lesbian families, will be in vanguard." Trinidad Galván investigates the implications of Ecuadorian transnational mothering on family dynamics. In her chapter, "Changing the Gender Script: Ecuadorian Sons' Increased Domesticity and Emotive Response to Transnational Mothering," she draws from "the narratives of three sons who discursively manoeuvre and enact alternative masculinities around the migration of their mothers and transnational mothering." Both chapters illuminate a hopeful flexibility in what Einion considers to be "that most fundamental, and gendered, of social institutions," the family.

The next three chapters reconcile a feminist awareness with the effects of hegemonic male masculinities on heterosexual family dynamics and fatherhood. All three contributors are concerned with the consequences for women, mothers, wives, and femininities caused by particular heteronormative representations of masculinity—both popular and personal. In his chapter "TV's New Dads: Sensitive Fatherhood and the Return of Hegemonic Masculinity," Dwayne Avery employs a maternal lens in his exploration of postfeminist father representations "to determine how televisual images of postfeminist fatherhood relate to the institution of motherhood and maternal practices." His project is motivated by a feminist suspicion that "TV's new dads" are mere reincarnations of hegemonic masculinity. In his chapter "What's So Funny about Childbirth?: The Projection of Patriarchal Masculinity in Popular, Comedic Childbirth Guides," Jeffrey Nall draws from his personal experience of fatherhood, as well as his own research concerning "the mastery of women and childbirth," to investigate childbirth guides with a feminist suspicion similar to Avery's: "that patriarchy is capable of adapting to changing demands in ways that maintain sexist social norms." His project conclusively suggests that "pregnancy and childbirth must also be viewed as a crucial front for a revolutionary reevaluation of the value of female personhood." Whereas Avery and Nall critique popular representations, C. Wesley Buerkle critically evaluates his relationship with his wife in his chapter "Just Along for the Ride?: A Father-to-Be Searching for His Role." Like Nall, Buerkle refutes the trends around women's reproductive health in industrialized nations in which women are "treated as medical objects with directives for their care dictated by an androcentric medical tradition and the men with whom women have their children." He considers his varied familial tasks of "helper," "caretaker," "bystander," "parent," and "feminist" in an honest and brave attempt to find "his role."

Sexed-subjective experiences of pregnancy, birth, and lactation often work towards naturalizing motherhood as inherently feminine. In their chapters, Jack Hixson-Vulpe and A.J. Lowik both consider what Ruddick terms "natal reflection" ("Thinking Mothers") and what Frye (in her chapter) defines as "the *thought* that derives from women's bodily and social engagement in birth-giving," and each work to problematize the essentialized maternal body. Drawing on the experience of an abortion as a transman, as well as the work of Lee Edelman and José Esteban Muñoz, Hixson-Vulpe puts his queerness into conversation with queer critiques of straight time. His moving recollection and theoretical analysis join forces to advocate for the queer practice of "wondering" in place of the typical essentializing and categorizing often triggered by people's gendered and sexed bodies and behaviours. He concludes his chapter contemplating, "What would it mean for us to wonder at each other's actions and lives as opposed to defining and solidifying their meaning?"—a question that speaks to the driving force of this compellation. In "The Ties that Bind Are Broken: Trans* Breastfeeding Practices, Ungendering Body Parts and Unsexing Parenting Roles," Lowik analyzes the lactation experiences of Trevor MacDonald, a Winnipeg-based transgender dad, and argues for both the ungendering of body parts as well as the unsexing of acts of parenting: "When breasts are ungendered and when breastfeeding as a parenting practice is unsexed, trans* and cisgender parents alike will be freed from the ties that bind." Both Hixson-Vulpe's and Lowik's projects work to interrupt the essentialist links between reproduction, care, mothers, and women. These efforts challenge "the already tenuous connection between bodies, identities, and behaviours when it comes to parenting" and ultimately will benefit not only trans* parents "but will better reflect the complex ways in which parents of all sexes and genders relate to their children, engage in parenting tasks, and divide labour in their households" (Lowik).

Essential Breakthroughs concludes with Michael Young's chapter, a project that grows from the fruitful overlap of all of the collection's themes—a critique of gender-essentialized knowledges and practices of care, a mother's "nature," the utility of a feminist maternal lens for regarding male care, constructions of motherhood and fatherhood, queerness, a son's perspective of the mother/son relationship, paid childcare providers, male mothering, and soft/sensitive/relational and otherwise anti-hegemonic masculinities. In "Becoming Mother's Nature: A Queer Son's Perspective on Mothering in an Era of Ecological Decline," Young evaluates his relationships with the three significant mother-women who played primary roles in his upbringing. Additionally, he explores how he satisfies his "reproductive impulse with [a] green thumb." While he recognizes the essentializing potential embedded in his maternal advocating, he advocates anyway, for he has come to believe "the impetus to cultivate feels better than the impetus to dominate, accumulate, and extirpate." Young speculates, "I have the looming sense that I am becoming Mother." And it is likely that upon your completion of *Essential Breakthroughs: Conversations about Men, Mothers, and Mothering* you will have the looming sense that neither he, nor we, is particularly concerned.

WORKS CITED

Berlant, Lauren. "Intimacy: A Special Issue." *Critical Inquiry* 24.2 (1998): 281-288. Print.

Doucet, Andrea. *Do Men Mother?: Fathering, Care, and Domestic Responsibility*. Toronto: University of Toronto Press, 2006. Print.

Doucet, Andrea. "Taking Off the Maternal Lens: Engaging with Sarah Ruddick on Men and Mothering." *Motherhood at the 21st Century: Policy, Experience, Identity, Agency*. Ed. Andrea O'Reilly. New York: Columbia University Press, 2010. 170-180. Print.

Edelman, Lee. *No Future: Queer Theory and the Death Drive*. Durham: Duke University Press, 2004. Print.

Gibson, Margaret F., ed. *Queering Motherhood: Narrative and Theoretical Perspectives*. Toronto: Demeter Press, 2014. Print.

Harris, Rob. "Why Do Male Seahorses Give Birth?" *Animals*. Whalerock Digital Media. n.d. Web. 3 May 2015.

Hood, Kate. "The Sea Horse: Our Family Mascot." *New York Times*. 31 Oct. 2008. Web. 3 May 2015.

Mortimer-Sandilands, Catriona and Bruce Erickson, eds. *Queer*

Ecologies. Sex, Nature, Politics, Desire. Bloomington: Indiana University Press, 2010. Print.

O'Reilly, Andrea. "Ain't I a Feminist?: Matricentric Feminism, Feminist Mamas, and Why Mothers Need a Feminist Movement/ Theory of Their Own." iffr development Word Press. Mar. 2014. Web. 3 May 2015.

O'Reilly, Andrea. "Outlaw(ing) Motherhood: A Theory and Politic of Maternal Empowerment for the Twenty-First Century." *Twenty-first-Century Motherhood: Experience, Identity, Policy, Agency.* Ed. Andrea O'Reilly. New York: Columbia University Press, 2010. 366-380. Print.

Park, Shelley M. *Mothering Queerly, Queering Motherhood: Resisting Monomaternalism in Adoptive, Lesbian, Blended, and Polygamous Families.* Albany: State University of New York Press, 2013. Print.

Rich, Adrienne. *Of Woman Born: Motherhood as Experience and Institution.* New York: W. W. Norton & Company, 1986. Print.

Rosenblum, Darren. "Unsex Mothering: Toward A New Culture of Parenting." *Pace Law Faculty Publications* n.d. Web. 3 May 2015.

Ruddick, Sara. "Maternal Thinking." *Feminist Studies* 6 (1980): 342-67. Print.

Ruddick, Sara. *Maternal Thinking: Toward a Politics of Peace.* New York: Ballantine Books, 1989. Print.

Ruddick, Sara. "Thinking Mothers/Conceiving Birth." *Representations of Motherhood.* Ed. Donna Bassin, Margaret Honey, and Meryle Mahrer Kaplan. New Haven: Yale University Press. 29-45. 1944. Print.

"Seahorse." *National Geographic.* n.d. Web. 3 May 2015.

"Seahorse Victoria." Seahorse Victoria Inc. n.d. Web. 3 May 2015.

Spade, Dean. "About Purportedly Gendered Body Parts." *Dean Spade.net.* 12 June 2014. Web. 3 June 2015.

Stephens, Julie. *Confronting Postmaternal Thinking: Feminism, Memory, and Care.* New York: Columbia University Press, 2011. Print.

Vincent, Amanda. "A Seahorse Father Makes a Good Mother." *Natural History.* Dec. 1990. Web. 3 May 2015.

Wallace, J. "Seahorse Papas Are Everywhere in San Francisco."

Visibly Transparent. 29 Aug. 2009. Web. 3 May 2015.

Warner, Michael. "Introduction: Fear of a Queer Planet." *Social Text* 29 (1991): 3-17. Print.

1.
Parental Thinking

What Does Gender Have to Do With It?

JOANNE S. FRYE

OVER THREE DECADES AGO, Sara Ruddick called feminists to attention with her compelling and controversial essay "Maternal Thinking." She concluded that essay by projecting a vision of future parenting: "There will be mothers of both sexes who live out a transformed maternal thought in communities that share parental care—practically, emotionally, economically, and socially. Such communities will have learned from their mothers how to value children's lives" (362). In such a world, she says, "There will be no more 'Fathers'"—no more people who have power over women and children while not engaging in "the work of attentive love" (362). Instead, there will be both men and women who engage in "maternal thinking" based on that crucial work committed to providing children with preservative love, nurturance, and training.

Three and a half decades later, this early call continues to provoke complicated response. Do men mother? Must mothers have an ongoing central role in children's development? Do children require the specific contributions of fathers? What are the appropriate expectations for gay and lesbian parents, transsexual parents, and single parents in thinking that has been largely based on heteronormative nuclear families? What values might we derive from the thought developed through caring for growing children? *What does gender have to do with it?*

I can't, of course, answer these questions definitively. But I do want to engage in my own speculative inquiry into parenting, gender, and cultural change using a lens that is both feminist and maternal—that is, an approach grounded in my own experiences as a mother and my ongoing commitment to feminist change.

Like many feminist thinkers about motherhood, I have taken much guidance from Ruddick's probing analyses. That early essay, "Maternal Thinking," through which I first encountered her work, was her initial foray into the thinking that emerges from caring for children and the ways in which that thinking relates to our understandings of gender. But it was also a provocation to her further work, in which she continued to wrestle with her overarching questions about mothering, gender, feminism, and peace politics. She went on to develop these ideas into a book, *Maternal Thinking: Toward a Politics of Peace* (1989). In subsequent years, she persisted in teasing out the difficulties and contradictions: in the preface to the 1995 edition of the book; in a 1994 essay, "Thinking Mothers/Conceiving Birth"; and in a 1997 essay, "The Idea of Fatherhood."

In the spirit of her willingness to revisit difficult questions, my own approach here embraces the value of "maternal thinking" even as it resists embracing its gendered construction. In doing so, I want to begin by drawing some definitions from Ruddick's work. First, the idea of "maternal thinking"—a practice generated by caregiving that is attentive to children's needs, yielding a mother's work to satisfy the "demands for preservation, growth, and acceptability" ("Maternal Thinking" 348). These concepts then develop into key chapter titles in *Maternal Thinking: Toward a Politics of Peace*: preservative love, fostering growth or nurturance, and training (Chapters 3-5). Second, the idea of "fatherhood"—the cultural expectation to fulfill three somewhat different functions: provision, protection, and authority ("Idea" 207). Finally, "parenting"—in her words, "a complex, ongoing *work* of responding to children's needs" ("Idea" 206). Though these three definitions are not in parallel form, together they open up the space in which to consider the idea of "parental thinking" as a practice deriving from the ongoing and active commitment to caring for children, shaped by current constructions of gender but available to both men and women. I do so in full awareness that the concept of "parental thinking" faces the hazard of what Ruddick calls "safe-speak" ("Idea" 218)—denying the ongoing presence of gender imbalance and the fact that the actual work of parenting continues to be done largely by women.

The first sticking point in any such analysis is the reproductive body. Ruddick's work in "Thinking Mothers/Conceiving Birth" is extremely helpful here. She speaks of her concerns as an inquiry into "the concepts of a social/bodily ego and sexed subjectivities" (42). She asserts that this inquiry is still in process but identifies four "organizing ideas" by which we might identify "natal reflection": the *thought* that derives from women's bodily and social engagement in birth-giving. These organizing ideas are 1) active waiting, 2) chosen pain, 3) a complex concept of control, neither "despairing passivity" nor "total control," and 4) "a distinctive construction of self and other" (42-43). She identifies such natal reflection as a "weave of mind and body" which is social (41), experienced within the distinctive historical, personal, and social environment of the pregnant and birth-giving woman. Intriguingly, she does not limit "natal reflection" to the reproductive bodies of women, though it is derived from specifically female experience; instead she asserts that a woman's close companions are "able to participate in natal reflection through imaginative, attentive listening" (41).

Note that the emphasis remains on *thinking*, the cognitive capacities that derive from a particular kind of maternal activity, in this case, thinking that changes a parent's understanding of relationships, especially "control" which neither governs nor yields and "self and other" as potently interconnected. Note, too, that she leaves open the idea that men—as attentive listeners and empathetic companions—might also participate in this sort of thinking, thus changing their ways of relating and drawing them into more intimate interactions than are apparent in the idea of fatherhood.

I share the overarching understanding that men in partnership with a birth-giving mother might well engage in "natal reflection," though not without a good deal of effort. I also share Ruddick's emphasis on the importance of "bodily involvement with infants and children after birth" ("Thinking Mothers" 36)—something available to fathers, as well as adoptive parents, nongestational parents in gay and lesbian couples, grandparents, and other caregiving adults. But like Ruddick, I am aware that the social/cultural assumptions in essentially all cultures link birthing, bodily care-giving, and reproductive bodies nearly inextricably with *mothers*. Like her, I am also inclined to separate our assumptions about birthing from our assumptions about mothers, hoping to free us from the idea that women are defined by reproductive roles. But none of us can deny that it is from a woman's body that children are born. In *Do Men Mother?*, a richly textured ethnographic study of 118 Canadian primary-caregiving fathers, most of whom are in partnered relationships with women, Andrea Doucet makes this point: "Both fathers and mothers assert the influence of female em-bodiment—pregnancy, birth, breastfeeding, and post-birth recovery ... as having greater weight in emotional responsibility" (239).

This leads to a second sticking point in a move from maternal thinking to parental thinking: the intensity of the association of *mother* with both femininity and primary caregiving. We have gone some distance in separating the idea of *woman* from femininity—that is, women are now more than ever engaged in activities of all kinds, including those traditionally seen as men's domain. But when we say *mother*, the link to femininity tightens. This is something that is deeply gendered. Consider, for example, the negative judgments on women who choose not to have children and are characterized as "unfeminine." Recall Freud's association of what he labelled feminine traits—especially passivity and masochism—with the cultural assumptions about birthing and women's reproductive capacities. Or think of the many images of women with infants who are seen as quintessentially feminine. In her classic analysis of "woman," Simone de Beauvoir begins her chapter on "The Mother" by recalling this link between motherhood and cultural femininity: "It is in maternity that woman fulfills her physiological destiny; it is her natural 'calling,' since her whole organic structure is adapted for the perpetuation of the species" (484).

The bodily link to reproduction—enacted through pregnancy and breastfeeding—becomes the foundation for assuming that caregiving in general is a female domain. Tina Miller points out the importance of "the very different starting places from which journeys into fatherhood and motherhood begin, one embodied as the pregnancy is physically carried and one more detached and seeking ways in. These differences are reinforced through the gendered, societal and individual expectations … [and] further shaped and reproduced through the structural features of paid work" (173). More colloquially, one father asserts, "Dads can't get pregnant or give birth or produce milk from our nipples.… In a sense, we're sort of obsolete" (Tobey). Very often, women as well as men draw on birth-giving to make this assumption: "A child needs the care of a *mother*." In both public policy and individual decision-making, "*maternal* care is prioritized" (Miller 190).

From this nexus of associations derives a third sticking point: defensive masculinity. Many men, even while giving care to children, seem to need to assert that they are "different" from women, that their manhood is not threatened or compromised when they give care to children. I think here of a series of father essays broadcast in 2011 on National Public Radio in which men say such things as, "The stork paid us a visit, but we're still guys here.… Manhood is not lost" (Bronson). Doucet's more grounded analysis ties the notion of masculinity back to the question of embodiment: "Father's embodiment also comes to figure in the ways that men focus on physical activities, being outdoors, playing, and doing sports with their children, all drawing on the notion of masculine embodiment as strong, physical, and muscular" (239). Doucet further claims "fathers' narratives are marked by hegemonic masculinity, evidenced mainly in their devaluation and concurrent distancing from the feminine" (118). As Joan Williams says in her compelling analysis *Reshaping the Work-Family Debate* (2010), "While women's lives have changed a lot since 1970s, men and masculinity have changed very little" (217).

Doucet's study of fathers who are primary caregivers sheds further light on the complications of gender surrounding any move toward "parental thinking." Her interviews with caregiving men often emphasize the difference in their parenting from women's parenting; in their self-descriptions, they are more inclined to physicality, more supportive of risk-taking, less emotionally expressive than mothers. Doucet points out that "men … have hegemonic masculinity at their backs, reminding them that they are men operating in traditional female worlds. Most men … cling to the view that … they can never be mothers or replace the *mothering* done by women" (123). Indeed, one of the overarching arguments of her book is that men do *not* mother; even when they are primary caregivers, they enact this role as *fathers*.

But this cultural failure to change masculinity in conjunction with the commitment to changing women's lives creates significant difficulties for re-opening our understandings of parenting or for thinking clearly about how the care for children actually shapes thinking. Perhaps a strong, physical, muscular engagement with children could also make a valuable contribution to the parental thinking in which women engage—learning through parental embodiment, male or female, both the closeness of physical embrace *and* the stimulation of physically active encounters. Note in this regard that Doucet's interpretation of fathers' narratives, while acknowledging that they rely on distancing and disparaging femininity, omits the ways in which female embodiment can also be strong, physical, and muscular; and women's engagement with children can equally draw on physical activities and the encouragement toward independence and risk-taking.

Susan Rubin Suleiman calls our attention to the importance of play in the development of a human subject. "Playing," she asserts, "is the activity through which the human subject most freely and inventively constitutes herself or himself. To play is to affirm an 'I,' an autonomous subjectivity that exercises control over a world of possibilities" (280). What's more, she affirms this importance in the context of her overall claim on the importance of valuing play in *mothers*, as she calls for "a displacement, from what I call the patriarchal mother to the playful mother" (273). From this, I think, follows the notion that the apparently distinctive contributions of fathers can and should also be made by mothers: play as a part of parental thinking—by both men and women—that engenders the child's subjectivity and opens the gendered boundaries of parental roles.

The importance of play has intriguing resonance in Jennifer Finney Boylan's parenting memoir, *Stuck in the Middle with You*, in which she traces her experience as a parent who transitions from male to female after the birth of two sons in a heterosexual marriage. Boylan thus claims the gendered experience of both father and mother in a complex set of experiential understandings. Like the fathers in Doucet's study, Boylan recalls being especially playful as a father, even citing a supporting study suggesting "fathers spend about 6 percent more time in play with their children than mothers do" (31). She goes on to assert "goofiness—a kind of joyful foolishness—still feels to me like one of the more dependably gendered character traits" (31). Boylan struggles with the relevance of gender to her parenting experience, understandably not sure when her behaviour is still the fruit of having grown up as a boy, when it is simply the expression of her individual ways of being, and when it is shaped specifically by her gender, first as a father and then as a mother.

From Boylan's blurring of gender boundaries, from Doucet's caregiving fathers, and from Suleiman's rethinking of how women might elude the strictures of "patriarchal motherhood" through play, I want, then, to claim my own position: play and risk-taking may well be more prevalent, at present, among fathers than among mothers. But through these incursions on the gender boundaries of parenthood we can go on to locate more complex sources of parental thinking as it exceeds gender assumptions.

Still, the gendering of parenting is deeply entrenched, evident even in dictionary definitions. Parts of the definitions of both *mother* and *father* have evolved in conjunction with broader social moves toward what Esther Dermott calls a "loosening of the connection between fatherhood and masculinity" (8). But differences grounded in gender persist even in the most recent *American Heritage Dictionary of the English Language* (2011). After initial recognition of male/female differences via sperm, egg, and birth-giving, the definitions look like almost exact parallels until we come to this distinction: unlike the definition of father, the definition of mother as a noun includes "tenderness" and as a verb "nourishing." Definitions of both mother and father refer to "create, originate, found"—and the mother is "protective"—but the father as noun is essentialized as "protector." In short, the connotations of mother remain closely tied to nourishment and tenderness; the connotation of father retains the sense of a stalwart and more distant "protector." Dictionary meanings continue to embrace this distinction: "'Distance' is a general characteristic of Fatherhood; the closer, the more intimate the parental work, the more likely it is to be assigned to women" (Ruddick, "Idea" 207-208).

Two recent collections of personal essays also suggest the persistence of gender imbalances in ideas of parenting, even in the face of apparent cultural change: *Mama, PhD: Women Write about Motherhood and Academic Life* (2008) and *Papa, PhD: Essays on Fatherhood by Men in the Academy* (2011). Although these essays are limited by the class position of highly educated parents, they nonetheless seem to participate in an ongoing entanglement of parenting with gender. My own overview of the essays by mothers suggests that these highly educated women continue to experience the sense that their presence is imperative for the wellbeing of their children. They frequently succumb to guilt that they are failing at one or the other of their two primary roles: professional achievement and parenting. Their concern with a life of the mind seems only to heighten a sense of mind-body split: as academics they are devoted to intellect, as mothers they are bodily bound to children. They feel ongoing anxiety about being a "good mother," even as they seek to achieve in their chosen profession. A significant portion of them choose to drop out of academic life—or are pushed out—because of their status as mothers. The "mind/body weave" in Ruddick's analysis seems to dissipate in the face of the cultural split between work and parenting, at least for women. The idea, even, of "parental thinking"—with its explicit focus on cognitive development through parenting—disappears.

By contrast, the essays in *Papa, PhD* reveal very little guilt or anxiety about the capacity to be both fathers and academics. Though they often trace an engagement with parenting that might suggest "parental thinking," they tend more toward assimilating parental thoughts into academic insights rather than developing insights that are grounded in experiential life with children. That is, the essays—in contrast to the mothers' essays—are much more cerebral than emotional. Most of these fathers are heterosexual and partnered, and even in embracing fatherhood they rely heavily on the women in their lives for emotional guidance in parenting. These men often show a good deal of fear that they are compromising their careers, and they also fear the stigma of caring for children, though some are defiant of such concerns. For these fathers, as for the fathers in Dermott's study, "'thinking about' fatherhood results in the adoption of familiar patterns of action rather than radical change" (Dermott 13). Similarly, these fathers may well be inadvertently shaping their fathering behaviours, as Miller suggests many fathers do, to "men's privilege and power" (172).

In short, although both of these collections suggest the possibility of "parental thinking"—certainly all of the essayists are thoughtful about their parenting—they nonetheless reveal a continuing gender divide in how this group of men and women experience their parenting. And neither gendered group probes the actual complexity of thought that develops from actively engaging in caregiving for children, haunted as they are by the gendered structuring of both their work lives and their parenting lives.

On an anecdotal level, I want to cite an administrator at my home institution who has noticed that parental leave, available to both mothers and fathers, is often used by fathers to advance their research projects, while mothers are much more fully immersed in their experiences as new parents. Joan Williams cites more extensive evidence of a similar pattern. Drawing on a study of parental leave at a law school, she concludes, "While women used the leave for child care, men took a different tack—one went to Mardi Gras during his leave (without the baby); another published a long article he wrote during his leave" (113). This is not, of course, to say that all fathers take such advantage of gender-neutral parental leave, but it is worth noting that gendered behaviour often persists even in the face of gender-neutral policies. These academic fathers participate in a broad cultural pattern: "parenthood has relatively little impact on men's involvement in paid work" (Dermott 17).

Clearly the cultural distinctions between mothering and fathering remain deeply entrenched. But the question persists: are they indelible? Must we continue to embrace gender differences at the heart of our understanding of parenting? Are either mothers or fathers fully disposed to embrace *parental thinking*, grounded in finding, even in the midst of cultural change, sustained ways of addressing the needs of children for preservation, growth, and training—and also for provision, protection, and a perhaps redefined authority?

For a potent first step in providing empirical evidence for moving beyond gender at the heart of parenting, I turn now to a recent neurological study of "the brain basis of human fatherhood, its comparability with the maternal brain and its sensitivity to care-giving experiences" (Abraham et al. 9792). This study measured "parental brain response to infant stimuli using functional MRI, oxytocin, and parenting behavior in three groups of parents (n=89) raising their firstborn infant: heterosexual primary-caregiving mothers (PC-Mothers), heterosexual secondary-caregiving fathers (SC-Fathers), and primary-caregiving homosexual fathers (PC-Fathers) rearing infants without maternal involvement" (9792). The preliminary results of this study of brain, oxytocin, and parenting behaviour indicate "the central role of actual caregiving behavior as an important pathway to the parental brain" (9795). Both "mothers and primary-caregiving fathers exhibited greater parent-infant synchrony, a style marked by provision of the human parental repertoire in accordance with the infant's social signals" (9795).

Using MRI data, the study concludes that primary-caregiving fathers' brains become more like those of primary-caregiving mothers and that both secondary-caregiving fathers and primary-caregiving parents of both sexes experience changes in brain structures linked with oxytocin: "Overall, our results describe a global parental caregiving brain network that was mainly consistent across parents and involved vigilance, salience, reward, motivation, social understanding, and cognitive empathy" (9795). The authors also conclude that "assuming the role of a committed parent and engaging in active care of the young may trigger this global parental caregiving network in both women and men, in biological parents, and in those genetically unrelated to the child" (9795). The study does not claim that primary-care mothers and primary-care fathers develop identical brain responses—"somewhat different pathways seem to underpin maternal and paternal caregiving" (9795)—but it does uncover a remarkable similarity in the brain's adaptation to caregiving responsibilities: "Although only mothers experience pregnancy, birth, and lactation, and these provide powerful primers for the expression of maternal care via amygdala sensitization, evolution created other pathways for adaptation to the parental role in human fathers, and these alternative pathways come with practice, attunement, and day-by-day caregiving" (9795).

I have necessarily oversimplified the results of this study, which the authors recognize is preliminary though significant. But their overarching conclusion is compelling: "Findings underscore the common neural basis of maternal and paternal care, chart brain-hormone-behavior pathways that support parenthood, and specify mechanisms of brain malleability with caregiving experiences in human fathers" (9792). Note that "time spent in direct childcare" becomes the foundation for specific changes in parental brains. The suggestion is that our longstanding assumptions about gender differences in parenting must yield to a reality of gender similarity among people who actually engage in primary caregiving.

This study focuses on caregiving of infants, but I would like to suggest further that changes in thought continue to develop through primary commitment to the nurture and guidance of growing children. Elsewhere, I have written about apparently gendered parenting in the narrators of two novellas by Jane Smiley, *Ordinary Love* and *Good Will*. Here I want to affirm a conclusion I reach in that essay: the ways in which we tell stories are often themselves governed by gender constraints, but if we learn new ways of understanding and interpreting parenting experiences, we might also elude some of those constraints and recognize parental thinking that develops from the needs of each specific child. The two novellas seem, at first, to be differentiated by the gendered narrative and parenting approaches of a mother narrator and a father narrator. But by the end of the second novella, the father narrator seems to have developed a different kind of parental thinking more similar to that of the mother narrator, that is, parental thinking based on "'fragments,' a resistance to wholeness, a need to incorporate contradictions"—an attunement to the changing needs of a growing child, an openness to changes required by life events, and a readiness to understand multiple perspectives (Frye, "Narrating" 74).

Let me now return to Doucet's investigations of primary-caregiving fathers, most of whom are in partnered relationships with women. My earlier references to what these fathers claim about their "masculine" parenting do not fully represent Doucet's interpretation of their self-descriptions. For one thing, she recognizes that "personal transformations that men undergo as a result of being highly involved in caregiving may ... be the key to the way gender changes, for this generation and the next" (242). And she emphasizes that "positive and nurturing parenting by mothers and/ or fathers is the critical issue" (249). Intriguingly, her investigations draw on a methodological and epistemological shift "from subjects to narratives; that is, I did not attempt to *know* fathers but, rather, I attempted to *know something about their narratives*" (225). In this I hear echoes of Sara Ruddick's initial approach via philosophy: an inquiry into not who mothers *are* but how they think about what they do. I also hear a resonance with Ruddick's repeated emphasis on the importance of *stories* in how we experience and think about parenting, as I too have just suggested in my reference to Smiley's parental narrators.

The question returns: is there such a thing as "parental thinking" or must we continue to differentiate "maternal thinking" from "paternal thinking"? I agree with Doucet that saying that men engage in "maternal thinking" doesn't work; it is too fraught with a re-emphasis on the femininity of parental commitments: men do not mother. And while I value recent attention to the importance of *fathers* because I believe that children benefit from the active involvement of caring parents, I do not believe that children require both a mother and a father in order to grow into their full range of capacities, nor that we need to differentiate the contributions and approaches of mothers from those of fathers. I see real value in renewed attention to the importance of fathers—as in the 2012 White House report on "Promoting Responsible Fatherhood" and other initiatives supporting "a positive, ongoing role of the father in the life of his children" (Pruett 4). But to me that value lies in encouraging all parents to invest in the wellbeing of their children rather than in asserting a gender-specific need that can only be met by male parents.

Indeed, I spent thirteen years as a single parent to my two daughters, both of whom have grown into amazing women. In those years, I usually called myself a "single mother" but sometimes, seeking to avoid the stereotype I saw embedded in "mother," I would call myself a "single parent woman." In my memoir of that time in my life, I voice my sense of how I saw myself as a single mother/parent: "independent, self-sustaining, responsible to children and to work, making a family from shared lives, not from assumed roles" (Frye, *Biting the Moon* 6). Non-normative parenting becomes a resistance to gender definitions.

Similarly, I find gender-resistant understandings of parenting in a series of blog posts by gay and lesbian parents who respond to the questions posed to fellow parent-bloggers: "Do you think of yourself as a 'mother'? A 'father'? Something in between? Why?" The questions were posted by a gay stay-at-home parent of a young child. In his own response, he suggests an initial anxiety that perhaps his son needed a "'mother' ... that I'd later find out we had engaged in a horrible experiment" (Josh), an "experiment" he feared might deny his son the necessary nurturance associated with mothering. But rather than wrapping himself in any kind of defensive masculinity, he instead pursued what was available to him: the rich and close association of bodies as he cared for his young son. Like many new mothers, he "had the experience of losing my bodily autonomy and my independent self." But when he is with groups of mothers, he does not feel like a mother any more than he chooses to embrace the notion of "father." He sees these mothers as "performing mommyness instead of just being themselves."

Although he is only one anecdotal example, I hear in his resistance to "mommyness" a quality similar to what Rachel Cusk describes in her mother memoir, *A Life's Work: On Becoming a Mother*, in which she identifies her own sense of alienation from groups of mothers gathered on the playground or in "mommy" activities. In both instances, and in my own experience as a single parent, I recognize a stance of standing apart, resisting the gendered norms of parenting, as well as an active engagement in daily caring for and thinking about young children: parental thinking.

Another blog, this one by a lesbian gestational parent, also repositions parenting in resistance to gender labels: "I like the moniker 'pomo' for myself. It feels like a hybridization of 'papa' and 'mom.' ... And since it's only mine it doesn't come saddled with linguistic baggage that builds constraints and/or expectations into its usage." In her view, "It's not about two men, two women, or a man and a woman; it's about two individual people working together as a team to foster the health and development of a child" (jlg). One gay parent—a friend of mine—suggests that perhaps those of us who resist gender-normative parenting, regardless of sexuality, are "gender outliers." To that I would add, perhaps through parental behaviours that are "gender outlying," we can begin to break down some of the stereotypes that continue to enforce the norms of gendered parenting. According to Dermott, gay fathers—and, I would add, parents in non-normative family situations of many kinds—are "more likely to think critically about the meaning and practice of contemporary fatherhood [parenthood]" (132). In non-normative parenting circumstances, both mothers and fathers may be particularly attuned to the development of parental thinking.

Once, when I was at the playground with this same friend and his young son, he paused and pointed out the sound of the train in the distance. I asked him about this alertness and he told me that his son had very acute hearing and that he had learned from him a new attentiveness to the sounds around him. As parents, attentive to children, I believe we expand our sense of the world through learning to hear with their ears, see with their eyes, sense with their skin. From this alertness, I believe we also develop distinctive strategies for attending to that particular child's needs for preservation, growth, and social acceptability. Though I believe that this capacity is usually differentiated by a parent's gender, I am convinced that this is because we live in a society in which most men are not trained to be alert to children's needs and most women have been taught to expect that they will make the caregiving of children a major part of their lives. These differences become the foundation for parenting that is differentiated by gender.

Ruddick says as much in "The Idea of Fatherhood": "If men now appear to be less effective than women in some aspects of parenting, this is a consequence of different preparation for parenthood. The insufficiencies of male parents are also exaggerated by sentimental, mystifying views of the talents of female parents" (206). But so too with the "*abilities* and 'functions'" ("Idea" 206) male parents are alleged to bring to parenting: provision, protection, and authority. Increasingly, women have developed these qualities in part through their participation in the workplace and in part through a general opening out from feminist change. And they bring these qualities to parenting. They are even, I submit, often ready to encourage children to risk-taking and to the development of independence—tasks generally assigned to fathers.

From these cross-over behaviours, I believe that men and women both are beginning to enrich their capacities for "parental thinking"—thinking that is grounded in the full range of activities required for taking care of children, thinking that attends to bodies, to the need for play and risk-taking, to constantly changing lives as a child grows, and to a child's variable needs for going out into a larger social world. These needs differ by race and class and social communities, just as individual parents differ in their strategies for addressing these needs. But to my mind, these differences are individual differences, not the differences between men and women as categories.

Still, as Sara Ruddick insists, as feminists we must not overlook the ways in which childcare has historically fallen to women or the fact that "parents almost everywhere lead highly gendered lives" ("Idea" 216). Nor should we overlook the urgency of developing what she calls "an *ethics* of sexual difference, an ethics which contests longstanding misogyny and heterosexual bigotry" (218). Furthermore, I believe that we need to take into account the ways in which workplaces act as "gender factories," in Joan Williams' phrase (88), enforcing gender divisions in complex and material ways outside the home, often marked strongly by class and race as well. And we must continue to work for the institutional changes that support parenting: paid parental leave that also takes into account the distinctive requirements of pregnancy, childbirth, and breastfeeding; universal free early childcare; and affordable after-school care for older children. In Ruddick's terms, "We must work to bring a *transformed* maternal thought into the public realm, to make the preservation and growth of *all* children a work of public conscience and legislation" ("Maternal Thinking" 361).

But I do not believe that we can wait until we implement the necessary changes in institutional structures to take on the deeply entrenched gender stereotypes that harm us all. Instead, as with most efforts toward feminist change, I believe we must act simultaneously on many fronts. Central among those efforts is the need to develop the full richness of non-gendered "parental thinking": understanding and incorporating the thinking of many different kinds of parents and embracing the full human complexity of each caregiving parent, regardless of gender. In this commitment, I again join Ruddick in affirming the importance of thought that derives from caregiving and in acknowledging the importance of "an *ethic* of sexual difference." But I choose instead to see a future of *parents* "who live out a transformed [*parental*] thought in communities that share parental care—practically, emotionally, economically, and socially" ("Maternal Thinking" 362).

Transformed parental thinking becomes a significant step toward nourishing all children as it encourages in both men and women the full range of human capacities that we can develop through caring for children: greater empathy, attunement to intersections of self and other, flexibility that attends to changing needs of growing children, responsibility for protection and provision, authority that does not involve dominance or control over, and a richer capacity for both nurturance and play. Through active parental engagement, both men and women, then, participate in breaking down the barriers erected by masculinity and femininity and alert us all to just how fluid and complex our own subjectivity can be.

ENDNOTES

[1] An earlier version of this paper was presented at the Sara Ruddick symposium, MIRCI conference, Toronto, October 2011.

WORKS CITED

Abraham, Eyal, Talma Hendler, Irit Shapira-Lichter, Yaniv Kanat-Maymon, Orna Zagoory-Sharon, and Ruth Friedman. "Father's Brain Is Sensitive to Childcare Experiences." *Proc. Acad. Sci. U.S.A.* 111.27 (2014): 9671-9672. Web. August 2014.

The American Heritage Dictionary of the English Language. Boston: Houghton Mifflin, 2011. Web. 30 Oct. 2014.

Beauvoir, Simone de. *The Second Sex.* New York: Vintage, 1989. Print.

Boylan, Jennifer Finney. *Stuck in the Middle with You: A Memoir of Parenting in Three Genders*. New York: Broadway Books, 2013. Print.

Bronson, Po. "Want to Be a Macho, Macho Man? Be a Daddy." National Public Radio. 22 Jul. 2011. Radio broadcast.

Cusk, Rachel. *A Life's Work: On Becoming a Mother.* New York: Picador, 2001.

Dermott, Esther. *Intimate Fatherhood: A Sociological Analysis.* New York: Routledge, 2008. Print.

Doucet, Andrea. *Do Men Mother? Fathering, Care, and Domestic Responsibility.* Toronto: University of Toronto Press, 2006. Print.

Evans, Elrena and Caroline Grant, eds. *Mama, PhD: Women Write about Motherhood and Academic Life.* New Brunswick, NJ: Rutgers University Press, 2008. Print.

Frye, Joanne S. *Biting the Moon: A Memoir of Feminism and Motherhood.* Syracuse: Syracuse University Press, 2012. Print.

Frye, Joanne S. "Narrating as a Mother: Experience, Cognition, and Narrative Form in Jane Smiley's *Ordinary Love* and *Good Will.*" *Maternal Thinking: Philosophy, Politics, Practice.* Ed. Andrea O'Reilly. Toronto: Demeter Press, 2009. 64-78. Print.

jlg. "you can call me pomo." *Breaking into Blossom.* 11 Apr. 2012. Web. 1 Nov. 2014.

Josh. "Josh's response: am I a 'mother' or a 'father?'" *Regular Midwesterners: Two Perspectives on Gay, Parenting, and Life in the Midwest.* 6 Sept. 2011. Web. 8 Sept. 2011.

Marotte, Mary Ruth, Paige Martin Reynolds, and Ralph James Savarese, eds. *Papa, PhD: Essays on Fatherhood by Men in the Academy.* New Brunswick, NJ: Rutgers University Press, 2010. Print.

Miller, Tina. *Making Sense of Fatherhood: Gender, Caring and Work.* Cambridge: Cambridge University Press, 2011. Print.

Pruett, Kyle D. *Fatherneed: Why Father Care Is as Essential as Mother Care for Your Child.* New York: The Free Press, 2000.

Ruddick, Sara. "The Idea of Fatherhood." *Feminism and Families.* Ed. Hilde Lindemann Nelson. New York: Routledge, 1997. 205-220. Print.

Ruddick, Sara. "Maternal Thinking." *Feminist Studies* 6.2 (1980): 342-67. Print.

Ruddick, Sara. *Maternal Thinking: Toward a Politics of Peace.*

Rev. ed. Boston: Beacon Press, 1995. Print.

Ruddick, Sara. "Thinking Mothers/Conceiving Birth." *Representations of Motherhood*. Eds. Donna Bassin, Margaret Honey, and Meryle Mahrer Kaplan. New Haven: Yale University Press, 1994. 29-45. Print.

Smiley, Jane. *Ordinary Love* and *Good Will*. 1989. New York: Fawcett Columbine, 1992. Print.

Suleiman, Susan Rubin. "Playing and Motherhood; or, How to Get the Most Out of the Avant-Garde." *Representations of Motherhood*. Eds. Donna Bassin, Margaret Honey, and Meryle Mahrer Kaplan. New Haven: Yale University Press, 1994. 272-282. Print.

Tobey, Matthew. "Letter to Dads: Stop Letting Moms Win at Parenting." National Public Radio. 22 Jul. 2011. Radio broadcast.

Williams, Joan. *Reshaping the Work-Family Debate: Why Men and Class Matter*. Cambridge: Harvard University Press, 2010. Print.

2.
Does the Manny Mother?

GARY LEE PELLETIER

THE MANNY AND I

THE FIRST CHILDCARE ADVERTISEMENT that I responded to explicitly called for a "manny." However, due to the keyboard's positioning of the "m" beside the "n," compounded by the reality of a relative lack of men in childcare in North America, I was skeptical as to whether the author of the ad was truly looking to hire a man. Preempting the poster's probable paranoia around gender, I decided to downplay my maleness, just in case, and signed the reply, "Sincerely, an experienced sitter." To my surprise the person who placed the ad—a forty-year-old, professional, single mom living down the street from me in Sunset Park (a neighbourhood in Brooklyn, New York) with her five-year-old son—was indeed in search of a male childcare provider. She told me she had been reading up on "the manny thing" and was attracted to the idea. I got the gig because I was the only male out of a dozen applicants to respond to the ad within the first twenty-four hours of its posting.

In the fall of 2009, this five-year-old Brooklyn boy became my first charge in what would bloom into a fruitful childcare career. A move from New York to Toronto—doubly motivated by my love for a charming Torontonian and my acceptance into a Toronto-based graduate program—would eventually lead to introductions to a slew of families whose children would be placed in my care. Admittedly, I did not become a manny on purpose. Prior to my experience in New York City, I had never cared for, or about, children. Infants and toddlers generally terrified me, I think, because they threatened to expose my own childish, queer, insecure, and sensitive self; I would eventually learn from both the kids in my care, and from theorists like Kathryn Bond Stockton, that children are the queerest of queers out there (*The Queer Child*). My new immigrant status and the limited employment prospects that Canada offers to "international students" were facts of life that led to my dependence on the "under-the-table" manny wage. What I thought would be a one-time job in New York became something of a way of life in Toronto. Wiping bums, washing dishes, doing laundry, and pulling a wagon full of tiny humans to parks throughout Toronto quickly became staples of my employed existence. In the midst of this exhausting job, I struggled to find the time and to summon the energy to be a graduate student.

The manny's genesis and rise to mainstream prominence is wrapped up in a complicated history of masculinities and, as Miriam Forman-Brunell shows in *Babysitter: An American History*, femininities as well. R.W. Connell's classic positing of masculinity as a relational concept is validated throughout popular discourse around the manny, whose masculinity is persistently propagated through its dichotomous relationship to the nanny's femininity. In popular culture, the manny signifies more than "childcare provider" and brings with him credentials that extend well past CPR certification and diaper-changing skills. I witnessed the manny as a trend, a status indicator, a husband/boyfriend/partner replacement, a good male role model, a buddy, a sexy accessory, a jock, a handy man, a chill dude from down the road, and a nanny replacement. Stereotyped and scrutinized, the manny is assumed to be strong and athletic. He is expected to excel in sports and motivate the children in his care to also excel physically. Due to his inherently active body, the manny is presumed to be a good fit for families with young boys. The manny is believed to be exceptional at preserving the child, specifically through physical protection. He is also often assumed to be handy. Just as female childcare providers' supposed inherent abilities to do domestic chores—like laundry and ironing—may be taken advantage of, the manny is at risk of falling prey to stereotypes of his own gender and co-opted into the role of husband/father replacement. When he is not acting as the stand-in husband, he is acting as the rare positive male role model in the child's life and is, therefore, representative of his entire gender. The assumed superior strength of the male physique is a significant part of the childcare transaction, but it is not the only object of consumption: the manny's sexuality is also an integral part of the purchase. His desiring and desired body is fantasized as heterosexual by some and assumed to be gay by others. Male childcare providers' sexualities are active sites of speculation and projection, as can be witnessed in the sexual abuse discourse that engulfs men in North America who care for children.

Holly Peterson's *The Manny* encapsulates the trend well in that the manny's prized physicality and purchased masculinity, rather than his methods of childcare, are the featured subjects of the novel. Identified as a "gutsy heroine" on the cover, the protagonist Jamie Whitfield is a mother in a powerful white family living on "the wealthiest acre of real estate in Manhattan"; she hires a manny to take care of her nine-year-old son. "A status symbol for some mothers is a male nanny who takes boys to batting cages and basketball courts when their fathers can't get away from their high-flying jobs in law or finance," one reviewer of *The Manny* observes (Harayda). The publisher sells the book with this enticing hook: "Will the new manny in [Jamie's] life put the ground back beneath her feet, or sweep her off them?"

A fantasy for caring men is traceable through American television shows and films from the 1980s through to 2000, starting with manny ancestors *Charles in Charge* (1984-1990) and *Who's The Boss* (1984-1992) and followed by *Mr. Belvedere* (1985-1990), *Mr. Mom* (1987), *Three Men and a Baby* (1987), *Kindergarten Cop* (1990), *Mr. Nanny* (1993), and *Mrs. Doubtfire* (1993). From *Charles in Charge* to *Modern Family*'s manny "Andy," what seemingly manifested from a cultural wish for caring men on the screen is now trending off it as well. John Brandon, arguably the trend's poster boy, has been featured in numerous stories about men's growing presence in childcare (Hoffman). Brandon gained international acclaim when he opened his first manny business, NYC Mannies.

> What I have done is put a name to something that has been around for thousands of years. When a man steps

up and becomes a mentor to a child ... he is a manny.
Many mannies work free of charge. They come in forms
of neighbors, cousins, coaches, teachers. But what about
those families who don't know any awesome guys in their
area? What if there were a company that could help you?
(Brandon)

As it happens, there are now myriad companies one can turn to
for help to secure a manny, such as London's My Big Buddy and
its competition Manny Poppins, which "provides experienced,
qualified and completely vetted male nannies to families throughout the UK" (*Manny Poppins*). And Brandon's most recent manny
venture, the New York City-based MyManny, boasts, "Most of our
mannies have college degrees and can tutor an array of subjects.
We also have mannies that teach: musical instruments, languages,
dramatic arts, outdoor activities, and much more!" (*MyManny*).
Although the United States and the United Kingdom are leading
the trend, apparent through their groundbreaking launch of
manny-specific companies, the manny has gained popularity in
the last fifteen years, swimming his way into mainstreams around
the world. I found traces of him in Japan, Australia, Ireland,
Germany, South Korea, China, England, France, Canada, and
the United States in novels, newspapers, magazines, tabloids,
children's books, young-adult books, romance novels, erotica,
pornography, comedy skits, childcare and feminist blogs, online
community forums, film, and television.

My critical interest in the manny was initially spawned by my
anxiety about the heavy acclamation of certain "masculine" components of male childcare practice that reinforce counterproductive
stereotypes in conversations about men and women in childcare. I
was concerned about the ways in which these conversations can sap
the maternal and feminine of some of their real and proven power.
Culturally speaking, comparing the manny to the nanny can be
like comparing masculinity to femininity; it can lead observers to
attribute the manny's childcare capabilities to his maleness while
simultaneously locating shortcomings in the nanny's performance
in her femaleness. The manny is commonly praised at the expense
of female childcare workers and mothers, whose ability to raise

children has been and is—perhaps now more than ever—questioned and challenged (Nathanson and Tuley). Drawing from research on the discursive intersections of men and masculinities, care, popular culture, and feminisms, this chapter facilitates a dialogue between my analysis of the manny and Andrea Doucet's work on primary-caregiving fathers (*Do Men Mother?*; "Taking Off"). I wonder if the manny mothers, while Doucet asks if men mother—questions that led me to consider what defines a maternal lens and query what such a lens is good for. Through an engagement with Sarah Ruddick's theories of maternal practice, I contemplate the capabilities of maternal theory and endorse a maternal lens for viewing male care.

"FORCED TO HIRE A BLOKE"

As Forman-Brunell displays, the gender of female babysitters has been historically vilified, while the manny is touted for his innate ability to raise children in a "masculine" way that hiring parents are citing as uniquely effective. The manny's mainstream progression has not occurred in a vacuum, but rather his profitable migration is largely a result of essentialist and combative discourses around gender. "They are very responsible and not as emotional about things," explains Susan Schindel who, in 2009, was the placement director for the central southern region of a childcare company called AuPairCare, where at the time one out of ten au pairs were male (Rouvalis). Schindel continues, "The female au pairs need to be nurtured and need to feel a part of the family. The male au pairs do their jobs and they take things in stride more" (Rouvalis). A male childcare provider's inherent ability to remain calm and rational in childcare situations is often pitted against a female childcare giver's lack of control over her emotions. This positioning recolours the female childcare worker into the "bitch" or the "ninny," as exemplified in these words from one mom in the United Kingdom: "For parents who may have suffered at the hands of a hormonal female nanny, prone to touchiness, a straightforward chap who takes orders without taking offence could prove to be a breath of fresh air" (Woods). The manny will figure out how to bake a batch of cookies if necessary, but his real value comes in his emotional restraint, which acts as a foil to the "holding" nanny or maternal figure (Ruddick).

Ruddick explains that "holding" involves "negotiating with nature on behalf of love, harassed by daily demands, yet glimpsing larger questions, mothers acquire a fundamental attitude toward the vulnerable, a characterlogical protectiveness" (79). "To hold," she continues, "means to minimize risk and to reconcile differences rather than to sharply accentuate them" (79). Manny discourse regarding overly emotional female childcare providers capitalizes on the ugliness that can result from a holding mother who has lost control. Ruddick acknowledges that "there is no doubt that holding can drive adolescent children crazy. Protectiveness characterized by holding is no one's idea of 'adventure'—a quintessentially mother-free notion" (79). Ruddick is not condoning the behaviour of the holding mother, rather she is providing an explanation of this character's genesis, illuminating how holding mothers are a result of their context.

Clover Stroud, a single mother, hired Giovanni (a model in his teens from Paris) for her three- and six-year-olds. Stroud claims she cannot live without her manny and describes him as her "friend, fashion assistant, IT expert, confidante and life-coach all rolled into one." She also claimed that her first two au pairs, who were both girls, "arrived with well established eating disorders and serious attitude issues." She elaborates:

> Work as an au pair was an easy passport to another world, and neither of the relationships were very satisfactory. And frankly, with three females in the house, my son would have drowned in a sea of hormones. Apart from anything else, living with a female au pair gave me a startling insight into how difficult, irrational and moody women are to live with. Thank goodness I don't have to....What could be nicer than living with a handsome boy who loves your kids, keeps the house tidy, will offer you an insight into the mysteries of the male mind, but who has absolutely no agenda whatsoever, other than to speak fluent English?... Manny or nanny? Girls, it's a no-brainer.

Another manny-hiring mother justifies her choice in an interview on ABC's *Good Morning America*:

> My personal preference is always young, enthusiastic, and energetic, because my daughter, that's what she likes. When it comes to male babysitters or mannies or whatever you want to call 'em. They just try a little harder, it seems, you know, they just make an extra effort to prove that they're awesome. ("'Mannies' On the Rise")

I wonder if the "extra effort" this mother has observed in her manny's work ethic is a result of the pressure of negative societal expectations of men in caring positions. As with the subjects of Andrea Doucet's research on father's mediated public displays of care, I suspect the manny is pressured by public surveillance and scrutiny. Does he feel he must be seen to be working harder than his female childcare-providing peers in order to be trusted and to keep his job ("It's Not Good")? Or is the perceived "extra effort" simply a discursive form of justified sexism against female childcare providers?

Popular discourses pit the adventurous, carefree, and risk-taking masculine manny against the holding maternal and feminine nanny, which in effect ignores the distinct ethos that these caregivers operate within. "Protective mothers often take on themselves the task of holding together relationships—with Father, lover, grandparents, teacher—on which their children depend," and "such holding has its risks," risks that the manny's gender exonerates him from, ironically resulting in the perception of the "risk-taking" male childcare provider (Ruddick 79). The trend is duped by the illusion that the manny's masculinity—as opposed to his greater social agency as a masculine being—is responsible for the "risk-taking" in his childcare practices (Ruddick 79). Therefore, if the manny's predominant characteristics are connected to his masculinity, they are only in so much as they are enabled by the relationship of his particular gender to the society in which he lives, as opposed to the direct effect of any inherent trait.

Furthermore, a manny is often hired to fulfill certain responsibilities that a hiring mother believes she is unable to fulfill as a woman, her husband refuses fulfill, or the lack of a husband or male role model prevents her from fulfilling. Stroud explains:

> Living with Giovanni means that I have all the pleasure of uncomplicated male company, without the angst that I associate with romantic cohabitation. My marriage was exciting and very eventful, but also quite short, as I split from my children's father just after Dolly was born. I maintain a friendship with him, and he is an important and constant part of the children's lives. He is their dad, and I'm not suggesting that a manny can in any way replace him. But at the same time I know that they benefit from having a man about the house as much as I do, and it's only through a process of elimination that I have come to this conclusion.

Summoning the manny as role model can be destructive because it acts as yet another example where men in childcare are considered to be doing something other than or in addition to caring. I have yet to witness an instance in which a family admittedly hires a female childcare provider to act as a good role model for their children. For families hiring mannies, however, such justification is extremely popular. Expanding male performance in the domestic sphere is not an uncommon feminist constructive suggestion. As journalist Charlotte Alter posits, "Maybe the future of feminism is less about women learning how to 'have it all' than about training a generation of men to help us do it." Nevertheless, the male role model discourse is often used as a misogynist and disabling tactic against lesbian, empowered, and/or feminist parents (Epstein, "Our Kids"; "Queer Parenting"; Clarke and Kitzinger). While it is important for children to experientially witness that men are in fact capable of nurturing care, the manny trend is contributing to popular discourses that work to displace female childcare providers and, more broadly, degrade feminine care practices overall. An aerial view of the manny phenomenon depicts a hopeful scene of men joining the ranks of care labour, but upon a grounded analysis it is obvious that the trend is indicative of antiquated yet intact sexist, essentialist, and heteronormative gender ideologies and norms, as opposed to progressive social change.

After Madonna had a falling out with her nanny, she was unable to find a suitable replacement and, as one tabloid put it in 2007, "Madge [was] forced to hire a bloke as baby carer" ("Mad Gets Man Maid"). Another article commented on Britney Spears' supposed manny hire:

> After a female nanny let baby Sean Preston fall on his head from a highchair, and Britney herself nearly took a tumble while carrying him out of a toy store, Spears resorted to strong, stable Perry Taylor, a Naval Academy graduate, to try to redeem herself as a mother. And she wasn't the first to come up with the idea. New York moms, especially those with young boys, have been hiring mannies for years. (Piaza)

Such discourse, regardless of its veracity, accurately reflects the manny's pervasive storyline: mannies are welcome when nannies are not. As women's methods of childcare continue to be scrutinized and deemed inadequate, more men are entering the childcare field. "Move over Mary Poppins," or some variation on that theme, has been repeatedly expressed in articles and news clips featuring the manny. The maleness of the manny, or his "male enrichment," is his major selling point; it's what distinguishes him within the childcare field (Erikson). The effect of this discourse on female childcare providers is socially damaging, not to mention bad for business.

THE MATERNAL LENS

I was initially seduced by the manny because I believed he had the potential to radically change our childcare systems through some sort of contagious presence that would help bridge the stigmatized gap between men and care. I believed the manny was enacting male mothering, a concept I first inhaled from Sarah Ruddick and which seemed quite radical. In *Maternal Thinking: Towards A Politics of Peace*, Ruddick argues children demand preservation, growth, and social acceptability; maternal practice is summoned into fruition to satisfy such demands. Ruddick contends that anyone can be a mother if they answer to the demands of maternal practice (40). I initially set out to prove that the manny engages in maternal practice or, in the words of Patricia Hill Collins, "mother work." Collins uses "mother work"

> to soften the existing dichotomies in feminist theorizing about motherhood that posit rigid distinctions between private and public, family and work, the individual and the collective, identity as individual autonomy and identity growing from the collective self-determination of one's group. (313)

Politically aligned with Collins, Ruddick, and other maternal theorists, I set out to analyze the manny's labour through a maternal lens. Evaluating men's childcare via maternal lenses is both common and contested in motherhood and fatherhood studies. Andrea Doucet's engagement with primary-caregiving fathers has served as a significant contribution to the intersection of gender and care. Her book *Do Men Mother? Fathering, Care, and Domestic Responsibility* is set up as a direct response to Ruddick's scholarship; the project is a thorough analysis of the efficacy of using a maternal lens on primary-caregiving fathers. Doucet identifies Ruddick as the "the most frequently cited proponent of the men and mothering position" and highlights theorists from the last thirty years, such as Diane Ehrensaft, Barbara Risman, Ann Crittenden, Sarah Balffer Hrdy, and Marny Jackson, who have been proponents of the men and mothering research category (9). Doucet also draws from opponents to the male mothering position, consisting of mainstream gender commentators, difference feminists, father's rights activists, and some fatherhood studies theorists.

It is worth noting that male childcare providers are almost entirely absent from the conversations about male care, both within Doucet's project and more generally throughout the literature. This dearth produced some initial ambivalence for me about whether the manny—who engages in paid childcare of someone else's children—could effectively enter these discussions. Perhaps parental status seems to be taken for granted in much of the research around mothering because Ruddick distinguishes between care labour and maternal practice in *Maternal Thinking*. In her defense of the use of the "maternal idiom" as opposed to broader categories of care, Ruddick conveys that despite the advantages of speaking generally of care labour (gender neutral, non-essentialist, and conducive to feminist labour politics), it is too broad a category and therefore blurs important nuances between different labours of caring (46-47). She explains:

> Similarly [to the tight-knit relationship of teaching to caretaking], mothering may be inseparable from, but it is not the same as, homemaking, feeding, teaching and nursing. If we don't distinguish these kinds of work we will not be able to see their differences or specify their connections. (47)

Ruddick offers the example of "patience," which she asserts takes on "distinctive meanings" amongst care workers. Reflecting on my own experience as a manny, I can attest to the distinction between summoning patience for one's charge versus one's own child. Money brings with it a different set of stakes.

Considering Ruddick's definition of maternal practice, the manny engages in various forms of care work under which mother work cannot effectively be grouped. Although I concur that maternal practice has its own particularities and is not adequately represented through the umbrella categorization of "care," I nonetheless agree with Amy Mullin that we should not foreclose maternal practice to paid childcare providers (52). She explains:

> We must recognize that multiple people can be maternal thinkers in response to one child, that these caregivers can stand in complicated relationships of power to one another, and that inauthenticity threatens not only mothers in relation to fathers but also paid caregivers. (52)

Although outside the scope of this article's purview, it is worth acknowledging the large number of transnational nannies who are also mothers to children of their own; therefore, the potential for maternal practice and maternal thinking to comprise these nannies' care labour practices is realistic and should not be dismissed. While *Maternal Thinking* primarily focuses on unpaid maternal practice, Mullin insists that Ruddick's analysis "makes it possible for us to think about the thought, skills, and virtues demanded to care well in other circumstances," such as with multiple and/or paid caregivers like the manny (62).

Whether we liken manny labour to mother work or not, a maternal lens has proved invaluable to my research due to its crucial detections of heteronormative, essentialist, and sexist ideologies within popular discourse of men in childcare. Such characteristics of the manny trend are covert unless observed up close. Although my thinking about whether the manny engages in maternal practice has morphed as I have become more acquainted with him, the significance of the maternal lens in relation to my overall project has not wavered.

Despite Doucet's appreciation of the scholarly contributions of Ruddick, and of others who support the male mother position, and despite her acknowledgement that men "can develop ways of being and thinking that emulate what we consider stereotypical mothering behavior" ("Men and Mothering" 15), she purports that a maternal lens limits our understanding of male caregiving ("Taking Off" 177). Doucet posits that fathers do not mother because the "everyday social worlds," the "embodied experiences of women and men," and the "larger 'gender regime' prevent the 'eliding' of the institutions of motherhood and fatherhood" (*Do Men Mother?* 224). In other words, men are capable of engaging in maternal practice but are socially prevented from doing so (or being regarded as doing so).

I discovered that the manny trend is similarly informed by social forces that keep femininities distinct and at bay. Regardless of what his childcare practices resemble, the manny is regarded as a man whose care methods are a function of his masculinity, and consequently his labour is distanced from mother work and quintessential notions of feminine care. This perception is perhaps exacerbated by one of the popular justifications for hiring a manny: the substitutive qualities he is predicted to bring to families lacking a male presence. Furthermore, the manny's presence is frequently designed as a combative response to the nanny: a change, an alternative, an upgrade, a new trend. There is motivation, therefore, for his methods of care to be perceived in corresponding opposition to the nanny's care and, by extension, feminine and maternal care.

Audre Lorde's conceptualizations of western classic myths of mother-son relationships—"Jocasta/Oedipus, the son who fucks his mother, and Clytemnestra/Orestes, the son who kills his mother"—are particularly apt here (76). As O'Reilly observes:

> These ancient myths are continually retold and reenacted in Western culture and function, in Louis Althusser's terms, as ideological apparatuses that interpolate mothers and sons into specific relationship positions that are most fully dramatized in the narratives of Clytemnestra and Jocasta. The sanction against mother-son closeness and connection is signified and achieved by the incest taboo, while the enforcement of mother-son separation is represented and enforced by the murder of Clytemnestra. Both patriarchal narratives are enacted through the denial and displacement of the maternal presence. (305)

Fuelled by the "denial and displacement of the maternal presence," these narratives are greatly responsible for the "big brother" and "big buddy" discourses of the manny trend, discourses which shield the manny's masculinity from maternal femininity. He is distanced from female childcare providers, such as the feminine nanny and doting mother. The common preference to use the labels of "buddy," "mentor," "big brother," or "coach" rather than "babysitter" or "manny" reveals a wish for manny care to more closely resemble male bonding and male leadership than care work—labour still typically regarded as inherently feminine. This gender dichotomous discourse ultimately inhibits the manny from reaching certain levels of intimacy with his charges.

In addition to Doucet's claim that gendered social realities prevent men from mothering, she suggests that using a maternal lens to regard men obscures and hides other ways of nurturing ("Taking Off" 177). She states:

Rather than comparing fathers to mothers, we require novel ways of listening and theorizing about fathers' approaches to parenting. More effective questions to be grappled with are ones that explore how fathers enact their parental responsibilities and ultimately how they reinvent fathering. (*Do Men Mother?* 225)

Doucet argues that "with regard to the issue of emotional responsibility, a maternal lens misses the ways that fathers promote children's independence and risk taking, while their fun and playfulness, physicality and outdoors approach to caring for young children are viewed only as second best, or invisible ways of caring." And, in terms of community responsibility, Doucet argues that a maternal lens is blind to the "creative ways that fathers are beginning to form parallel networks to those that have traditionally been brought into existence by and for mothers" ("Taking Off" 177). These characteristics of father care that Doucet has observed are almost identical to the "masculine" qualities the manny is praised for exhibiting in his childcare methods:

Along with baking cookies with the children, straightening up the house and helping with homework, male nannies can provide a more adventurous experience for children. While women are more nurturing and protective, men encourage children to push their boundaries, to take risks. And the benefits of male role models extend beyond the playground. While women tend to comfort frustrated children, men usually encourage them to deal with frustration. (Stoddard)

Such tired stereotypes do not come across as particularly revolutionary in either the context of primary-caregiving fathers or the manny. While I concur with Doucet regarding the importance of reinventing fathering, I disagree that taking up male care through a maternal lens is a hindrance to doing so, especially if its use has not been adequately explored.

Furthermore, I question whether the maternal lens can be uninstalled for, as Ruddick reminds us, "We cannot at will transcend a gender division of labor that has shaped our minds and our lives" (41). A maternal lens is a commitment to a historical feminist consciousness. Once we are aware of the gender damage that the institution of motherhood has caused, and continues to inflict through contemporary manifestations like intensive mothering, we cannot unlearn such knowledge. Although a woman is no more "naturally a mother" than a man and no more "obligated" to or capable of maternal work, and despite the reality that "many women now refuse maternal work and many more would do so if they could without penalty," women and mothers are "conceptually and politically linked" because "most of the people who have taken up the work of mothering have had female bodies" (Ruddick 41). The history of motherhood is, therefore, inherently part of the history of women. Abandoning the maternal lens feels like forgetting and burying this history.

Allowing for the space to "reinvent fathering," as advocated through Doucet's ethnographic research, is not antithetical to maternal theory. Like the manny, the fathers Doucet interviewed are susceptible to discourses that exceptionalize men in childcare. Although personal, these narratives are not inherently progressive. A maternal lens does not miss or ignore the specificities of such narratives, nor does it promote them. When operating efficiently, a maternal lens detects oppressive forces like hegemonic masculinity and patriarchal motherhood. Doucet flags the sometimes detrimental impact maternal discourse has on fathers and their methods of care, as exemplified through her discussions of "maternal gatekeeping," as well as how fathers often feel compelled to rigidly fashion their parenting in relation to their children's mothers' care (*Do Men Mother?*). These critiques of the essentialist nature of some maternal theory and maternal lenses are, of course, insightful. However, while Doucet claims that physical, outdoorsy, risk-taking, and independence-promoting fathering styles were too frequently observed in her research to ignore, I contend that such characteristics too closely resemble gender-essentialist stereotypes to ignore and are more evident of the gender confines of these fathers, and consequentially their limited abilities to parent, than they are indicative of the reinvention of fathering.

While I maintain that using a maternal lens does not hide men's ways of caring, I wonder if an obscuring of male characteristics is precisely what is needed to encourage men to adopt other, less gender-obvious childcare methods. Taking a child to the hockey rink *is* "second best" childcare if the experience is void of any sensitive, relational, and nurturing care. The social forces that hinder father work from resembling mother work (or comfortably being called so) are the same social forces that limit fathers and male childcare providers from redefining their methods of care. I believe a maternal lens is essential to making this discovery. Rather than abandoning the maternal lens as a method to promote caring men, I suggest we use it to continue to deconstruct hegemonic gender norms in an attempt to encourage the development of alternative masculine methods of care.

CONCLUSION

Paralleling Doucet's stance on primary-caregiving fathers, I maintain that although men can mother, the manny—given the gendered social restraints embedded in his trend—usually does not. However, such a stance does not preclude the maternal lens, an analytical tool to which I am indebted for helping me to arrive at such a conclusion. Despite my critique of the gender inequalities in popular discourses surrounding men in childcare today, I do not deny that I have benefited from such circumstances. Working as a manny is a job that provides me with an income when I desperately need one. In the words of one manny, "This job gives me a nonthreatening, male role-model high—a high from teaching kids some self-assurance and decency before adolescence comes around to fuck up their heads; from demonstrating that being male doesn't have to mean the same things I thought it did" (Bow). He then cheekily asks: "But is this high good enough to make me turn down some lucrative night-janitor position if one should come up? Ask me when the economy evens out" (Bow).

Like the strapped-for-cash boysitters who flooded the babysitting scene after World War II, the manny has arguably given this "exotic" career a chance because of recent economic hardship (Forman-Brunell). The need for financial stability has sutured the characteristic of temporariness to male childcare, as exemplified by the brief shelf life of the manny, which is bolstered by the mannies as well as their hiring families. One of the mothers I used to work for said she admired the fact that I was doing this kind of work until I would be able to get back on my feet. Mannies seem to be riding this upscale trend and, in some instances, are getting paid more than their nanny counterparts; mannies with engineering degrees are unapologetic about this being a work experience blip on their resume—a random job until they find something more suitable to their education and/or gender. A manny is given temporary clearance to the private realm with the condition he is en route to the public sector.

Ultimately, this project advocates less for the manny and more for maternal theory as an effective mode of critical inquiry. I consider the development of the maternal lens an important feminist function, one the mainstream would be wise to adopt in pursuit of a stronger societal ethic of care. As Ruddick contends:

> Although maternal work can, in principal, be performed by any responsible adult, throughout the world women not only have borne but have also disproportionately cared for children. Since most of the people who have taken up the work of mothering have had female bodies, mothers, taken as a class, have experienced the vulnerabilities and exploitation as well as the pleasures of being female in the ways of their cultures. Although some individual mothers may be men, the practices and cultural representations of mothering are strongly affected by, and often taken to epitomize, prevailing norms of femininity. (41)

Ruddick argues that such a history cannot be transcended, for "in most cultures the womanly and the maternal are conceptually and politically linked" (41). My analysis of the manny justifies why a feminist scrutiny embedded in a maternal lens is necessary. The manny, who initially appeared to me as a mighty harbinger of social progress in the arenas of gender and care, is ultimately exposed as a conduit of sexist discourse.

Initially, I was most concerned with the gendered and sexualized commodification of the male childcare worker and his resulting transformation into a posh trend, which I found resulted in negative consequences for female childcare providers and in a degradation of femininity more broadly. Nonetheless, I discovered men who are passionate about childcare as a career choice and clearly showcase nurturing love and care. Sydne Didier, a mother from Massachusetts who penned an eloquent portrait of her experience with her male babysitter, Trevor, comes immediately to mind. She hired Trevor when he was twelve to help mind her son, who was almost three. When Didier wrote her reflection in 2013, her son was twelve and Trevor was twenty. She describes the strong friendship the two still have, despite Trevor moving away to college and seeing her son less frequently. Now that Trevor is older, she is even more grateful she made the decision to call him over from across the street nine years prior:

> As much as I want Trevor as a playmate for my son, I also want him as an example of how a young man can be kind and capable with children. I have never wanted him to have only female childcare because in so many ways, it perpetuates the mythology that women are inherently more adept at caring for children, and men simply sub when a woman is not available. Not having boys take care of children leads to men like my husband who had never held an infant before our own child, never changed a diaper, never been entrusted to care for a baby, and never been taught how to do so. He learned quickly, is an incredible father, and always hated the refrain that too often greeted him when he was out with our young child. "Giving Mommy a break?" people asked, to which he always wanted to answer, "No! I am parenting my child." But he is aware that there was a steep learning curve for him because of all he missed when he was younger.

Although Didier plays into some essentialist thinking, her account is moving and hopeful.

The film *Mr. Mom* debuted in 1983. Four years later, I was born. *Mr. Mom*, along with *Cinderella* and an animated version of *The*

Little Prince, was a significant part of the rotation of movies I watched as a young child. In addition to operating the VCR, my mother predominantly raised me. My father was giving, but distant. He was the breadwinner while I was growing up, so our relationship was orchestrated by his conventional father role. I am not exactly sure why I enjoyed *Mr. Mom* so much as a child, or why I became a manny, or why I care so much now about those who care. It is likely that my fascination with caring men is a concoction congealed by—exact proportions unknown—my mother's care, my father's care, my sexuality, my parent's relationship, my relationship with my sister, my politics, and the millions of idiosyncrasies that coloured my experiences growing up. As I continue to grow sideways, filling out my boundless queerness, my theoretical hard-on for caring men stands stronger than ever.

WORKS CITED

Alter, Charlotte. "No, Girls Are Not Natural Babysitters." *The Wall Street Journal*. 10 May 2013. Web. 5 Oct. 2014.

Bow, Dave. "I'm a Male Daycare Worker: Tales of Straight White Male Caregiver Who Is (Surprise!) Not a Pervert." *The Portland Mercury*. 15 Sept. 2011. Web. 1 Feb. 2013.

Brandon, John. "Why Mannies Matter." *Mommybites*. 25 Feb. 2015. Web. 29 Feb. 2015.

Clarke, V. and C. Kitzinger. "'We're Not Living on Planet Lesbian': Constructions of Male Role Models in Debates about Lesbian Families." *Sexualities* 8.2 (2005): 137-152. Print.

Collins, Patricia Hill. "Shifting the Center: Race, Class, and Feminist Theorizing about Motherhood." *Mothering, Ideology, Experience, and Agency*. Eds. Evelyn Nakano Glenn et al. New York: Routledge, 1994. 45-66. Print.

Connell, R. W. *Masculinities*. 2nd ed. Berkeley: University of California Press, 2005. Print.

Didier, Sydne. "Why I Hired a Male Babysitter for My Son." *Role Reboot*. 3 Jul. 2013. Web. 10 Jan. 2014.

Doucet, Andrea. *Do Men Mother? Fathering, Care, and Domestic Responsibility*. Toronto: University of Toronto Press, 2006. Print.

Doucet, Andrea. "'It's not good for a man to be interested in other people's children': Fathers and Public Displays of Care." *Displaying Family: New Theoretical Directions in Family and Intimate Life*. Eds. Esther Dermott and Julie Seymour. London: Palgrave MacMillan, 2011. 81-101. Print.

Doucet, Andrea. "Men and Mothering." Father Involvement Research Alliance Conference. 2008. Web. 16 Aug. 2015

Doucet, Andrea. "Taking Off the Maternal Lens: Engaging with Sarah Ruddick on Men and Mothering" *Motherhood at the 21st Century: Policy, Experience, Identity, Agency*. Ed. Andrea O'Reilly. Newcastle upon Tyne, UK: Cambridge Scholars Press, 2010. 170-180. Print.

Epstein, Rachel. "Our Kids in the Hall: Lesbian Families Negotiate the Public School System." *Mother Outlaws: Theories and Practices of Empowered Mothering*. Ed. Andrea O'Reilly. Toronto: Women's Press, 2004. 131-144. Print.

Epstein, Rachel. "Queer Parenting in the New Millennium: Resisting Normal." *Twenty-first Century Motherhood Experience, Identity, Policy, Agency*. Ed. Andrea O'Reilly. New York: Columbia University Press, 2010. 90-104. Print.

Erikson, Chris. "Yes, Sir, that's My Manny!" *New York Post*. 14 Jun. 2011. Web. 17 Mar. 2012.

Forman-Brunell, Miriam. *Babysitter: An American History*. New York: New York University Press, 2009. Print.

Harayda, Janice. "Review of Holly Peterson's 'The Manny': The Worst Sex Scenes Ever Published in a Novel Excerpted by Newsweek?" *One-Minute Book Reviews*. Word Press, 26 Jun. 2007. Web. 11 Nov. 2013.

Hoffman, Meredith. "Male Nanny Agency Gains Global Fame." *DNAinfo New York*. 25 Jul. 2013. Web. 27 Apr. 2014.

Lorde, Audre. "Man Child: A Black Lesbian Feminist's Response." *Sister Outsider: Essays and Speeches by Audre Lorde*. Berkeley: Crossing Press, 2007. 72-80. Print.

"Mad Gets Man Maid." *Mirror.co.uk*. Mirror Online, 28 Apr. 2007. Web. 27 Apr. 2013.

"'Mannies' on the Rise in New Trends for Child Care." *Good Morning America*. ABC News, 30 Nov. 2013. Web. 15 Dec. 2014.

Manny Poppins. 2008. Web. 5 Jan. 2015.

Mullin, Amy. "Paid Childcare: Responsibility and Trust." *Maternal Thinking: Philosophy, Politics, Practice.* Ed. Andrea O'Reilly. Toronto: Demeter Press, 2009. 52-63. Print.

My Big Buddy. 2014. Web. 2 Jan. 2015.

MyManny. 2013. Web. 10 Dec. 2014.

Nathanson, Jessica, and Laura Camille Tuley, eds. *Mother Knows Best: Talking Back to the "Experts."* Toronto: Demeter, 2009. Print.

O'Reilly, Andrea. "In Black and White: African-American and Anglo-American Feminist Perspectives on Mothers and Sons." *Mother Outlaws: Theories and Practices of Empowered Mothering.* Toronto: Women's Press, 2004. 305-327. Print.

Peterson, Holly. *The Manny.* New York: The Dial Press, 2007. Print.

Piaza, Jo. "IT'S JERRY POPPINS! He's Sweet, He's Sensitive, and He Loves Your Kids. For New Yorkers, the Manny Is a Must." *New York Daily News.* 8 Jun. 2006. Web. 10 Dec. 2012.

Rouvalis, Cristina. "The Manny: Czech Au Pair Puts New Face on Child Care as a Male Nanny." *Lifestyle.* Post-Gazette, 9 May 2002. Web. 13 Sept. 2013.

Ruddick, Sarah. *Maternal Thinking: Toward a Politics of Peace.* New York: Ballantine Books, 1989. Print.

Stockton, Kathryn Bond. *The Queer Child: Or Growing Sideways In the Twentieth Century.* Durham, NC: Duke University Press, 2009. Print.

Stoddard, Teri. "Gender Equality: Men in Child Care, the Last Frontier?" *TheExaminer.com.* 24 Feb. 2010. Web. 10 Mar. 2011.

Stroud, Clover. "Why I Love Male Nannys." *Mail Online.* The Daily Mail, 12 Feb. 2007. Web. 5 Jan. 2015.

Woods, Judith. "How I Met the Manny of My Dreams." *The Telegraph.* 5 Jun. 2008. Web. 4 May 2013.

3.
"Is He the Son of No One?"

A Son's Relational Narrative on His Mother

NICK J. MULÉ

THIS CHAPTER FOCUSES on the ongoing complex relationship between an immigrant, Italian-Canadian woman and I, her queer, pro-feminist son.[1] The parallel trajectory of our lives is explored in narrative form from the perspective of a caring and sensitive son who has at once come to recognize my mother as a heroine, indeed one of the greatest influences of my life, yet also a woman with many limitations and whom I had to adapt to learning and unlearning from. This iteration of my relationship with my mother is consciously temporal in its reflexive process in that I am very cognizant of the shifting roles each of us have played throughout our relational lives, shifts partly based on age and maturation, partly based on the fluidity of social positionality. The importance, special status, and intensity of a relationship between a mother and child have long been known, yet rarely are such relationships, especially between mothers and sons, delved into. What little attention the literature does give to the mother-son relationship tends to be from the perspective of the mother.

This chapter reverses the focus to that of my relational experiences with my mother, recognizing all the limitations that memory, emotions, character, and bias bring to it. This reversal serves to provide a subjective and discursive perspective, offering insight to the literature on feminism, mothering, masculinities, gender, and queer studies. Importantly, I encourage sons to think about, reflect upon, and possibly positively influence their own relationships with their mothers. I urge that the importance of the mother-son relationship be two directional.

What I hope to impart in this chapter are a set of inevitable temporalities between my mother and I, merely one of countless mother-son relationships, yet one that demonstrates the vast plains she and I have covered and that still remain between us. In keeping with the permitted space, I have structured this chapter by means of a series of vignettes drawn from memories that have seared themselves into my conscience—sometimes with meaningful significance, other times mysteriously in absence of great importance, yet with a poignancy that can only be parsed with subsequent and reflexive analysis. These memories are linked to themes that underscore the dynamics of the relationship between my mother and me, themes that brought lessons for us both to learn, themes and lessons open to all for the learning. This relationship is further specified by the unique experiences of an immigrant mother and her queer-identified son—from the perspective of the latter—that I hope will provide insights into the challenges of growth and love in the sustenance of meaningful bonds.

I was motivated to write this chapter as, increasingly, I have been giving thought to the incredible complexity of my relationship with my mother, which the literature on mothering and feminist thought, through its various transitions, has not fully captured. Herein, I provide insights into a lived, relational experience that is ongoing. This is a relationship in which I experience admiration, respect, love, honour, humour, shock, anger, frustration, and disappointment towards the woman who is greatly influential for me. I have come to learn to be grateful for all of these experiences, as my life lessons would be diminished in the absence of any one of them. On the subject of diminishment, in no way do I intend to diminish my mother by writing this from my perspective only, as my intention is to redress a spectrum-gap in the literature. Similarly, given the focus of this anthology, in no way do I intend to diminish my father, a man I love and respect deeply and who can rouse the same aforementioned experiences yet in different ways and who too, as a result, has provided me with invaluable life lessons.

Apart from personal motivation, I write from an interest in offering a tempered approach in which theory and unique, real-life experiences need to be balanced. I exercise such tempering regularly when I wear my psychotherapist's hat, lest I be accused of "analyzing everything." Admittedly, this is an academic chapter written wearing my academic hat—but not entirely. My subjective perspective at the core of this iteration of my relationship with my mother provides both the foundational narrative and acts as a counterbalance to theory itself. The point here is that we can turn to theory to help guide us in our understanding of complex experiences and relations, but we need not over-theorize them either, lest the accusation of "theorizing everything."

OUR BACKGROUNDS:
INTERSECTIONS, PARALLELS, AND DIVISIONS

This narrative is contextualized via my mother's historical background: she was raised in a large family in a small, Sicilian town, had limited formal education, and had a desire to escape by immigrating to Canada, where she married my father (also an Italian-Canadian immigrant). They in turn provided my background as a second-generation Italian-Canadian raised in a blue-collar, mid-size city with three straight, male siblings. Yet, in the centre of this testosterone-driven household, my mother—despite her petite stature—stood like a towering figure of impassioned, Sicilian, feminine strength that you would dare not cross.

As Liamputtong has highlighted, mothers such as mine were disenfranchised twice, on the one hand for being female in a highly patriarchal society, and on the other for being a migrant who immigrated to Canada with very limited education, next to no formal work experience outside of domesticity, and very little knowledge of the English language (198-199). Despite these limitations, during her first few years in Canada, my mother made a series of conscious decisions as the sole migrant of her family of kin. Although she worked with a sister-in-law at a jam factory for eight months, she left that job, opting instead to devote herself to motherhood and domesticity, a decision mutually agreed upon by my parents and partially influenced by their respective gendered and cultural expectations and partially by the fairly secure labour job my father held in a steel factory, which afforded them a good income with corresponding benefits.

REFLEXIVE NARRATIVE THEMES:
CULTURE/RACE AND ETHNICITY

Without the presence of kin from her family of origin, my mother needed and contributed to a new family in her new land (my father's side, involving three of his siblings, all brothers, two of whom had immigrated to Canada years earlier, and their Canadian-born wives). Another conscious decision my mother made was to try to learn the English language, which she did through a brief stint in an English course, ongoing communications with her sisters-in-law, and, importantly, via radio and then television. This is noteworthy, as my mother to this day stands out as one of the few of the immigrated family members to commit herself to learning the language, albeit a broken English, despite for the most part not working outside the home. Temporally, all of my siblings and I were initially raised in a household in which the Sicilian dialect of Italian was spoken first and English, broken at best, was secondary. This order of language preference would eventually reverse itself based on the influence of my siblings' and my education, yet all of us to this day speak part English and part Sicilian dialect when communicating with our parents.

Learning the language was a formidable task that contributed to the social construction of my mother becoming an Italo-Canadian. Yet she retained Italian cultural values, such as the importance of family and food. Regarding the former, my mother holds family—especially extended family—to a high level of respect. Paradoxically, this lends itself to endless gossiping and strategizing between my parents on how best to relate to their respective siblings. As for the latter, my mother fully embraces the multiple values Italian culture places in food, such as nutrition, health, nurturance, a nucleus for social gathering, and relationship-building. The importance of food is pronounced by her being an amazing cook, impressing all who are fortunate enough to taste her food. Being a great cook has become part of her identity to the point that she will deliberately cook in abundance to ensure care packages for all following each holiday gathering.

Although lessons have been learned from these values, they have also contributed to growing tensions experienced by me and my siblings. We questioned, particularly at moments of family strife, family being seen as first and foremost in Italian cultural social relations, with an underlying distrust of those outside family. If anything, my siblings and I have had to teach the value of friendships to my parents. In particular, my experience as a queer person who is not fully supported by family and has racialized friends challenged my mother's socialized racism. The heavy importance placed on meals can negatively impact people's personal diets (she loves to fatten people up), relational manners (her persistent pushing of food on people), major time investment (elaborate meals can throw off schedules at time-sensitive social events), and sharing of duties (her difficulty in reducing, let alone relinquishing, this role as she ages).

Immigrants often attempt to straddle two lands, that of the "old country" and that of the new. Like most immigrants who obtain citizenship status and settle into the "new country," my parents retained a knowledge base premised on their respective memories of Italy as it was when they left. My parents took my younger sibling and me on a trip to Italy, which was also my father's return thirty-one years after immigration and my mother's return twenty-four years after immigration. It was on this trip that I came to appreciate a new side of my mother, as I learned of her place and family of origin, in essence her history (this in addition to an amazing two-week tour of Italy and meeting many aunts, uncles, and cousins for the first time). At the time, I was among the youngest of four generations on my mother's side, which included a great grandmother, grandmother, and mother. I came to revere the strength of these women, yet also witnessed the tensions among them.

I now recognize how such tensions become repeated patterns through familial generations, particularly when some of us personify strength that can easily lead to controlling behaviour. It was also here that I could see how much my mother had become a North Americanized-Italo-Canadian, from playing the interpreter for me and my sibling to her stylish presentation, for which she was exoticized in this small Italian town. On an emotional level, I witnessed and learned the importance of memory and reconnection in a pathos-infused image of my mother and her older and closest sister. They were at the latter's cottage, laughing and crying together over their past memories while making fresh pasta, and I repeatedly brought toilet paper, in place of unavailable tissues, for them to wipe their tears.

FEMINISM, GENDER EXPECTATIONS, AND MALE CAREGIVING

Rich (qtd. in Liamputtong 195) offers two meanings for motherhood: women's potential to bear and rear children, and motherhood as an institution with prescriptions and conditions on how women experience the former. Feminism has challenged the institution of motherhood, as opposed to mothers and mothering. Richardson (cited in Liamputtong 195) points to the role of motherhood as a site of "power, creativity and insight." Theoretically, motherhood has been critiqued as culturally constructed (Butler, *Gender Trouble* 136; *Bodies that Matter* 3, 15) and further critiqued for not adequately acknowledging the embodied value of mothering (Hughes and Witz 56). This latter perspective sums up my mother's feminist sensibilities as a woman who is unapologetic regarding her choice to make motherhood and mothering a primary focus of her life. Although she did not have access to an education that could lead to a career, she takes her role as a mother and wife seriously, as defining her occupation and her identity. Most noteworthy is the internal importance my mother imparts to motherhood, an innate sense of who she is and to whom she is unquestionably devoted, which is very much informed by her cultural, generational experiences and socialization in the absence of formal education.

My mother, who is minimally educated, has very low literacy skills, and does not engage in activism, has committed herself to being a wife and mother with domestic responsibilities, yet as a woman she clearly stands her ground in our male-dominated society. My mother embodies what Ruddick calls "works of preservative love, nurturance, and training" (17). Her strong commitment to such values of motherhood could seemingly contrast greatly with her strong and paradoxical personality. She has a tough exterior that does not suffer fools gladly but a sensitive interior with strong intuition and feelings easily hurt.

She is highly task oriented, confident, and impatient, with a fiery temper that is easily ignited. She has a sarcastic sense of humour with a sharp and cutting tongue, sometimes venturing into the ribald. She has a piercing, loud voice in the midst of her anger, which contributes to escalating matters, and a distinctive laugh that is infectious and furthers the hilarity in comical situations. In many ways these paradoxes epitomize the "double voice" of many mothers, premised on the culturally constructed and the maternally embodied woman, is subject/object, passive/active, and resistant/conforming positions (Kruk 35-36). Through her personality, these are the ways that my mother staked out her stance as a stealth feminist and embodied mother.

It was in my mother's interactions with others that through my childhood eyes I could see what I now understand to be her feminist leanings and steadfast stances. With my father working outside the home, often doing shift work, my mother became the point person dealing with servicemen who would visit for repairs, and she would directly involve herself in such "male tasks" as understanding the issues and costs involved in matters like TV repairs and dealing with a malfunctioning furnace. This was always done in a polite and respectful manner, but no less a manner that let it be known that because she was female did not reduce her responsibility regarding such "male tasks."

More pointed is witnessing my mother's interactions with my aunts, who varied in their sense of self-agency in relation to their respective marriages to my uncles. My mother always confidently takes the position of the empowered woman in the world she occupies as wife, mother, sister, sister-in-law, and aunt, challenging others who are quick to acquiesce to male dominance, encouraging an equal and equitable team-like part- nership (the kind she and my father have), and making it clear she would not tolerate anything less. She also does this with her female friends and neighbours. I have also witnessed my mother being empowered by some of these same women over the years as a means of mutual support towards living more self-fulfilling lives. My mother, now a grandmother of five, three of whom are granddaughters, carries forward this feminist perspective and support to the next generation.

What is telling about the kind of stealth feminist life my mother is living is that in her social circle of women for which motherhood and domesticity are primary, a micro level of feminist sensibilities are taken up, embodied, and lived. This may be far removed from the mezzo and macro level of feminist activism that became prominent during her lifetime, but its effects were felt, absorbed, and integrated in my mother's growth and development. The feminist knowledge exchange between my mother and the women in her life happens in the sidewalk and over-the-fence conversations with neighbours, kitchen talks with her sister and sisters-in-law, and sometimes spirited dining room discussions with my uncles. These dialogues paralleled news stories regarding the advancement of women's liberation and facilitated my mother's growth, including being initially challenged and, in turn, her challenging of others.

Although Berridge and Romich focus on boys' household work from the perspective of single-mother households, their findings point to a de-gendering of household tasks, albeit a de-gendering that remains based on traditional family values of raising such boys to be "good husbands" (158). My experience, in which my parents demonstrated team effort in carrying out household work, was no less delineated by gender lines, yet was somewhat complicated by my mother being the only female in the household. Based on my personal interests and my sequential positioning in the family (I am the third child four years apart from both my closest older sibling and my younger sibling; my older siblings are two years apart), my father would often draw upon my older brothers for "male-oriented" household assistance, such as grass cutting, car washing, and do-it-yourself renovations. For a number of years I was deemed too young; during this time I demonstrated a propensity towards indoor domestic household chores—such as food preparation, baking cookies, drying dishes and putting them away, dusting, cleaning, and preparing snacks for guests—by watching and emulating my mother. Although my older siblings and I all contributed to sibling care by order of our positioning, I soon became the one my parents could rely on to carry out what would be stereotypically deemed feminized domestic household chores. This would sometimes create resentment between me and my siblings, with mutual feelings that the other was not pulling their weight in the chores that we were expected to do.

This form of socialization has primed me well for the independent life I lead, a life in which I am responsible for all household tasks of living in a condominium setting and for which indoor domestic chores are primary. Yet, to this day, my mother will state sympathetically that my lifestyle has me charged with the duties of both a man and a woman, to which I respond in my non-gendered sense of independence that these are the duties of a household.

As O'Reilly ("A Mom and Her Son" 190), a Canadian feminist scholar, discovered in her relationship with her son, I too have discovered in my relationship with my mother that gender can indeed be fluid. Similarly, an African-centred feminist approach (Lawson Bush 388-389) also emphasizes the importance of blurring the gender lines. I learned this early on when my siblings and I half-joked that the true powerhouse in our household (back when we were all living there) was my mother, and this is still the case today. In such a testosterone-fuelled setting, she has consistently and unwaveringly staked out her place as a power to be reckoned with and one not easily crossed. Ironically, I continue to cross her on her rigid views of gender and gender expectations, yet not surprisingly I am the only son (the queer one) that does so. To further the irony, I see my mother with all her paradoxes as a pillar of strength, even if somewhat flawed, that I admire and have aspired to.

Yet my mother herself has learned of the fluidity of gender, particularly how it is performed (Butler, *Gender Trouble*) through nurturance, via her two younger sons. Both my older brothers followed the traditional masculine route of working in the same industrial factory my father had, whereas I went into the female-dominated field of social work and my younger brother went not just into teaching but teaching at the primary level, making him highly sought-after. My mother has come to see that my younger brother and I engage in much nurturance in our respective professional careers. Social workers are charged with providing nurturance (Myers 42) to service recipients who present with an array of human suffering. Teachers nurture interest, knowledge, and growth in their students (Anderson 70). My younger brother extended such skills towards his own children, as do I in all aspects of my multi-varied work (teaching, research, psychotherapy, community development, and activism). This has taught my mother that nurturing is not essentially maternal or feminine (Ruddick 40). She has come to see through the work and lives of her two younger sons a kind of male caregiving that is not only possible but is also a positive contribution both personally and societally.

CLASS MOBILITY AND EDUCATION

At the time of my birth, my parents had moved into middle-class status, with a nice, modest home in a good, quiet neighbourhood, clothes on our backs, plenty of food, and a car in the garage. As both of my parents were raised during the depression and wartime era (my father's upbringing was an impoverished one), they have always been economically focused, with a tight grip on money. This issue came to a head for me when, in my teens, I came into direct conflict with most of my family, immediate and extended, regarding my desire to attain a higher education. Despite my family's middle-class status, the blue-collar, labour-based ideology reigned supreme. They could not understand why I would forego an opportunity to work full-time at the steel company where my father worked for a decent wage and good benefits in favour of an expensive education that would only produce a career that potentially paid less. My arguments—personal interest, contributing to society, and that money was not a high priority—fell on deaf ears. Yet my mother slowly came around and began to support me, a difficult task in direct opposition to other family members and even while postsecondary education was completely foreign to her. Through her support she brought others around. This has meant a lot to me.

Nevertheless, my return home post-master's degree, following two years (sans the summer in between) of living in residence in New York City, was a particularly conflicted one for me. For my parents, this involved having an adult son move back into the household while I tried to become financially independent (getting my first full-time social work job, paying off my school debts, and saving for independence). Although I represented the first wave of graduates moving back in with parents, at the time my parents took solace in reasons having to do with my expensive education outside the country and my need to resettle. For me, it was like returning to a sheltered existence, coming from New York City where I blossomed intellectually, physically, socially, and sexually. It meant living a closeted existence under my parents' rules based on their traditional, closed-minded values and incessant worrying. Despite my physical reconnection, a disconnection became increasingly apparent as I challenged many of their views through my social work education. My mother once frustratingly declared, "I swear, the more you're educated, the stupider you're becoming."

All the same, growth and progress are not necessarily linear. On one of my home visits from New York University in the midst of my graduate studies, while we were drying the dishes, my mother raised the issues of my change in class status via the master's level education I was receiving and the new people I was meeting. She recognized that I was maturing, disconnecting somewhat, and becoming my own person. Interestingly, I recognized that as I continued to grow with my career and further studies at the doctoral level, my mother changed, oftentimes mimicking my matured, logical, methodical, and sensitive ways of addressing matters when relating to me. This is an example of growth undertaken on both our parts.

Many of the tensions between my mother and I are co-constructed (Schwartzman 232) in that we feed off each other's mutual generosity, a generosity that simultaneously offends, given our differing educational, cultural, and class perspectives. An example of this is my mother's attempt at soothing social issues each of us may be facing with what I consider simplistic explanations rife with stereotypes, and to which I counter with what she must consider complicated descriptions that dispel stereotypes producing endless potentialities. Both of these responses are difficult for respective recipients to receive but, ironically, I am left feeling somewhat assured: whatever social issue we are discussing will find its way and she will have learned a broader perspective not previously considered.

NICK J. MULÉ

HETERONORMATIVITY AND THE GAY-QUEER SON

My coming out as gay proved to be a major rupture in my family relations, particularly with my parents. It resulted in trust being shaken between the three of us and definitely between me and my mother, a form of trust-breakdown Miller and Boon found in one fifth of their study participants (56). My mother's initial reaction to the news had an indelible effect on our relations that triggered a period of anger and non-communication, followed by tentative communication before renegotiation of the relationship and a slow return to rebuilding trust between us. During the difficult coming-out period, I was grateful for my parents' weak ties to the Catholic Church. They were far more concerned about their own discomfort with the notion that one of their sons has same-sex desires, and, importantly, what the family and neighbours would say, than how the Catholic Church would view me. My parents had enough knowledge to recognize being gay (which is how I identified then) as a sexual orientation but urged that I remain closeted so that family, friends, and neighbours would not find out. As an activist committed to effecting change, I refused to repress a natural part of myself. This has taken some time to deal with and my parents to this day are uncomfortable with any public exposure I get as a queer (how I currently identify myself) activist.

In its own strange and perverse way, it was my parents' concern about anticipated suffering on my part in a heterosexist world (as if I had not already experienced this and what drove my counteraction by coming out) that in time softened their stance. At the point in their transition towards renegotiating our rela-tionship, my mother said to one of my sisters-in-law, "È il figlio di nessuno?" which translates as "Is he the son of no one?" The thought of completely casting out a son was even too painful for her, a disavowal of her motherly "instincts." This utterance is also highly symbolic of a shift from offense, anger, and rejection to one of recognition that my sexuality, although an important part of me, is but one part of me. My parents came to realize that losing a son over one aspect of his being is extremely problematic and would be a severe affront to the high premium placed on the value of family in the Italian culture. Therefore, the rejection of my being gay was replaced with the renegotiated relationship and re-established family ties, ironically without straying from heteronormative assumptions—a set of conditions from which my parents could undertake a form of acceptance (Bertone and Franchi 72). I made a determination in the midst of this crisis that I could either laugh or cry and decided that enough tears were shed up to that point in my life, being socialized in a society that was either outright hostile or ignorant, that I would instead laugh at the ludicrousness of closed mindedness and place my confidence in the passage of time to heal while demonstrating that my life need not be one of suffering for being gay.

Although my mother shows subtle signs of progress (my father is far more difficult to assess, based on his silence regarding the issue), such as wincing less and not abruptly becoming defensive on the topic of LGBTQs, she nevertheless maintains a resolute disagreement and rejection, as if to hang onto a traditional stance that she is not willing to give up. Even when considering positive themes, such as positive emotions, activism, personal growth, social connection, and closer relationships (Gonzalez et al. 333), my mother has only shown signs of progress in the latter three of these themes at a very micro and non-public way. As people who identify as LGBTQs are increasingly represented in popular culture and accepted by society, my mother has developed a better understanding, although she is still far from acceptance.

(DIS)CONNECTION: DISTANCED/INTIMATE COMMUNICATIONS

Just as it has been noted that mother-daughter relationships are characterized as fluctuations involving separation and connection (Gerber 10), such characterizations also apply to mother-son relationships, particularly those of the kind I have with my mother. It is a process that I believe any mother-child relationship endures, as on the one hand there is a desire to maintain a degree of symbiotic connection (Benjamin 18) yet on the other a desire to pursue separation in order to permit personal growth (Silverstein and Rashbaum 150). The latter is essential, as it would not be in anyone's interest to simply replicate their mother. Rothman emphasizes the importance of parenting, whether mothering or fathering, yet critiques the differences therein due to the patriarchal society in which we live (143). It has been argued that feminism has failed the mother-son relationship (Smith), yet O'Reilly has questioned (*Mother Outlaws*) and challenged this (*Maternal Theory*; "A Mom and Her Son") from an empowerment perspective that can positively influence the growth and development of the son. Hirsch, based on the study of works by African-American writers, furthers the concept of a "double voice" to the positioning as subject/object, passive/active, and resistant/conforming (57). My mother and I have taken up such positioning, both independently and in relation to each other. Relational closeness has been theorized to include both developmental and interactional involvement with the parties in question (Fehr 280), or premised on what Prager notes as intimacy (230). Within such relations are critical incidents which can shape, shift, and define relationships, incidents that Morman and Whitely identified in their study with mothers (31-34) and sons unrelated to each other (28-31), critical incidents that I can relate to in terms of both sets of participants. Such incidents, in essence, created the subheadings of this chapter: the personal closeness that was developed through social support (my learning of my mother's history during the important trip to Italy, my mother's eventual support of my decision to further my education in an unsupportive familial environment, my teaching her how to drive); physical distance (my moving away to pursue graduate studies, my moving out of the city to pursue my career aspirations); maturing of a son (which for me happened in my post-secondary years of study and the launching into my career); conflict (my coming out); and family crises (marital breakdowns among my siblings). All of these critical incidents represent crucial and influential experiences in the development of my relationship with my mother and were exacerbated by my choice to live independently—hence my not having a partner to turn to for emotional support yet being cognizant not to burden or overwhelm my mother with my needs.

Yet disconnection is intricately woven with maintaining connection/closeness. This is recognition of a fundamental difference between us as independent beings, despite my being an outgrowth of her existence, made possible by life experiences:

> The mother-son relationship is subsumed within a dialectic in which the mother's directness of expression may generate distance in the son. Dialectic here refers to an ever-present tension within a process that is a pull by opposing tendencies in contradictory directions. (Schwartzman 227)

Dialectical past and continuing challenges between us mutually push our boundaries, at times creating difficult tensions, and force us to stretch, yet ultimately feed our development. Such tensions can involve the theme of disappointment felt and experienced dialectically: "In the co-construction of the mother-child relationship, issues of attachment, separation, and autonomy that emerge in early childhood may continue or be revived at crucial times in adulthood" (Schwartzman 227). An interesting temporal contrast is my disappointment in my mother's absence at small experiences (but meaningful to me at the time) during my early childhood, such as picking me up after school or attending my field trips as a parental assistant. She was restricted at the time due to having to care for my younger infant sibling. More recently, she expressed disappointment for not being able to be there for me during recent hospitalizations I experienced. I discouraged her company, given the difficulty she would have travelling in and out of the city in which I reside. Both of these events address the further theme of independence; as a young child I needed to learn that life sometimes needs to be lived on one's own, and as an adult my mother needed to learn that sometimes we simply live our lives on our own.

The strong influence mothers exert in the lives of their sons calls for us to better understand the ways in which mothers and sons relate, provide support to each other, and negotiate closeness (Morman and Whitely 36), for the impact of these relationships is not only felt between us as sons and mothers but by all those who share space in the familial/social relational circle. To this end, I am cognizant of the difference I represent among my siblings and the need to maintain relations with my mother for both our sakes. Of her four sons, I am the one who identifies as queer, has gone furthest in education, lives independently, and is geographically most distanced. Due to the demands of my career, my visits home are reduced to the major holidays and odd visits, if that.

Yet my mother and I have supplemented this scenario with our Sunday-night phone calls. Each week we make a point of being in touch and providing each other with updates on our respective lives and the lives of my siblings, their families, and other relatives and friends. We discuss news items, store sales, and timely issues of relevance. Some of these conversations are lengthy and meaty, with involved discussion, challenging of perspectives, and some tension. Other conversations are short and merely a check-in. These weekly discussions, taking place for over two decades of my living independently, are a form of communication that keeps us connected with the goal of sustaining intimate relations. This serves to redress the geographical distance between us, regardless of whether distancing is experienced in the context of the discussions we have.

REFLEXIVE DISCOURSES

When a son takes up the values his mother embodies, as I have, it creates a "mothering son" (Kruk 43), one who projects preservational love, nurturance, and training towards others, disrupting "gender scripts" while furthering fluidity between the genders and, importantly, values the mother stands for. On my part, this requires a form of resistance against the social pressures of what is expected of the North American man, just as my mother resisted the cultural constructivist critique placed on her (and all mothers) in embracing her maternal role. Therefore, an underlying strength that has developed in our relationship is a form of reciprocal alliance (Kruk 43); I have learned from, respect and carry forward in my behaviours, and will hopefully pass on to the future generation, values my mother has embodied. As a childless person, I do so in all aspects of my work. Simultaneously, she has witnessed and learned from the possibility that an opposite-sex offspring she produced is capable of replicating such values in respect to her and for the benefit of society.

Yet I am fully cognizant of the fact that I would not have arrived here if it were not for my mother's hope to raise relational sons.

My evolving relationship with my mother is one that involves connection, disconnection, and new connection (Dooley and Fedele 185-187). From a macro perspective, I can say my relationship with my mother has ebbed and flowed in this sequential order. At a more micro level in which I take into consideration the ups and downs of daily life, the cycle of connection, disconnection, and new connection is far more circular. Although I can generally say I am at a stage of new connection with my mother, given our respective stages in life, I still experience times of connection and disconnection, sometimes based on our direct relations and other times due to external forces. I also know this to be true of my mother, whose more overt points of distraction become apparent when she reveals issues or problems she initially chose to withhold from me.

Another point of connection that is somewhat more subtly related is my mother's feminist stance in a male-dominated world and my queer stance in a heterosexist world. Watching my mother's growth and development as a self-confident woman with agency has fuelled my own sense of respect for the feminist position in a world that unfairly devalues women. This, in combination with what I have learned by working with feminists in the community, the social work profession, and academia, has helped me identify as a pro-feminist. I do not pretend to know all realities that women face but I am consciously sensitive to such realities and constantly challenge myself as to new and developing realities that may undermine those who identify as female. This kind of sensitivity links well to my also identifying as queer, the importance of ongoing resistance against heteronormativity, and the kind of inner strength and personal agency required to do so, which is similar to that demonstrated by my mother and her feminist sensibilities. Yet this is a subtle connection at best, between my mother and me, as she continues to struggle with my being queer. Like her, I think I have demonstrated my abilities despite being disenfranchised, but her personal discomfort and worry regarding the perceptions of others (although this latter point is helped by society's growing acceptance of LGBTQs) continues to be a work in progress for us.

A real benefit of my reflexive process at this time in my life as a matured adult is the ability to see my parents as adults themselves (albeit aging) who continue in their parental roles. Within such a role, it is currently my mother who leads in this process, as my father is experiencing the challenges of older age with corresponding health deficits. The literature has revealed important internal dialectic dimensions for parents of adults: connecting and separating emotionally; the child as an extension of the parent and the parent's desire for the child to individuate; increased importance of familial connections and addressing the perceived generation gap; parents' balancing personal and children's needs; and maintaining both a hierarchical and an equal stance (Levitzki 232-233). Recognizing this is the reality of my mother's current relationship with me; as an adult child who often takes on the parental role, I will oftentimes self-censor aspects of my life to protect her from worry (which she and my father have a propensity towards) or being overwhelmed with the complexities in my life (such as my career), experiences that may simply be far too foreign for her to grasp or know how to respond to.

CONCLUSION

I conclude this chapter inconclusively, as any ongoing relationship that ebbs and flows with ever-evolving life circumstances, aging, and, most importantly, ongoing growth and maturation is a fluid and polysemous process. As with all important relationships, that between me and my mother is a worthy work in progress that herein I have reflexively deconstructed based on our relational experiences, yet from my perspective as a means of infusing a son's view in the literature. I have drawn upon theories to ground my reflections; some of these theories lend themselves well, others less so. A balance of what theory can contribute and what real-life experiences teach provides for an informative learning experience. Finally, all of this was complicated by the lived, cultural differences between my mother and me, her Italo-Canadian, immigrant, stealth feminist sensibility and my second generation Italo-Canadian, educated, queer sensibility. My mother's cultural positioning is bred by her country of origin, her immigration experience, her Canadian citizenship, and an informal stealth feminism that she embraces and exudes in response to her environment. Although this may contrast with my being the son of Italian immigrant parents, formally and internationally educated and consciously adopting a politicized queer position, what we share is a resistance towards any attempts at homogenizing what we respectively stand for within the status quo. Ironically, this can also contribute to tensions between us regarding my proud queer stance versus her generational heteronormative values. All of these elements infuse our relationship and combine the saliency of her maternal role and my male caregiving with patterns and intersections of dis/connection, separation/intimacy, stagnation/challenges, and maturation/new connection that have and continue to contribute to this complex mother-son relation of meaning-making and development.

ENDNOTES

[1] I identify as queer based both on my same-sex sexual orientation and politically resistant stance against homonormative notions of "gay." I also identify as "pro-feminist," a man that is sensitive to and supports feminist values and perspectives, yet is living within a male embodied and socialized existence and thus cannot fully experience what a woman does.

WORKS CITED

Anderson, Rae. "Empowering Students through Feminist Pedagogy." *Voices from the Classroom: Reflecting on Teaching and Learning in Higher Education*. Eds. Janice Newton, Jerry Ginsburg, Jan Rehner, Pat Rogers, Susan Sbrizzi and John Spencer. Aurora, ON: Garamond Press. 2001. 68-74. Print.

Benjamin, Jessica. *The Bonds of Love: Psychoanalysis, Feminism and the Problem of Domination*. New York: Pantheon, 1988. Print.

Berridge, Clara and Jennifer Romich "'Raising Him ... to Pull His Own Weight': Boys' Household Work in Single-Mother

Households." *Journal of Family Issues* 32.2 (2011): 157-180. Web. 6 Oct. 2014.

Bertone, Chiara and Marina Franchi. "Suffering as a Path to Acceptance: Parents of Gay and Lesbian Young People Negotiating Catholicism in Italy." *Journal of GLBT Family Studies* 10.1-2 (2014): 58-78. Web. 6 Oct. 2014.

Butler, Judith. *Bodies that Matter: On the Discursive Limits of Sex*. New York: Routledge, 1993. Print.

Butler, Judith. *Gender Trouble*. New York: Routledge, 1990. Print.

Dooley, Cate and Nikki Fedele. "Raising Relational Boys." *Mothers & Sons: Feminism, Masculinity and the Struggle to Raise Our Sons*. Ed. Andrea O'Reilly. New York: Routledge, 2001. 185-216. Print.

Fehr, Beverley. "Intimacy Expectations in Same-Sex Friendships: A Prototype Interaction-Pattern Model." *Journal of Personality and Social Psychology* 86.2 (2004): 265-284. Web. 30 Oct. 2014

Gerber, Nancy. *Portrait of the Mother-Artist: Class and Creativity in Contemporary American Fiction*. Lanham, MD: Lexington Books, 2003. Print.

Gonzalez, Kirsten, Sharon Rostosky, Robert Odom and Ellen Riggle. "The Positive Aspects of Being the Parents of an LGBTQ Child." *Family Process* 52.2 (2013): 325-337. Web. 7 Oct. 2014.

Hirsch, Marianne. *The Mother/Daughter Plot: Narrative, Psychoanalysis, Feminism*. Bloomington: Indiana University Press, 1989. Print.

Hughes, Alex and Anne Witz. "Feminism and the Matter of Bodies: From de Beauvoir to Butler." *Body and Society* 3.1 (1997): 47-60. Print.

Kruk, Laurie. "Mothering Sons: Stories by Findley, Hodgins and MacLeod Uncover the Mother's Double Voice." *Atlantis* 32.1 (2004): 35-45. Print.

Lawson Bush, V. "How Black Mothers Participate in the Development of Manhood and Masculinity: What Do We Know About Black Mothers and Their Sons?" *The Journal of Negro Education* 73.4 (2009): 381-391. Print.

Levitzki, Naama. "Parenting of Adult Children in an Israeli Sample: Parents are Always Parent." *Journal of Family Psychology* 23.2 (2009): 226-235. Web. 30 Oct. 2014.

Liamputtong, Pranee. "Motherhood and the Challenge of Immigrant Mothers: A Personal Reflection." *Families in Society: The Journal of Contemporary Human Services* 82.2 (2001): 195-201. Print.

Miller, Jeff R., and Susan D. Boon. "Trust and Disclosure of Sexual Orientation in Gay Males' Mother-Son Relationships." *Journal of Homosexuality* 38.3 (2000): 41-63. Web. 30 Oct. 2014.

Morman, Mark T., and Marianna Whitely. "An Exploratory Analysis of Critical Incidents of Closeness in the Mother/Son Relationship." *Journal of Family Communication* 12.1 (2012): 22-39. Web. 30 Oct. 2014.

Myers, Niall "An Exploration of Gender-Related Tensions for Male Social Workers in the Irish Context." *Critical Social Thinking: Policy and Practice* 2 (2010): 38-58. Web. 26 Jul. 2015.

O'Reilly, Andrea, ed. *Feminist mothering*. Albany, NY: SUNY Press, 2008. Print.

O'Reilly, Andrea. *Maternal Theory: Essential Readings*. Toronto: Demeter Press, 2007. Print.

O'Reilly, Andrea. "A Mom and Her Son: Thoughts on Feminist Mothering." *Journal of the Association for Research on Mothering* 2.1 (2000): 179-193. Print.

O'Reilly, Andrea. *Mother Outlaws: Theories and Practices of Empowered Mothering*. London: Women's Press, 2004. Print.

Prager, Karen J. "Intimacy in Personal Relationships." *Close Relationships: A Sourcebook*. Eds. Susan S. Hendrick and Clyde Hendrick. Thousand Oaks: Sage, 2000. 229–242. Print.

Rich, Adrienne. *Of Woman Born: Motherhood as Experience and Institution*. London: Virago, 1977. Print.

Rothman, Barbara Katz. "Beyond Mothers and Fathers: Ideology in a Patriarchal Society." *Mothering: Ideology, Experience, and Agency*. Eds. Evelyn Nakano Glenn, Grace Chang, Linda Rennie Forcey. New York: Routledge, 1994. 139-157. Print.

Ruddick, Sara. *Maternal Thinking*. Boston: Beacon Press, 1989. Print.

Schwartzman, Gertrude. "The Subjectivity of the Mother in the Mother-Son Relationship. Attachment, Separation and Autonomy." *International Forum of Psychoanalysis* 15.4 (2006): 226-232. Web. 30 October 2014.

Silverstein, Olga and Beth Rashbaum. *The Courage to Raise Good Men*. New York,: Viking Press, 1994. Print.

Smith, Babette. *Mothers and Sons*. Sydney: Men and Unwin, 1996. Print.

4.
Why Isn't Everyone Celebrating Me?

My Mom, Bankruptcy and My Ego

JUSTIN BUTLER

I T WAS THE RECESSION of the early 1990s: my mother had just
finished a difficult divorce, had been forced to declare bankruptcy, was unemployed, and her four-year-old son (me) was both
concerned and oblivious. Amidst this relatively common American
scenario, significant parts of my personality were formed. I'm now
a fairly resilient, moderately funny, and periodically depressed
social worker, with some self-diminishing caretaker tendencies
and a useful, though sometimes dysfunctional, grandiose sense
of self, which often has me wondering, "Why isn't everyone celebrating me?"

Using memory and imagined dialogue (all of which have been
approved by my mom), this personal piece explores the development
of a son's sense of self via his relationship with his single-parenting
mother. About the remembered/imagined/reconstructed dialogue: it
is based on real memories that are fuzzy. They all take place when
I was three to four years old and were written in consultation with
my mother, Judy Mandel. They are intended to capture the spirit
of our interactions and serve as a beginning place for analysis.
Moreover, this piece does not claim that parents are the only factor
in establishing who we are, nor does it seek to blame mothers; it
instead attempts to offer one more anecdotal lense through which
to view this often seminal relationship. Here I ask: How do economically stressed son-mother dyads survive? What ego defenses
did my mother foster in me that she might have needed herself?
And what discrepancies exist between the world she created for
me and the world I must live in as a relatively functional adult?

Mom: Honey, I'm not sure what we're going to do.
Son: Do?
Mom: Don't worry about it, sweetie. Just know that we're
going to be fine.... And you're so smart—do you know
that? You can literally do anything that you want to do.

The above dialogue excerpt is a fairly common twist of phrase for strapped parents. Faced with an acute stressor, my mom defaulted to extreme praise. She had just lost her part-time job and was worrying: "Paying the rent, buying enough food, losing healthcare coverage, and saving enough money to someday send you to college ... in that order.... And building your self-esteem was the one thing I had control of" (Mandel, "Interview"). This is an apt statement about capitalism and emotions: in financial peril, one of the few factors we can master is our intimate relationships and, in rare moments, our feelings. This puts an immense amount of pressure on the low-income parent to succeed at the one thing she feels capable of impacting in her child's life (hooks 138). And still, even with this emotional project, she must find ways to materially provide for her family.

My mother feels that this praise was sometimes for her, as well as for me. Her memory of this is one of symbiosis and reciprocity: "I am sure I indirectly relied on you for support. We were like a team. You bolstered me and kept me striving to make a better life ... and you always were a comfort. There is nothing like a little boy hug!" (Mandel, "Interview"). She clearly received some sustenance from our interactions. It was a laboratory of sorts, where positive words were possible and dreams wouldn't be dispelled. It was the first time she had such total control over an environment with another person. And by telling me I could do anything and deserved the world, she felt a certain amount of support and comfort herself.

In psychodynamic terms, her verbal acrobatics described above seem to involve sublimation, projection, and a little denial. She sublimated her feelings of stress and anxiety into an expression of encouragement and love—mostly as a way to redirect her own catastrophizing thoughts and to stop herself from panicking. In a recent interview, she explained this as "translating stress into creating a kind of oasis of security for you" (Mandel, "Interview"). While she was feeling the pressure of countless limitations, she wanted me to feel none. This mention of limitless possibilities—that I could be anything I wanted to be—*has* been an oasis for me and has, I think, helped me recover from defeats. In later years, her statement about my abilities became more specific: "You're so good at everything: you could be an actor, a lawyer, an architect—whatever, sweetie." I still carry these words with me, almost literally. I often think the only thing keeping me from being a professional rugby player or brilliant mathematician is practice time and maybe some genetics.

The projection in her words is important too. She is praising me in a more comforting way than she was praised as a child; she is also projecting the uncertainty of the moment, and her uncertainty, onto me. It's likely that reassuring me that everything was going to be okay alerted me to something I wasn't even aware I needed to worry about—which could have been both reassuring and troubling to the four-year-old me. And this anxiety may have been magnified by any uncertainty in her voice. This projection process relates closely to her denial: it's almost as if her faith in me would save us from our woes (which, she would argue, it did). She says today that some momentary denial was necessary to enjoy life at all at that time (Mandel, "Interview").

Who knows if or how these interactions contributed to my current functioning; many studies have been conducted to prove the developmental significance of children's peer and non-parental relationships (Harris 142). That said, it has been useful for me to analyze my central caregiver relationship—not looking for absolute causality, but for connections.

For example, this centrality of praise as reassurance can help to explain why I always seek refuge in it as an adult by telling myself, "I'm a great poet," or "Even if that person gets published before me, I probably had something better to say," or "It's okay, I'm probably the most effective therapist on the team," or "There's no reason to feel self-conscious talking in class; people hang on my words and cherish my contributions." Of course these fantasies are hardly grounded in reality and often rely on comparison. They serve as defenses against a much more complex reality and self-image.

Yet, it can be useful for us to feel like we're omnipotent when we're young. Especially as infants, this narcissism gives us a sense of security: we want food and we get fed, we want to be picked up and we are—almost as if we willed it to happen. Without this irrational sense of our own power, we would be faced with a much more frightening scenario: that we must depend on these incomprehensible giants to take care of us (Kohut and Wolf 414). But, of course, this omnipotence is challenged immediately by parents' benign delays in attending to cries, the deliberate and tragic attempts to "let them cry it out," and in more severe circumstances of abuse or neglect. In this frame, the moments when our grandiosity is challenged are also crucial to our development, as they allow us to test and adjust our perception of our omnipotence while hopefully still maintaining a sense of security in our caregivers or other figures: "By merging with calmness and competence of the selfobject, those qualities can be established within the self" (Flanagan 175). This, some think, is how our personalities are formed: in moments of uncertainty, which traits from our caregivers and peers do we internalize as our own? This can also be when our capacity for reality-testing is formed and how our sense of security and self-worth is established: by learning and coping with the discrepancies between our infancy and inevitable harshness of the years that follow.

Maggie Nelson elegantly describes this dance of the child's needs being met in varying degrees and their close entwinement with the mother's demands on the child, which are sometimes to "fill a lack, or soothe an egoic wound" (96). And, as the mother/parent proves she is a separate person, and naturally fails to meet some of the child's needs, the child's separate sense of self is gradually formed. Nelson is deliberate about not pathologizing mothers in any aspect of this process: "So far as I can tell, most worthwhile pleasures on this earth slip between gratifying another and gratifying oneself. Some would call that an ethics" (Nelson 96).

Challenges to our grandiosity further shape our worlds by awakening us to the needs of others—enabling us, with newfound empathy, to someday become humanists, feminists, and otherwise aware people. Without this process, unchecked self-esteem seems likely to lead to destructive self-absorption. In fact, narcissistic tendencies have been linked to higher rates of prejudice and discrimination (Hodson, Hogg, and MacInnis 688). It is no secret that prejudice is effective in superficially bolstering self-esteem. And you can hear an implication of discrimination in my own self-affirmations above. Is my brand of self-esteem therefore embellished, in part, with the self-serving premise of othering and oppression? Is the fostering of grandiosity in white children and adults, and all positions of power, unavoidably linked, at least in part, to preserving that power? In this way, perhaps challenges to grandiosity are part of the process of unlearning racism, sexism, ableism, classism, and other systems of domination.

Perhaps the way in which I cling to superiority is proof that I didn't experience enough optimal frustration, given the fact that I was likely praised like this for some time. I also had unchallenged access to my mother for the majority of my childhood. As an only child with a single parent, our relationship was central and without rival. It wasn't until she remarried many years later that I had to renegotiate the limits of our bond and the nutrients it provided me, including that sense of grandiosity. And still, beneath this grandiosity is fragility, or, more accurately, a fear of fragility. Perhaps because my parentified caregiver traits (discussed below) were highly encouraged, I was never able to be fully dependent on my parents and was therefore hindered in my task of becoming an independent, secure, spontaneous person, who is able to tolerate his own fragility (Miller 23). It is also necessary to situate this climate of praise within my other privileged identities; as a white, cisgender, non-disabled, documented, North-American male, my sense of security was further reinforced by society.

But it wasn't pure praise. There is also fear and uncertainty in the above quotation. In addition to the tone, which was likely one of worry, the juxtaposition of ideas is jarring. It's almost equational: you are wonderful because we're struggling. It's as if my grandiosity were constructed in tandem with doubt about my place in the world and the stability of our family. Therefore, the implication was—and still is today—that in times of self-doubt, my excellence is the solution. It also establishes the premise that my success is conditional and contingent upon some stress. Judy tells me today that she knew "the world would trample you enough when you got out there.... I felt it was my job to bolster you when I had the chance—you needed security and protection to weather what might come" (Mandel, "Interview"). Of course, *she* was being trampled at the time and needed some protection herself, so it was quite resilient and adaptive of her to attempt to bolster both of us during hard times.

There is also an implication of an opposite whenever someone is too profuse—the "doth-protest-too-much" phenomenon. Much like Jean Liedloff's theory that children likely intuit that the applause they receive for not falling or dropping something means it was *expected* they'd fall or drop something (102), perhaps some part of me interpreted my mother's applause as signs of a deficit. This, again, sheds some light on my fragile self that now exists below my grandiose one: it's as if I suspect my greatness to be untrue, the way I block out all other thoughts—as if a single acknowledgment of my inadequacy will undermine my very existence and I'd be left alone, without identity.

Many adults' annihilation anxiety or intimacy challenges may be rooted in an unintentionally overwhelming parent, one who excessively exposed their child to their own needs and desires. The child becomes the "vulnerable container for parental excitement … and a container for the unbearable" (Atlas-Koch and Benjamin). Atlas-Koch and Benjamin argue that this early dynamic can lead adults to seek out extremes, like control and domination or obsession and dependency. Similarly, I often fluctuate between avoiding intimacy and desperately seeking it out. It seems that many of us are constantly attempting to master this early dynamic throughout our lives. While the following dialogue isn't invasive (it's in fact a great example of affect-joining), it depicts another dynamic that I continue to reenact in my adult life.

> Mom: *We're going to Chuck E. Cheese!*
> Son: *Yess!*
> Mom: *You can play the alligator game! And maybe you've saved up enough tickets to get that weird light thing!?*
> Son: *And pizza?*
> Mom: *Yeah! You've been so good this week!*

My mom made sure trips to Chuck E. Cheese—an American restaurant/arcade chain with cheap pizza, animatronics, and skeeball—were a monthly treat. Today, she's always quick to point out that it was also the only kid-friendly place where I could play for a few hours while she had a cheap beer. It was treated as a celebration for another great week—which it always was, no matter how much we fought or yelled at each other. She seemed to find any excuse for celebrating: MacDonald's after the first day of school each year, "grape cones" (literally just grapes in tinfoil shaped like an ice cream cone) on the first warm day of the year, or simply her excitement when picking me up from daycare.

My mom grew up in a household she describes as "loving and laugh-filled" (Mandel, "Interview"). Her mother and father were first-generation Hungarian-Jewish and Russian-Jewish immigrants respectively, and both prioritized their family despite working tirelessly. But she often had to take a backseat to the urgent medical needs of her sister and was inadvertently excluded from the family unit because she was born after a tragic accident that defined the family (a plane crashed into their apartment, killing one daughter and badly injuring the other). She tells this story in detail in her own book, *Replacement Child*. She explains further:

> Because of grief over losing a child and heartache about my sister who needed so much care, my parents did the best they could to give me attention and love. As a replacement child, I inherited a confused sense of myself, never being able to live up to expectations—especially of my dad, [who] was distanced from me by his grief, and probably unconsciously resented that I was here when his eldest daughter was taken from him. I never felt I fit in with the family, having missed the pivotal event in all of their lives but mine. ("Interview")

By her own analysis, growing up in a family where she sometimes felt invisible inclined her toward constant praise of me and her conveying that I was exceptionally special and valuable. She continues: "I wanted to be more fully present for you than either of my parents was able to be, for various reasons—grief, guilt, resentment.... Correcting that parental relationship might have been unconsciously my impetus" (Mandel, "Interview"). Such "corrective emotional experiences" offer an opportunity to master a past conflict or hurt, and this one perhaps allowed my mom to reorient her relationship with herself and the world by forming new attachment relationships and attachment dynamics (Fairbairn 74).

Again, my mother sublimated her insecurity into support of me. In her periodic exclusion from her family, she was denied some real chances for twinship as a child (Flanagan 178), and denied again in an emotionally invalidating marriage, and then again in her struggle as a single parent—and likely in other relationships in her life. These cycles have a way of repeating themselves, deriving nourishment from past moments of worthlessness and the powerful feelings of worthlessness and uncertainty that are left behind (Wachtel 27). Not coincidentally, these are some of the same feelings her parents felt after the death of their child in the plane crash. Family therapy theorists like Kaethe Weingarten would argue that this intergenerational transmission of trauma was somehow perceptible to me and present in our interactions (47). So, while her celebrations and love helped me feel validated (and still do today), I likely metabolized her reassurance within our family memory of epic, senseless loss, wherein the world is frighteningly unpredictable. I speculate that I, in my child under-standing, could feel the holes in her certainty and maybe in her own self-confidence. This may help explain why I now defend my own worth so ardently.

She also agrees today that her financial and personal stresses at the time dramatically influenced the way she tried to shape my world for me. Like most parents dealing with any kind of stress, she tried to protect me from it and wanted me to think the world was a perfect, benevolent place. In addition to being the sole wage earner, she was doing the triple duty of caring for me materially and emotionally (hooks 37; Weis 78). As mentioned before, the emotional aspect of this endeavour included shielding me from the realities of her labour struggles—from the realities of a system of wage-toiling that left her with no savings, a constant hunt for a job that paid enough, and a near-constant feeling of worry about how we would survive as a little family. So, this melancholy can be viewed, at least in part, as a product of her alienating experience in the free labour market (Fromm 86). To this end, Judy says, "I didn't want you to feel less than, or responsible for any of our hardships" (Mandel "Interview"). She sought to spare me the truth about the practical source of her struggles (the daily activities of capitalism) and the emotional effects of those struggles (the fallout of capitalism).

In concrete economic terms, she was rationing out the monthly budget. For her, it was sometimes a choice between Chuck E. Cheese and lunch for herself that day or a badly needed interview outfit. She calls the tight budget strategy she used "the envelope method": "From my paycheck, I would take whatever money I designated for food and put it in an envelope, and one for gas, and on and on. I had a calendar for the big bills and kept a list of how much each month had to be saved for each expense. It was a lot of work" (Mandel, "Interview").

For all of her brilliant shielding and scheduling and celebrating, there must have been holes in her performance, because I also grew up wanting to protect her. Perhaps I sensed that, underneath her efforts to convince me that all was well, she needed comforting— which she of course did (Mandel "Interview"). And today, while I often crave celebrations like a trip to Chuck E. Cheese, especially in periods of depression, I am usually skeptical of them, as if they carry the whispered message that all is *not* well—with me or the world. Sometimes, when I come home after a few days away, I expect my partner to be ecstatic—to throw the laptop, yarn, and scissors down and hug me passionately, relieved to be reunited with me. Other times, a similarly joyous welcome will feel like proof of my alien-ness and pushes me further into despair and isolation.

> *Son: I think Miss Martense is sad.*
> *Mom: What do you mean?*
> *Son: She told me all during preschool that her husband's mother doesn't like her, and they've been fighting.*
> *Mom: Oh boy, she does sound sad, huh . . .*
> *Son: Yeah...*
> *Mom: You know, you really have a special gift. You can get anyone to talk to you. For some reason people have always wanted to open up to you. Even since you were younger. You're such a good listener.*

There is some miraculous mirroring and empathy in this exchange, as well as encouragement for a young boy to express his emotions and to tolerate and appreciate when women do the same. And here, a parent is acknowledging such emotional tolerance as a skill her child is demonstrating. In this way, she is modelling empathy—and does so again when she assesses my tone of worry and responds directly to it with an affirmation: "She does sound sad."

This example of praise is specific to my skills as a caretaker—a listener, a counsellor, a toddler-sized social worker. Here, praise, the currency I'd then come to expect, was given because I had taken care of someone. This positive reinforcement is a smart way of encouraging desirable behaviours and seems much more effective than, say, hitting me when I didn't properly empathize with someone. So, this particular praise for my caretaking, along with the unavoidable exposure to my mother's needs, may have helped to hardwire me for empathy and listening. I may also have received the message that my age-appropriate needs and selfishness were, in contrast, less desirable (Miller 14, 34).

Whatever the exact equation was, it seems that my penchant for listening to other people's stories was already developing at this age. This dialogue also shows the significance of the other relationships in my life. There are at least ten other Miss Martenses (men and women) from my childhood whom I remember by name; all of them excessively poured their worries out to me.

It may have also set a tone of prioritizing the needs of others before my own. As an adult, I am often accused of "getting other people to share" long before I say anything about myself. Often, friends will get to the end of a long conversation with me before they realize that I dodged every question they asked about my life. And of course, this therapy mode often leaves me feeling depleted from listening and lonely from not sharing.

In later years, as I began to understand other people's suffering more consciously, I perceived a discrepancy between their need to talk and my own. This, along with the praise I received for empa-thizing and the inherent rewards of caring for others, implied to me that it's somehow my duty to take care of people. As if she were aware of this internal process of mine, my mom says today that she was also wary of this phenomenon of adults unduly opening up to me. "You were always worrying about someone else, and I wondered if that came from me" (Mandel "Interview"). Perhaps she added, or could have added, something to this effect: "That's so sad that Miss Martense is going through all that. It's great that she wants to talk to you, and it's also okay for you want to play with the other kids. And she should also be finding some adult to talk to." In order to further foster my self-awareness and empower me to prioritize myself along with others, she could have said, "And how did you feel when Miss Martense told you all that?... What were the other kids doing? Does any part of you wish she didn't tell you?"

Perhaps my mother's words here somehow conveyed that I should be taking care of her in this way too—that if I could elicit such praise from her for counselling another person then she'd certainly appreciate receiving the same service herself. Like dropping a hint. And, as discussed above, I was likely primed for this kind of mom-care from the coded messages of worry and insecurity in her communication with me: "I tried not to burden you, but I'm sure you intuited the struggles, and also my loneliness many times" (Mandel "Interview"). And as she attests today, she was going through a time of deep craving for support and compassionate listening. When asked about her emotional supports, she paused, "Not that much, really.... My parents and sister were far away.... No, there was not a lot" (Mandel, "Interview"). Surely this craving was palpable to me in our small apartment.

Although our relationship provided her with comfort and fulfillment, she was still depleted. bell hooks discusses the complicated nature of this reward-deficit paradox of mothering, especially when the popular narrative is one of maternal bliss: "In spite of the difficulties of single-parenting in this society, the focus is on 'the joys of motherhood,' the special intimacy, closeness, and bonding purported to characterize the mother/child relationship" (135). This invalidation could have added to Judy's feelings of isolation and disempowerment.

SOME QUESTIONS I HAVE

Why do I think of my mother as the struggling mother? Why do

I sometimes think of her as having a loveless childhood (which is simply untrue)? Why do I locate her (our) economic strife in the center of our lives? Why do I attribute so much of my Self to my mother?

Maybe: I need to think of her struggling so that we survive together? So that I can save her? So that she can save me—to make her the hero? To simplify her struggles? To celebrate her? To exert some control and mastery over my childhood and over my mother? To create an organizing principle for understanding the most important and mysterious relationship in my life? To explain the miracle of how much love and care she gave me? To explain why I feel positively about my childhood, when so many people do not? To construct a foil for my privilege? To further reinforce my privilege? Because of my male, white, now middle-class guilt? Because I'm nervous about raising my own kids?

CONCLUSION

Some of my interest in writing this, I now realize, is to dispel the assumption that poor families have inadequate parenting or are too stressed to love and support their children's development. Even through my scrutiny in these pages, I hope it's clear that the parenting was remarkably good. Our economic stresses partly defined our experience as a family—forcing an incredible creativity and clearly shaping many of the messages communicated between us. And still, thoughtful and intuitive parenting somehow transcended the hardship. Of course my mother and I had access to the considerable advantages that come with whiteness, citizen-status, her undergraduate degree, and other privileges, which undoubtedly affected our experiences, from apartment applications to job interviews and daycare searches. Privilege tempered privation and is inextricably linked to her and our eventual ascendancy into the middle class.

Amidst stress and some deprivation, my mother filled our child-parent dialogue with limitless encouragement and praise. While over-encouraged kids have become a cliché of recent generations, I would like to make two important distinctions: such praise and admiration is still not the norm, as any mental health clinician who works with younger clients—scores of whom are diminished, derided, and abused by their parents—could attest; and a parent's belief in their child is different from a "spoiled" child who "never hears the word 'no.'" Discipline and praise are not mutually exclusive styles.

I keep returning to my fragile confidence. I don't know if I felt this somehow when I was small, but I cling to it so desperately now and still have a big reaction when it's challenged. The frightening truth, which I sometimes know consciously and sometimes completely deny, is that no one is celebrating me—a few people *do* care, but no one is impressed and no one is going out of their way for me. This has become one of the most difficult truths for me to comprehend. And such acceptance is hardest when I'm in my most insecure, confused, or defeated moods and crave a Judy-type response most deeply. The inflated self I described here is still an active defense against this reality: imperfect and problematic but very familiar.

Most childhoods involve being excluded from parental emotions—subjected to and invaded by them, yet also kept in the dark about them (Atlas-Koch and Benjamin). It is a mystery in which we are constantly immersed—the sensations of which (facial expressions, vocal tones, subtle and drastic actions) we cannot avoid and yet we are given no map or glossary to decode them. And often these maps and glossaries are withheld with the noble intentions of sparing children from the harshness of adulthood. This chapter and its analysis of mom-son interactions from over twenty years ago and the mom-son interview conducted twenty days ago has been an attempt to write one of those glossaries.

I tried here to better understand my mother and myself (not unlike the empathy she indirectly and overtly cultivated in me). My mother's praise and encouragement seems to have provided me with security, confidence, and a model for relating. It shaped the way I understand the world and find safety in it. Still, her parenting style is not the sole culprit in my development. My other relationships and experiences, and the myriad ways I processed challenges to and reinforcements of my earliest experiences, have also contributed hugely to my ways of being.

As my mom appropriately feared in 1991, the world's harshness has "trampled" me somewhat—in ways neither of us could have predicted. I feel that one of my biggest adult projects is learning the differences between the world I live in and the safe world she created for me—even as I still carry that safe, small world around inside me. And now, in times of stress and insecurity, like when I first started working as a social worker, I crave the kind of devotion and praise I got then. I pray that my partner will give it to me, but this rarely (sensibly) happens. I instead make my partner turkey-parsnip soup and clean the apartment and wonder why everyone isn't celebrating me.

WORKS CITED

Atlas-Koch, Galit, and Jessica Benjamin. *The "Too Muchness" of Excitement and the Death of Desire—Theoretical and Clinical Perspectives.* Institute for Expressive Analysis, New York University, New York, USA. 17 Oct. 2014. Lecture.

Fairbairn, Ronald W. "The Repression and the Return of Bad Objects." *Psychoanalytic Studies of the Personality.* London: Routledge & Kegan Paul Ltd, 1952. 59-81. Print.

Flanagan, Laura Melano. "The Theory of Self Psychology." *Inside Out and Outside In: Psychodynamic Clinical Theory and Psychopathology in Contemporary Multicultural Contexts.* 2nd ed. Eds: Joan Berzoff, Laura Melano Flanagan, Patricia Hertz. Boulder: Jason Aronson, 2008. 161-188. Print.

Fromm, Erich. *Marx's Concept of Man.* London: Continuum, 2004. Print.

Harris, Judith Rich. *Nurture Assumption: Why Children Turn Out the Way They Do.* New York: Simon and Schuster, 2009. Print.

Hodson, Gordon, Sarah M. Hogg, Cara C. MacInnis. "The Role of 'Dark Personalities' (Narcissism, Machiavellianism, Psychopathy): Big Five Personality Factors, and Ideology in Explaining Prejudice." *Journal of Research in Personalit,* 43: 4. (2009): 686-690. Print.

hooks, bell. *Feminist Theory: From Margin to Center.* Cambridge: South End Press, 2000. Print.

Kohut, Heinz, and Ernest S. Wolf. "The Disorders of the Self and

Their Treatment: An Outline." *International Journal of Psycho-Analysis 59*. (1978): 413-425. Print.

Liedloff, Jean. *The Continuum Concept: In Search of Happiness Lost*. Boston: Da Capo Press, 1985. Print.

Mandel, Judy. Personal interview. 1 Oct. 2014.

Mandel, Judy. *Replacement Child: A Memoir*. Berkeley: Seal Press, 2013. Print.

Miller, Alice. *The Drama of the Gifted Child: The Search for the True Self*. New York: Basic Books, 1990. Print.

Nelson, Maggie. *The Argonauts*. Minneapolis: Graywolf Press, 2015. Print.

Wachtel, Paul. *Therapeutic Communication: Knowing What to Say When*. New York: The Guilford Press, 1993. Print.

Weingarten, Kaethe. "Witnessing the Effects of Political Violence in Families: Mechanisms of Intergenerational Transmissions and Clinical Interventions." *Journal of Marital and Family Therapy* 30: 1. (2004): 45-59. Print.

Weis, Lois. "Gender and the Reports: The Case of the Missing Piece." *Feminist Critical Policy Analysis: A Perspective from Primary and Secondary Schooling*. Ed. Catherine Marshall. London: Falmer Press, 2005. Digital file.

5.
Lesbian Families, Sons and Mothering

Parenting Outside the Boundaries

ALYS EINION

THE EMERGENCE OF the widespread potential for lesbians to
become parents outside the heterosexual dyad has resulted
in a number of manifestations of the lesbian family, with
lesbian mothers occupying roles as biological and non-biological
parents. In the UK, with changes in the law since 2005, non-biological mothers now have legal recognition as step-parents or
as full parents, with their names on the birth certificates of their
children. As such, they can be seen as occupying a parental space
traditionally reserved for a gendered dyad of father-mother, which
becomes instead a mother-mother space. However, for lesbian
mothers of sons, this can present a specific challenge in the perceived issue of the absence of male role models and, for some
lesbians, the prevention of entry into or existence within lesbian,
female-dominated, or female-only spaces which oppose manifestations of heteronormativity. Parenting outside the boundaries
means parenting beyond the narrow definitions of motherhood,
fatherhood, family, and social life that restrict us so powerfully.
In this chapter, my aim is to consider how lesbian parents might
create their own models of parenting, particularly when faced with
the challenge of bringing up a son in a world of gender binaries,
where gender is the ultimate dividing principle. Lesbian mothers of
sons, in particular, address a gender dynamic, which is constructed
as problematic in external space, regardless of its dynamic in the
internal space of the family unit. Drawing on personal experience
and published work, this chapter explores the experiences of lesbians
parenting outside the boundaries and considers the unanswered

questions about the difficulties of transgressing the rules of that most fundamental, and gendered, of social institutions: the family.

I write this chapter from an insider perspective, as the lesbian mother of a son now in his mid-teens. That we have both survived thus far with minimal to moderate scarring is a mystery and a joy to both of us. I never set out to be a lesbian mother of a son. I had been a student and student feminist activist; I had been an activist for sexual health and secretary of the LGB society on campus. I had campaigned for the continued existence of a women's room on one university campus, a room which was by its very nature a male-free space. I believed in the need for lesbian separatism. I studied and wrote about feminism and maternal empowerment as a student nurse and, later, as a student midwife. I worked with lesbian parents within the maternity system and fought small but hard-won battles to promote their rights before the changes in the law in 2005. My identity was as a lesbian feminist, bordering the edges of separatism.

Then I became pregnant with a much-wanted child. I was single and my lesbian identity disappeared because everyone assumed I was a straight, single mother. I worked in the maternity care setting and did not disclose my sexuality or my politics, and when I left work to take up the mothering role, I was encouraged by the heterosexual and heterosexist world to continue keeping my lesbianism under wraps, hidden, relegated to an uber-private sphere into which my innocent, vulnerable, developing child would not be admitted. Despite this, I was surprised to find myself in a relationship that blossomed during the early months of his life, and I accepted the woman who had been my best friend for four years both as my lover and my co-parent, my son's other mother.

Our decision was that she would be a full co-parent and that her identity as his parent would be reinforced at every opportunity. Yet, from the outset, the question of lesbians parenting a son was raised in every possible permutation. Professionals asked about male role models. Family members discussed normative social relations, suggesting that he would not understand "typical" family relationships because he was not exposed to them. I argued that he would be loved by two committed and affectionate parents, who, regardless of any differences between us, placed his wellbeing as our highest priority for the duration of our relationship. My family responded by withdrawing, thus ensuring that, in the private sphere, he would indeed have limited exposure to heterosexual relationships, despite the fact that these pervaded every other aspect of his life.

It would be wrong to say that I did not share their concerns. It was a decade and a half ago that I was first challenged as a feminist because I had given birth to a son. My partner and I were almost completely isolated: with no childcare or family support, we had a very limited social life and little access to social spaces that reflected our lesbian identity. What we encountered when we did enter such spaces was a negative response to the presence of a small child, and in particular a boy in a women-only, lesbian-oriented space. Not wanting our son to grow up marginalised by our own community, we were unable to engage with it. Heterosexual spaces marginalised and even blatantly rejected us as a family unit. And so we were faced with this seemingly impossible paradox: two radically, diametrically opposed identities and seemingly little hope of crossing the boundaries between them. Within such a destabilising context, we were left to each create and hold the parenting space for the other, with no lexicon, no role models, and little or no support. Attempts to access "community" from the newly emerging social media were also less than satisfying, with one online lesbian feminist support group being particularly exclusive. One member asked me, "How does it feel to have given birth to a rapist?"

It was then that I started to address the issue of my own identity and the lived experience of lesbian parenting that I had, naively, assumed would be as natural as his birth had been. Part of the challenge appears to be the concept of the "good mother" which, gendered and socially constructed, pervades dominant parenting discourses. It appears difficult to equate the apparently oppositional social constructions of "lesbians" with social constructions of "motherhood." There are lesbian single mothers and lesbians who successfully co-mother, both of whom are biological mothers to one or other of their children (Biblarz and Savci 481-482). But I argue that regardless of the biology, the boundaries of heteronormative space are firmly entrenched in any notion of society because lesbians must parent within that society and find their peer group amongst an (unsurprisingly) essentially heterosexual social network. Suter, Daas, and Bergen discuss how lesbian mothers will encounter discriminatory and negative behaviour, as well as positive behaviour, in their encounters with the institutions that go alongside the mothering role, such as healthcare providers and education providers (29). This judgment of the lesbian parent as at best unconventional and at worst unacceptably deviant is associated with the social concept of what a good mother is and does.

As Green shows, mothers have been subject to scrutiny and judgment for centuries, with outside agencies and society defining the parameters of acceptability within this role (21-22). Green further states that mothering "includes the culmination of social structures and meanings that create conditions under which women are expected to parent, and thus, prescribe and shape the circumstances of women's lives" (24). She further argues that women must parent in accordance with the ideals and conditions of the dominant culture, thus finding themselves under pressure to be a "perfect" mother from the various social institutions and influences in their lives (24). This includes meeting "the mainstream Western standards of intensive mothering" and having this reinforced by family, friends, and work colleagues who "perpetuate the dominant expectations of motherhood through their attention/surveillance and unsolicited suggestions" (24). What is of greatest concern here is the *normalization* of these unrealistic standards, which, as Warner shows, are doomed to fail and to leave women bitter and disenchanted (58). I did not expect, as a feminist, to be so strongly influenced by these standards or to spend my motherhood journey in such a state of guilt and uncertainty. It was apparent to me that I was faced with a number of challenges, all of which centred on legitimising the status of my family and, in particular, compensating for the absence of a male role model within my son's life.

The concerns about lesbian mothers in the current context have moved away from issues relating to legal, social, or family status, or even from issues around custody (particularly in the UK setting). The issues lie within the wider social structures that define motherhood and which, in turn, create barriers to the successful marriage of lesbian identity and parenting. The paradox of representations and cultural constructs of motherhood is a challenge for any woman. Forna describes motherhood as "a state which is both revered and reviled, natural yet policed" (7). When one compounds this with the presence of a lesbian partner (lesbians, of course, being sexual beings above all other things in the eyes of society), one adds to the stigma. The lesbian parent, constrained by the social dimensions of "accepted" behaviour, will inevitably find herself doubly or triply challenged by her role because those boundaries may be much more visible to her (particularly if she is a feminist) and more difficult to address.

It appears that lesbian mothers are under even greater scrutiny than our heterosexual peers, and the level of surveillance and judgment of mothers in general is already unacceptably high. Forna states that "collectively we judge the mothers around us personally and through our institutions," arguing that the collectively and socially defined myths of motherhood that permeate all media and all institutions affect all women in cruel and limiting ways (23). So it may be that the lesbian who chooses motherhood must face greater challenges, both in exploding the general myths of how mothers should behave and should parent and in pushing the boundaries of the definition of mothering by taking that relationship beyond a biological or a socially sanctioned one. Mothering a son intensifies these challenges.

However, it is also clear that the literature which explores the impact and outcomes of lesbian parenting does not address this issue of lesbians raising sons in sufficient detail. The research by Leddy, Gartrell, and Bos, for example, does not address differences between responses of sons versus daughters. One of their participants discusses the lack of gender binaries or gender roles in tasks and playthings, but the gender of this participant is not identified (249). However, an essay by Lopez published online discusses the experiences of a male growing up in a lesbian family and highlights specific differences, including the failure to learn "all the unwritten rules of decorum and body language in their homes." Lopez further states that "they understood what was appropriate to say in certain settings and what wasn't; they learned both traditionally masculine and traditionally feminine social mechanisms." Certainly the fear of such limitations being a challenge in our son's life affected the ways in which I and my co-mother parented our son.

As Maushart (xix) shows, the transition to motherhood itself results in a significant identity crisis for women as they face the challenge and tedium of motherhood. "After the initial trauma of transition comes the painful process of re-evaluating life choices, of bringing to consciousness our most deeply embedded assumptions about the way things ought to be" (Maushart xix). For some women, the greatest shock is that they are now fully embedded in, and almost fatalistically shackled to, the gender roles they thought they had left behind in their assumption of a (deviant) adult female identity. Gender theory delineates the nature of these gender roles and of gender identity, whilst more recently, queer theory suggests that gender is much more fluid and flexible and that gender identity and sexuality in lesbian women is often much more diverse than we realise. Fox and Murray, for example, discuss the concept of parenthood roles as mothering and fathering roles that go beyond the genders of the person carrying out the role (1160).

I feel that there is a strong need to not define parenting roles according to gendered definitions—mothering, fathering—but rather as parenting identities and behaviours that can be applicable to all. It may be that social trends are moving this way for all families. However, I think it is unacceptable to assume that because lesbians may now have the protection of the law (as is the case in the UK) and can choose to parent legally and freely, they are automatically free of the problematic negotiations of lesbian parenting identity of the past.

Based on my own experience and that of friends and acquaintances, I believe this legal shift has not necessarily reduced the amount of homophobia in schools and other social institutions but rather only made it possible for legal challenges to be brought when it is discovered. It has not made it easier to be a lesbian parent but instead perhaps shifted the lesbian identity towards a more heteronormative expectation, putting pressure on lesbians to get married and have children. It has not changed the attitude of service providers, simply given them another set of rules within which to perform their roles. As such, it is limiting the definitions and freedom of lesbians to make choices outside patriarchal paradigms of family and is significantly challenging the identity of lesbians as something radical and oppositional to the base sexism and misogyny of Western social norms. Biblarz and Savci discuss the symbolic nature of the lesbian family in which multiple identities are negotiated but varying degrees of inequality exist, particularly in relation to biology, suggesting that superiority of biological relationship between parents and child remains both a personal challenge and a legal issue, particularly in America (489-492). Other authors have critically debated this issue, particularly Park in her book *Mothering Queerly, Queering Motherhood*, where every aspect of the assumed superiority of biological mothering is critically examined. Park proposes multiple perspectives on the emergent nature of family in a queer, gender-fluid and open social world. However, such models remain on the margins of the mainstream and those women choosing to parent as lesbians are still challenged if they parent within normative social spaces.

Thurer states, "Motherhood—the way we perform mothering—is culturally derived" (334) and suggests the way that we mother is defined by the context in which we find ourselves mothering. And outside of the privileged spaces of so-called "lesbian community," the standard models of motherhood remain heterosexist, sexist, and more challenging than ever before for women. There is no traditional role to step into, particularly when one is not the biological mother of the children. Lesbian parents are subject to multiple social forces, requiring them to be both the perfect mother and somehow retain the "normative" identity of lesbianism, which is fully (and rightly) equated with their sexual nature and the nature of their primary affections. Lewin argues that the history of lesbian parenting is dominated by the kinds of utopian images of resistance played out within a changing family dynamic in which lesbian parenting was outside traditional family forms (371). For many lesbians, this may seem like an ideological goal, but the lived experience of lesbian parenting may be far from this ideal. As Lewin so ably states, "The achievement of lesbian mothers would both counteract the notion that lesbianism and motherhood are inherently contradictory and in fact, redefine and desexualise what it means to be a lesbian" (372).

Yet I argue, as does Judith Butler, that within the family dynamic, there remains a gendering of parental roles that is not easily avoided or resisted (17). It is about the pervasive heteronormativity of the world of family in which the underlying assumption is that all families are constructed around "normative" gender roles. Buying into this normative format was a conscious act for our family in order to limit the negative impact of our "deviance" on our son's life experiences and opportunities. This normativity is related to what O'Reilly describes as the "ideological assumptions that cause motherhood to be oppressive to women" and that define and limit motherhood through patriarchy and gender essentialism (64). These ideals include normalisation, biologicalisation, and naturalisation, ideals in which motherhood is strongly linked to the "natural" and to biology and which deny the mothering that takes place in the absence of biological relationships (O'Reilly 65). Many lesbian women choose to parent in non-biological relationships, through adoption, fostering, and co-parenting, and it is possible to equate lesbian parenting with O'Reilly's definitions of the performance of empowered mothering simply because lesbian parenting is a fundamental transgression of assumed heteronormativity (66).

However, I believe that lesbian parents, and in particular lesbian mothers raising sons in a gender-obsessed world, are either more strongly influenced by the need to mother in a more socially sanctioned way or else take a more radical step away from these gendered norms and therefore, by necessity, must push the boundaries of gendered roles. De-gendering parental roles appears to leave a kind of identity void for the parents themselves and, in particular, the "other mother." This lack of "official" status affected my son's other mother during our whole relationship. Regardless of my constant validation of her role, my emphasis on it in private and public space, this difference could not be overcome. For example, her role as one of his primary carers (an equal co-mother) was not valued or validated in her workplace, despite it being a feminist organization whose sole function was the support of women experiencing life challenges and despite the fact that she worked part time in order to be available for child care, as I was the family breadwinner. When stating that she could not attend a meeting after hours due to the need to be home with our son, the response was "Can't his mother have him?"

In this case, it seemed that our transgression of typical gendered mothering roles, in which I was both the biological mother and the primary wage earner with a committed and challenging career, was more difficult for those outside our family circle; this brought more challenges into our family dynamic. We constantly questioned our ability to parent effectively, collectively and individually, and parenting decisions, behaviours, and ideals were the most common source of tension in our relationship. We had both internalised the doubts raised by our transgression of the rules and this resulted in an overly self-critical approach to parenting in which neither one of us found validation or support outside of our circle of three. Speziale and Gopalakrishna echo this, arguing that there is "scant social recognition and validation" of the lesbian-led family in the outside world (174-175).

In this context, it is clear that the parental role for the lesbian mother occupies a place outside the boundaries of typical parenting dynamics. The very act of asserting herself as a mother is a form of resistance for the co-mother that forces a redefinition of parenting roles beyond simplistic gender binaries but accepts that the relationship is also defined by the absence of a male father-figure. Speziale and Gopalakrishna state that lesbian, nuclear-type families function in much the same way as heterosexual families, but these authors also highlight the difference:

> [Heterosexual families] are secure within patriarchal society's organizations and institutions. Safeguarded by their privileged status, heterosexual parents do not ordinarily fear that they or their children will be treated negatively by persons with authority or power within neighbourhood schools, places of worship, or health care settings. (179-180)

Speziale and Gopalakrishna also recognise that there is increased stress in the parenting relationship and on identity in lesbian parents (180).

Whilst much of this is true for lesbian parents regardless of the gender of their children, the challenge is more acute for those lesbians with sons because, in many cases, this takes them outside the boundaries of their own social spaces. I do not argue that the lesbian world is an island of tranquillity entirely devoid of men or masculinity. But, as Aragon suggests, lesbians are very capable of defining who is worthy of the privileges of inclusion in lesbian community, and one of the categories of membership is adherence to a specific set of lesbian norms (3). Atkins argues that sexual practices define who is *not* a lesbian; in the case of lesbian parenting, assuming the shape of the heteronormative, two-parent family, particularly in the parenting of male children, can be viewed by some as a practice that transgresses that boundary (2). This then shifts the focus to the queering of the lesbian family, which follows on from the current trends in queer theory and queer politics that step away from gendered binaries and instead view identity in a more fluid form.

The construction of parental identity, particularly for those parents for whom masculinity enters the parent-infant dyad, is a challenge. Fonagy, Gergely, and Target describe one way of understanding parental identity construction:

> The ability to give subjective meaning to psychological experiences becomes possible as a result of our developing ability for explicit and reflective understanding that others' (as well as our own) actions are driven by underlying mental states and the establishment of adaptive mentalising strategies to reason about interactive experiences in terms of such mental states. (288)

This psychological standpoint suggests that the understanding of our own identities comes from a set of specific mental processes and that these are socially influenced (288). The "queering" of the understanding of sexual identity and self-construct opens up new vistas of possibility with the blurring of the lines of demarcation between gender and identity, sexuality and self (Peel 34). But the dominance of the heteronormative social paradigm prevails in the world of the family, and those families constructing alternate identities beyond those boundaries remain marginalised. Thus, the risk remains that their children will suffer the consequences of that marginalisation.

These are fundamental questions for those women (and men) who struggle with the current trend of total acceptance, particularly within the UK, of the lesbian parenting dyad as a macro-social construct. When teaching the topic of diversity with my mid-wifery students, there is now less and less tolerance of arguments that lesbian parents are marginalised from both mainstream heteronormative society and lesbian society. Lesbian parenting, particularly for the younger students, is viewed as a given, just another manifestation of social life. There is good reason for this. Lesbians now have legal status; their relationships are sanctioned by marriage and a lesbian partner can now, by law, be included on the birth certificate as the parent regardless of her biologi-cal relationship to the child. Based on the perceptions of these students, who exist in the "normal" world (rather than my own somewhat invidious position as an academic, a lesbian, a parent, and a person with a challenging history), it would seem that there is no need for activism and that families, in their diversity, are becoming less problematic.

I argue differently. It is indeed much easier to negotiate one's lesbian identity in the current context. Lesbianism has become more accepted, more mainstream, and as an identity, is for many of us legislated in terms of equality and the right to live as any other socially responsible citizen. Biblarz and Savci show that part of this right is affected by the perpetuation of a subtle homophobia inherent in the constant fear of the absence of a male role model in the lives of lesbian families, particularly those with sons (491). But I believe that "mainstream" lesbianism is a *social* identity, socially defined and, as such, limited to acceptable dimensions and manifestations, not the activist identity I grew into as a teenager and young adult. Indeed, if I were to ascribe to the same values as mainstream society, I would not believe in any further need for activism. Yet it would seem that in achieving our mainstream status, lesbian parents in particular have lost both the personal imperative for activism and the understanding of how marginalised we remain from our own communities. Here, I suggest, lies the crux of the matter. We need our own communities in order to retain the distinctiveness of our identity that allows us to define ourselves, rather than be defined by a persistently and politically poor patriarchal society that has given us the nod and the wink to allow us to play with their ball. At the same time, my co-parent, my son, and I have experienced exclusion, marginalisation, and discrimination from such communities because the very act of parenting challenges lesbian-feminist ideologies, and parenting a son is viewed by many as one step too far. The fundamental issue is that bringing a male into lesbian space means bringing all the associations of what it means to be male, which could include gender privilege, heteronormativity, and even the need to distinguish between one gender and another. An accusation from an ex-partner that I was "not a feminist" because I cooked meals for my son, drove him to the station to get the train for his Saturday job, and engaged in typical maternal activities such as doing his laundry, emphasized my perception that boys in a lesbian-dominated social context must feel marginalised and excluded at some level. I would have carried out all of these parenting activities if my child were female, yet I was made to feel less of a feminist, and less of a lesbian, because he is male. Suter et al., in "Motherhood as Contested Ideological Terrain," discuss the discourse of essential motherhood and the discourse of queer motherhood. In the former, motherhood is denoted by biological relationship; in the latter, monomaternalism is confronted, which includes challenging the patriarchal assumptions that inevitably surround the concept of motherhood. If we are moving towards a non-gendered concept of pluralistic parenting, where "mother" relates to a more "permeable and malleable structure" (Park 12), then it is crucial that we start to explore how to challenge the deeply ingrained and internalised assumptions which can undermine our confidence in parenting our sons.

What is the challenge here? Why do I continue to struggle with these issues, like so many of my sisters? I think that the core challenge is the nature of lesbian identity, which has been sorely won by individual women and by the "lesbian community" as a whole and which still competes with the mainstream sexualisation of everything that is remotely lesbian. If, as Seif argues, sexual identification labels are socially constructed then it is no surprise to find that the lesbian mother finds herself facing a form of cognitive dissonance, wearing a sexual identity that must de facto include a social identity of mother that does not sit comfortably with being a sexual object (33). Perhaps it is the transgression of the defined labels of lesbian that results in their marginalisation within their own communities. Yet that marginalisation within the already fringe communities of lesbianism is accompanied by a paradoxical mainstreaming of their rights, visibility, experience, and roles within the dominant culture.

Despite the issues raised in this discussion, research shows that lesbian mothers can and do successfully co-mother their children of both genders, negotiating the difficult paths through gender binaries, family dynamics, and heteronormative social structures effectively (Millbank 541). Millbank summarises a range of research that shows varying family structures and dynamics, with and without involvement of sperm donors, with and without the boundaries of typical parenting dyads (541-576). Biblarz and Savci carry out a similar and very comprehensive review of literature that clearly shows the progress and continuing challenges inherent in pushing gender boundaries within heteronormative social spaces (480-497).

What this research does not address, however, is the gendered nature of parenting roles and how women may settle into such roles; nor does it address any specific differences relating to the gender of children. Research shows that in terms of breadwinning and household maintenance tasks, there is a much greater experience of egalitarianism and sharing within lesbian-parented families (Goldberg and Perry-Jenkins 297). Dunne demonstrates that lesbian families can be a more positive locus of development than heterosexual families (11). Thus, it appears that lesbians who struggle with the transition to parenthood may be suffering more than they need to, given that some families are perfectly able to achieve a positive family dynamic regardless of the limitations and influences of the predominantly heteronormative world of the family beyond their borders.

Hicks deals explicitly with the issue of gender socialisation within non-heterosexual families and suggests that all gender is performative (43-44). I cannot disagree. Gendered roles abound, and I had no reason to be concerned about my son's ability to distinguish gender identities sufficiently to function in "the real world." Upon entering into the family dynamic, the lesbian family is heterosexualised, particularly in places such as the UK where there are limitations on social and community inclusion in lesbian-dominated spaces. Although Millbank (547) and Bilbarz and Savci (481-491) cite a number of sources that suggest a great deal of fluidity in family form and structure within the lesbian household, and although research clearly indicates that the nature of the lesbian family is creative and diverse, it is clear that for the majority of lesbians, their family is assimilated into heteronormative space, rather than radicalising it or resisting it. The locus of resistance is within the home, within the identities of the lesbian parents themselves but not, I argue, within the performative dimensions of family. Those performative dimensions are, crucially, defined by the context in which the performance takes place. Thus, I conclude that my experiences as a lesbian mother of a son were affected by the inherent heteronormativity which is, oxymoronically, inherent in the lesbian-feminist paradigm that was the source of my personal liberation.

I was, as were many other lesbian parents, compensating for the lack of a father in my son's life by performing my parenting role within "normative" (heterosexual) social spaces rather than socialising in lesbian spaces, because within those latter spaces I was no longer viewed as an authentic lesbian. Biblarz and Savci identify a number of research studies that demonstrate the gender of children being an issue within lesbian families and that lesbian parents anticipate more challenges parenting a son than a daughter. They highlight the issues very effectively:

> Lesbian mothers raising sons may face unique tensions in wanting social and socioeconomic success for their sons when that may mean colluding with cultural ideas of hegemonic masculinity that encourage male achievement but involve the subordination of women. To teach their sons to reject dominant definitions of masculinity risks potentially subjecting sons to ridicule and obstacles in the extra-family environment. In turn, boys with lesbian mothers may also have more to lose in the way of homophobic abuse by

their peers finding out—in threats to traditional heterosexual masculinity—than girls do in threats to traditional
femininity. (482)

This echoes my own concerns and those of my co-mother. However, the reality is that our son has developed a healthy attitude
towards self and gender. I should have been more concerned about
the impact on his developing mind and identity of the rampant
homophobia displayed by the parents of his peers and within the
social spaces he was required to inhabit. Whilst his classmates
had no problem relating to him as just another boy in their peer
group, it was the parents of his classmates who vented their rampant homophobia and significantly limited understanding of life
on my son. It soon became evident that the social isolation of
lesbian parenting within heteronormative spaces was played out
in miniature in the social world of a boy seeking only acceptance
and friendship and who found, instead, incomprehensible rejection.
I certainly did not want him to model himself on the behaviours
and attitudes of the men he encountered in these spaces.

In her research on young people growing up with a lesbian or
gay parent, Fairtlough found that the challenges to such children
were not indeed issues with their parents but with the wider world
(15). She discusses "the young people's experiences of living in a
society where derogatory attitudes or institutional discrimination
towards lesbian and gay people was routine" and cites incidence
after incidence of such young people being on the receiving end of
homophobic discourse and behaviour (15). Other research shows
that lesbian, gay, bisexual, transgender, and queer (LGBTQ) children
of LGBTQ parents experience a particular pressure toward both
gender conformity and heterosexuality. In their research, Suter, Daas
and Bergen discuss the pressure for children of lesbian parents to
defend their family and the challenges of being constantly confronted
with heterosexism in the social institutions they encountered (43).
There is no differentiation in these studies between boys and girls,
sons and daughters, suggesting both are similarly affected. At the
same time, research by Bos and Sandfort suggests that children
of lesbian parents have less of a sense of pressure for gender role
conformity than non-lesbian families (120).

I am surprised that in all the research and literature on lesbian parenting there is nothing written about the way that child gender may contribute to the experience of lesbian parenting. In the study by Leddy, Gartrell and Bos, it appears that adult daughters and sons of lesbian parents cite many of the social issues I mention above, including the fundamental pervasiveness of heterosexism and the experience of social stigma as the child of lesbian parents (243). This study, however, does not address the ways in which lesbians may negotiate their relationships with male children, and I consider this to be an important area for future research and discussion. Research by Kuvulanka and Goldberg shows that having LGBTQ parents can positively foster the development of sexual and gender identity in children.

What is the future? How can lesbians remain true to their radical past and step outside the norms of social acceptability and legal status to continue to challenge the confines of normative roles, especially when so many of them do not even question those confines or realise their own enslavement to a heteronormative ideal of motherhood? As Donati (qtd. in Crespi 12) states, family defines the manner of how we live and, as Crespi posits, it is within the family that gender differences are constructed through social, relational, and biological processes (12).

If we accept that the family is in essence a "gender relation" (Crespi 12), we must remind ourselves that it is through the family that children learn to know and understand the world in the first instance. There are many families where children are nurtured by mothers without fathers, by female care groups, or by strong networks of extended family relationships without the confines of the traditional "nuclear" family concept and often without close males to act as role models. Yet, many families still feel themselves as being judged against, and falling short of, the false ideal of parenthood, which remains particularly true for lesbian mothers of sons. It is this ideal that forms the ultimate boundary of definition and identity, and parenting outside this boundary must be viewed as an alignment to queer politics. As Chevrette states, the emergence of the concept "'queer' disrupted the homosexual/ heterosexual binary, countered categorical models of sexual identity, and examined the cultural, historical, and political discourses around which sexuality is constructed" (172). I feel sad that I lacked the awareness of the ways in which I perpetuated gender difference through my own parenting. Had I possessed the conceptual understanding and the access to new discourses around gender fluidity and queerness, I like to think my approach to parenting would have been radically different.

Perhaps the answer lies in the re-definition of family as outside the boundaries of mother-father, parent-child, and instead as a community of development and mutual affection in which the child is not an achievement, a product, or a status symbol but is instead a person whom we love and cherish, protect, nurture, and support and, when the time comes, we let go. This includes stepping outside the self-defined boundaries of political and personal identity as lesbian and feminist, an identity which served me well but which is essentially challenged by the emergent discourses of queer theory, queer politics, and gender fluidity that now frame the landscape in which we perform our unique form of mothering. My son is growing away from me, spending the majority of his time with his male friends, his peer group, and I am delighted. My concerns about the effects of my choices on his development or ability to function "in the real world" were unfounded.

We are in a different extended family now, as separated parents, but the parenting decisions remain the core of any communication between us as co-mothers, regardless of our estrangement and of his other mother having no legal rights or status as his parent. She is and always will be his co-mother. We continue to parent across the boundaries. Perhaps a radical re-visioning of family within society will be led by those who see and move beyond the heteronormative, heterosexist, sexist, and limiting definitions of mothers and fathers, lesbian feminists and lesbian mothers of sons. And maybe lesbian families will be in the vanguard. Perhaps not. Perhaps we, too, will fall to the ideological power of the system and lose ourselves in the process, only to find ourselves later on when we have moved past the pressure to be perfect parents.

Perhaps the shifts in discourse and understanding, of which this chapter forms a small part, will aid the development of communities not based on segregation, communities in which lesbian and feminist activism and male gender are not seen as mutually exclusive. Perhaps viewing family in this way, as a social and communal enterprise, as part of the movement towards the queering of gender, identity, sexuality, family, and parenting, will not leave us destabilised by motherhood, or struggling with the concatenation of seemingly opposed identities, but liberated by our love for each other and our belief in the possibilities of a different future where such boundaries no longer exist.

WORKS CITED

Aragon, Angela Pattatucci. "Introduction: Challenging Lesbian Normativity." *Journal of Lesbian Studies* 10.1/2 (2006): 1-15. Print.

Atkins, Dawn. "Introduction: Lesbian Sex Scandals." *Journal of Lesbian Studies* 3.3 (1999) 1-9. Print.

Biblarz, Timothy J. and Evren Savci. "Lesbian, Gay, Bisexual and Transgender Families." *Journal of Marriage and Family* 72 (2010): 480-497. Print.

Bos, Henny and Theo G.M. Sandfort. "Children's Gender Identity in Lesbian and Heterosexual Two-Parent Families." *Sex Roles* 62 (2010): 114-126. Print.

Butler, Judith. *Gender Trouble: Feminism and the Subversion of Identity*. New York: Routledge. 1999. Print.

Chevrette, Roberta. "Outing Heteronormativity in Interpersonal and Family Communication: Feminist Applications of Queer Theory 'Beyond the Sexy Streets.'" *Communication Theory* 23 (2013): 170-190. Print.

Crespi, Isabella. "Gender Socialisation within the Family: A Study on Adolescents and Their Parents in Great Britain." 2003. N.p. Pdf. 1 Nov. 2014

Dunne, Gillian A. "Opting into Motherhood." *Gender and Society* 14.1 (2000): 11-35. Print.

Fairtlough, Anna. "Growing Up with a Lesbian or Gay Parent: Young People's Perspectives." *Health and Social Care in the Community* 16.5 (2008): 521-528. Print

Fonagy, Peter, George Gergely, and Mary Target. "The Parent-Infant Dyad and the Construction of the Subjective Self." *Journal of*

Child Psychology and Psychiatry 48.4 (2007): 288–328. Print.

Forna, Aminatta, *Mother of All Myths: How Society Moulds and Constrains Mothers*. London: Harper Collins. 1999. Print.

Fox, G. L. and V. M. Murray. "Gender and Families: Feminist Perspectives and Family Research." *Journal of Marriage and Family* 62 (2000): 1160-1172. Print.

Goldberg, Abbie E. and Maureen Perry-Jenkins. "The Division of Labour and Perceptions of Parental Roles: Lesbian Couples across the Transition to Parenthood." *Journal of Social and Personal Relationships* 24.2 (2007): 297-318. Print.

Green, Fiona Joy. "Moms under Surveillance: Noticing and Challenging the Idea of the 'Good' Mother." *What Do Mothers Need?* Ed. Andrea O'Reilly. Bradford, Canada: Demeter Press, 2012. 21-24. Print.

Hicks, Stephen. "Gender Role Models, Who Needs 'Em?" *Qualitative Social Work* 7.1 (2013): 43-59. Print.

Kuvulanka, K.A. and A.E. Goldberg. "'Second Generation' Voices: Queer Youth with Lesbian-Bisexual Mothers." *Journal of Youth and Adolescence* 38 (2009): 904-919. Web. 7 August 2015.

Leddy, Anna, Nanette Gartrell, and Henny Bos. "Growing Up in a Lesbian Family: The Life Experiences of the Adult Daughters and Sons of Lesbian Mothers." *Journal of GLBT Family Studies* 8.32 (2012): 243-257. Print.

Lewin, Ellen. "Negotiating Lesbian Motherhood: The Dialectics of Resistance." *Maternal Theory, Essential Readings*. Ed. Andrea O'Reilly. Bradford, Canada: Demeter Press, 2007. 370-389. Print.

Lopez, Robert Oscar. "Growing Up with Two Moms: The Untold Children's View." *The Public Discourse*. 6 Aug. 2012 Web. 7 Aug. 2015.

Maushart, Susan. *The Mask of Motherhood* New York: Penguin Books, 1999. Print.

Millbank, Jenni. "From Here to Maternity: A Review of the Research on Lesbian and Gay Families." *Australian Journal of Social Issues* 38.4 (2003): 541-600. Print.

O'Reilly, Andrea, ed. *Maternal Theory, Essential Readings*. Bradford, Canada: Demeter Press, 2007. Print.

Park, Shelly M. *Mothering Queerly, Queering Motherhood*. Albany, New York: SUNY Press, 2013. Print.

Peel, Elizabeth. "Moving Beyond Heterosexism? The Good, the Bad and the Indifferent in Accounts of Others' Reactions to Important Life Events." *Psychology of Sexualities Review* 3.1 (2012): 34-46. Print.

Seif, Hinda. "To Love Women or to Not Love Men: Chronicles of Lesbian Identification." *Journal of Lesbian Studies* 3.3 (1999): 33-44. Print.

Speziale, Bette and Veena Gopalakrishna. "Social Support and Functioning of Nuclear Families Headed by Lesbian Couples." *Affilia* 19.2 (2004): 174-184. Print.

Suter, Elizabeth A., Karen L. Daas, and Karla Mason Bergen. "Negotiating Lesbian Family Identity via Symbols and Rituals." *Journal of Family Issues* 29.1 (2008): 26-47. Print.

Suter, Elizabether A., Leah M. Seurer, Stephanie Webb, Brian Grew, and Jody Koenig Kellas. "Motherhood as Contested Ideological Terrain: Essentialist and Queer Discourses of Motherhood at Play in Female-Female Co-mothers' Talk." *Communication Monographs* (2015): 1-26. Web. 7 August 2015.

Thurer, Shari, L. "The Myths of Motherhood." *Maternal Theory, Essential Readings.* Ed. Andrea O'Reilly. Bradford, Canada: Demeter Press, 2007. 331-344. Print.

Warner, Judith. "Bait and Switch: Moving On from 'Mommy Madness.'" *What Do Mothers Need?* Ed. Andrea O'Reilly. Bradford, Canada: Demeter Press, 2012. 53-62. Print.

6.
Changing the Gender Script

Ecuadorian Sons' Increased Domesticity and
Emotive Response to Transnational Mothering

RUTH TRINIDAD GALVÁN

ECUADOR'S MIGRATORY HISTORY spans several decades, destinations, and the gender make-up of the traveller. While men and families led the migration stream to the United States during the 1960s and '70s, recently, women lead migratory flows to different countries in the European Union (Bonilla and Borrero; Jokisch and Kyle). Although these female-led migratory streams are becoming commonplace, they create unique circumstances in countries such as the Philippines and Ecuador where childcare and the overall function of the household is left to "other mothers" or women in the family (Bohr and Whitfield; López de Lera and Oso Casas; Salazar Parreñas "Mothering from a Distance," Children of Global Migration; Yepez del Castillo and Herrera).

If families rely on mothers to financially sustain the home by migrating and leaving the care of children to the spouse or extended family, how is the gender order of families altered at home and transnationally? In previous research that I conducted in rural Mexico, men and fathers initiated and, in many cases, migrated during the entire duration of their children's upbringing (Trinidad Galván "Global Restructuring"). Wives and mothers left behind were responsible for the entire care and education of the children, while fathers financed the wellbeing of the family. Male-led migration changed gender relations by repositioning women as heads of households and community leaders (Trinidad Galván *Women Who Stay Behind*). In most Latin American countries, where the burden of care, socialization, and education of children still falls primarily on women and mothers, female migration creates distinctive transnational parenting, social relations, and gender shifts (Bohr and Whitfield; Dreby; Salazar Parreñas "Mothering from a Distance," "The Care Crisis"). I concur with Salazar Parreñas who states that the "formation of transnational households threatens cultural parameters and institutional norms marked by material inequalities between men and women as well as ideology. Thus, transnational families in their institutional arrangement invite gender transformations in the level of interaction" ("The Care Crisis" 5).

How does migration and transnationality change gender relations and consequently gender norms in Ecuadorian families where mothers are the travellers and sons stay behind? With the widespread global movement of people, comes changes in social relations in both receiving and sending communities. One illustration is that of children parented transnationally and who grow up without their parents nearby. This family reconfiguration is especially prevalent in marginalized regions of Latin American countries that are highly migratory. I argue that the transnational relationship of mothers who migrate and sons who stay behind breaks gender relations that are traditionally enacted in patriarchal Latin American families where sons receive greater privileges in the home and society vis-à-vis girls and daughters. Moreover, given sons' incurred domestic responsibilities and the sense of loss and intimacy their mothers' migration produced, I contend sons' narratives reveal gender shifts and a refashioning of masculine constructions.

This narrative inquiry is part of a study aimed at investigating gendered migration in urban Ecuador (Hesse-Biber and Leavy; Savin-Baden and Major). Investigations that center on families and individuals not migrating but who are affected by the migration of loved ones continue to be sparse; even more infrequent are those focused on the refashioning and/or reproduction of gender constructions (Salazar Parreñas, "The Care Crisis"; Trinidad Galván, "Global Restructuring," "Renegotiating Masculinity"). Data for this study consists of oral history interviews with half a dozen men that document men's experiences with the migration of either their spouse or mother (Hesse-Biber and Leavy).

The qualitative interview study included two husbands and four sons. For the topic that pertains to this discussion, I focus on the narratives of three sons who discursively manoeuvre and enact alternative masculinities around the migration of their mothers and transnational mothering.[1]

INTERSECTIONALITY

Theories focused on the intersections of structure and agency reveal the myriad ways individuals straddle the tensions between large-scale societal structures and individual lived experiences (Collins; hooks; Hurtado and Sinha). I draw on intersectionality to understand the dialectical relationship between transnational familial relations and structures and sons' ideological disposi-tions and gender scripts. Theories of intersectionality inform my understanding of the overlapping axis of power and privi-lege, while simultaneously revealing moments of disadvantage and contradiction within young men's gender scripts (Collins; Crenshaw; Salazar Parreñas "The Care Crisis"). That is, social and institutional structures and the relations and patterns they create ultimately get reenacted or vie against acts or ideologies of resistance (Haywood and Mac an Ghaill, *Education and Mas-culinities*). Specifically, I draw on a decolonial conceptualization of intersectionality rooted in global South intersecting identities and ideologies along the axis of gender, race, class, sexuality, and other subjectivities (Collins; Connell; Crenshaw; López, "Racially Stigmatized Masculinities"). Decolonial conceptualizations of intersectionality attend to the colonial legacy of global North and South relations that manifest themselves in discourse (Hernandez Castillo and Suarez Navaz; Trinidad Galván, "Chicana/Latin American"). This is especially pertinent in examinations of global South relations where global North capitalist and imperialist structures impact and devastate the circumstances of Ecuadorian women and men who must migrate to financially provide for their families. It is within this context of transmigration, shifting familial structures, and the persistence of patriarchy that these theories help frame and examine the micro and macro relations of Ecuadorian transnational families in this study. As Noguera and Hurtado suggest, "Masculinity and its accompanying privileges are not the only dimensions of identity that Latino men use to negotiate society. Class, sexuality, ethnicity, and race also shape and influence the way Latino men are treated and their perceptions of social reality" (11).

The intersectional nature of Ecuadorian sons' positionality renders Salazar Parreñas' discussion of the gender paradox logical as it underscores the complicated, complicit, and contradictory nature of gender relations and scripts of young, raced, working class men. Salazar Parreñas refers to gender paradox in her analysis of husbands and children left behind as the "nuanced process of gender ... at work in these families, one that involves a struggle between change and tradition" ("The Care Crisis" 94). Noguera and Hurtado remind us that traditional socialization and enactment of gender norms occurs within Latino families: "The Latino family unit has historically played an important role in socializing children into gender roles and reinforcing male dominance through patriarchal cultural practices, values, and norms" (8). While patriarchal "traditions" predominate in many Latin American families, like those of this study, racial and social class inequities are also at work. Hence, Latino and Latin American masculinities are shaped by familial socialization as well as the structural inequities persistent in global South and North relations. Sons, for instance, are cognizant of the reasons and conditions that led their parents to migrate and the marginalization they suffer in the new country. The multiple subjectivities Latino men must contend with lead Hurtado and Sinha to claim that Latino masculinities intersect along an axis of power relations that limits their privilege "on the basis of their devalued group memberships. In other words, being a man of Color, gay, and working class or poor creates various obstacles to accessing the full range of male privilege" (337). An intersectionality framework provides the analytic tools to tease through such themes as sons' contradictory notions of domesticity and the marginal place of young, working class racialized men in the overall context of Ecuador's sociopolitical state. Hence, intersectionality helps explain the varying—and at times contradictory—ways men understand and respond to their roles.

RESEARCH DESIGN: SONS' NARRATIVES AND
CRITICAL DISCOURSE ANALYSIS

These findings are part of a larger Fulbright-funded research inquiry into Ecuadorian migration. After my initial queries with a non-governmental organization into the migratory conditions of the country fell through, I became interested in the growing trend of female migration (Salazar Parreñas, "The Care Crisis"; Yepez de Castillo and Herrera). Like previous gender-specific explorations of migration and families who stay behind in Mexico (Trinidad Galván, *Women Who Stay Behind*), my six-month stay in Quito led to a similar exploration that focused on men. As an outsider and female researcher in Ecuador, access to men was not easy. It ultimately required the assistance of a male community member familiar with the topic and families affected by migration. As a resident of a rural community on the outskirts of Quito, he became my point of contact to the young men (Savin-Baden and Major). Of the six men who shared their oral life histories and narratives, two were husbands of migrating women (whom I don't address here) and four were sons. I focus on the narratives of three sons left behind by migrating mothers because two of the sons were brothers (Mateo and Lorenzo Torrez) who narrated similar circumstances and issues surrounding their parents' migration. Although one of the sons was also a husband and father, it was the realities of his parents' migration that he featured in his narration. As in many South American communities with sizeable emigration, these sons form part of Ecuador's working class and darker-phenotype population who are forced to migrate to survive (de la Torre and Striffler).

I focus on two twenty-three-year-olds, Mateo Torrez and Samuel Lozoya, and twenty-four-year-old Alberto Lugones,[2] all of whom grew up and resided in a small community on the outskirts of the capital of Quito. Their parents migrated when these young men were between fourteen and sixteen years of age. Mateo was fifteen years old when his parents and youngest brother migrated to Valencia, Spain. During the time of the interview, Mateo lived with two brothers in their parent's home and in the same neighborhood where extended family resided.

In Alberto's case, his mother migrated first to Spain in 2000 and was followed six months later by Alberto's father and eventually by his sister. Samuel was the only married son and father of two children with no immediate family in Ecuador, besides his wife and children. His father initiated the family's migration to Spain; he was followed by Samuel's sister and eventually by his mother and younger brother. As his narrative reveals, although Samuel was encouraged by his family in Spain to migrate too, his experience as a son who was left behind and his roles as husband and father kept him from migrating without his wife and children.

I employ a discursive analysis in order to attend to the ideological meanings behind the narratives of this small group of young men. At the core of this discursive analysis is the dialectical nature of global structures impinging on and creating familial migratory conditions and sons' ideological understandings and reactions to their parents' migration. A critical analysis entails understanding that "power is both located in the structural advantage [or disadvantage] of individuals and also exercised partly through the construction of discourses" (Davies et al. qtd. in Reay 118). I utilize a critical discourse analysis (CDA) framework as presented by Fairclough and Wodak:

> CDA sees discourse—language use in speech and writing—as a form of "social practice." Describing discourse as social practice implies a dialectical relationship between a particular discursive event and the situation(s), institution(s) and social structure(s) which frame it. A dialectical relationship is a two-way relationship: the discursive event is shaped by situations, institutions and social structures, but it also shapes them. (259)

CDA reveals the operation of power/knowledge in communication through the ideologies it unveils. In the process of unveiling these ideologies, they are interrogated and denaturalized and understood within their sociocultural context (Fairclough).

Utilizing Fairclough and Wodak's CDA framework, I analyze spoken "language texts" to understand the "contested nature of gender identities" and ideologies impacted by transnational mothering (Dillabough 17). I am interested in examining gender shifts in traditional notions of masculinity as they were conveyed in the discourse of the sons of migrant mothers. Connell defines masculinity as "socially constructed and [it] has a material existence at several levels: in culture and institutions, in personality, and in the social definition and use of the body. It is constructed within a gender order that defines masculinity in opposition to femininity, and in so doing, sustains a power relation between men and women as groups" (454). I am particularly interested in what Haywood and Mac an Ghaill suggest when they state, "Approaches to the study of men need to think not simply about identifying the range of masculinities, but about moments where masculinity is resisted and the implications of this" (*Education and Masculinities* 117). The conditions that led to and are left by migrating parents set the stage for a range of masculinities that reproduce and resist the traditional Latino masculine script.

DOMESTICITY AND SHIFTS IN THE GENDER SCRIPT

Mothering practices from afar are influenced and enacted upon by numerous cultural and social practices that include, and are not limited to, the inequitable global relations that elicit migration, further marginalization of racialized working class peoples, and gender-specific demands that lead mothers to migrate. These global realities inform the discursive messages migrating mothers transmit to their children left at home. Even before parents migrate, children hear of the inequitable circumstances and conditions that force parents to leave. Children grow up with often contradictory messages of displacement, sacrifice, and opportunity (Salazar Parreñas, "Mothering from a Distance").

Mothering as a method of transmitting cultural and social beliefs and practices is highly discursive in the case of parents who are not present and must rely on long-distance communication (Parreñas, "Long Distance Intimacy"). What parents transmit via phone conversations, letters, or technologies impacts and shapes children's and young adults' understanding of their parents' migration and their own roles and responsibilities at home. Children of migration who are parented transnationally by one or more parents and raised strictly among siblings or extended family experience an array of emotional, social, and personal challenges and changes (Salazar Parreñas, "The Care Crisis"). Children at home experience, among others, feelings of neglect and newfound social and educational opportunities abroad and at home.

The conditions that lead to global migration, in and of itself, alter gender relations at home and abroad (Trinidad Galván, "Renegotiating Masculinity"). The waning power of migrating Latin American males who experience greater marginalization abroad and the increased financial independence of migrating women, for example, alter Latin American familial gender relations:

> Indeed, transnational families are significant because they pose a challenge to the maintenance of the ideology of separate spheres as well as the traditional gender divisions of labor.... These challenges include the removal of biological mothers from the domestic sphere, the increase in the income power of women, and also the parodic performance of mothering and fathering that is prompted by its recital over distance. (Salazar Parreñas, "The Care Crisis" 6; see also Hondagneu-Sotelo)

With the migration and absence of mothers, issues around domesticity were the first clear articulation of changes in the traditional gender script. Sons could no longer rely on their mother or other women in the family and, instead, were forced to tend to domestic chores on their own. Alberto's mother, for instance, left when he was fifteen years old and his sister was seventeen. As his narrative relays, as children left behind, they alone were responsible for their home and school duties. Hence, one shift in the enactment of "traditional" forms of masculinity is expressed in the level of freedom and acquired responsibilities left to sons. This is especially the case when mothers migrate and sons are required to take on household chores. Alberto expresses how being left behind forced him to mature at a younger age:

> Well, with my sister I think we have—*based on those things we have lived*—been forced to mature a little. Well in this

case we were responsible, they [parents] wouldn't let us do whatever we wanted. I think that helped us a lot, to become like now almost full-fledged professionals. *I think it has been one of the best things [being left alone] that* caused us not to deviate.

Alberto seems to imply, as noted in the italicized text, that his and his sister's increased level of maturity and responsibility would have been unlikely if their parents, especially their mother, were present. Although he certainly doesn't mean that his mother's absence was "the best thing that happened to him," it did require that he take on greater responsibilities "traditionally" left to Ecuadorian mothers or sisters. It is no secret that patriarchal family structures continue to determine sons' and daughters' roles in the home and family. In her book, *Hopeful Girls, Troubled Boys: Race and Gender Disparity in Urban Education,* Nancy López outlines the additional responsibilities handed to daughters in Latino families in the U.S. and the social repercussions this has on both daughters and sons. In her intersectional analysis, López also underscores the manner in which familial and school structures co-construct moments of male marginalization and privilege by simultaneously inferring and demanding less of men at school and home.

Alberto specifies what domestic responsibilities he and his sister shared in the following comment:

Well, in that respect, *we took turns* [to cook]; we organized ourselves. When she sometimes arrived early or sometimes I arrived early *we cooked, we cooked for each other....* In the matter of cleaning and clothes and stuff, we organized our weekends to send our clothes to wash, also my sister helped me with the ironing and *I helped her with other household chores.*

He provides an interesting turn when he states, "I helped her with other household chores." While Alberto does not enact "traditional" Latino masculinities that assume women's place in the home, there is tension around who holds the responsibility of household chores (Noguera and Hurtado). His comment that he "helped" his sister indicates they are not equally responsible for the cleaning, ironing, and other household chores prevalent in traditional masculine ideologies.

Alberto's reliance on his sister, however, is only temporary as he later narrates that once his sister marries, their household includes his brother-in-law and new niece. Alberto is then exposed to other realities as they get played out in his sister's relationship with her husband. It is the global realities of migration and the lack of professional opportunities in global South communities that shift the gender script. In his narrative, he shares how his sister eventually also migrates after the birth of her daughter and inability to find employment in Ecuador. Instead of her husband migrating and leaving stable employment, she joins her parents in Spain and leaves her husband and daughter behind. Alberto states:

> There's a bit of difference because my sister is an automotive mechanic, a technologist, and I think at one point [she and her husband] had problems because she couldn't find work. Also it was my brother-in-law's idea that my sister stay home and not work. But she, on the other hand, *had another philosophy to not stay home.* That I also believe, *forced her to leave, to have her own money.*

Since dominant forms of masculinity are certainly learned, they can be unlearned and changed (Connell and Messerschmidt). Sons vacillate between socialized dominant forms of masculinity and new forms they've had to learn as a result of being left behind and, thus, transnationally parented. "In this way, subjectivity is conceptualized as a process of *becoming*, characterized by fluidity, oppositions, and alliances between particular narrative positions" (Haywood and Mac an Ghaill, "Education and Gender Identity" 53). This fluidity and opposition is seen in Alberto's narrative as he relays his sister's difficult decision to migrate in order to meet her professional goals and her family's economic wellbeing in much the same way their mother was driven to migrate. This repositioning, however, is not disconnected from the intersectionality of race, class, and gender that characterizes not only sons' positionality but that of the entire family both in Ecuador and abroad. Even though his sister is an educated professional, their marginal position as working class and racialized people does not ensure her sufficient employment opportunities to merit staying in her home country.

Mateo, who was left with older and younger brothers at the age of fifteen, also discusses the changes in gender order upon having to take on "traditionally" female-oriented tasks in the home: "In the evenings when we have time *we cook ourselves* and sometimes *we ourselves wash our clothes or iron ourselves*. And then sometimes when we have time or sometimes we tell my aunt to wash our clothes or clean the house, but otherwise *we do it ourselves*. We each do something."

While Mateo's narrative consistently reiterates the many tasks he and his brothers are required to do, he emphasizes doing domestic labour "*ourselves*." Since domestic labour is generally not the responsibility of males in the family, the fact that they must do for themselves obliges young men like Mateo to underscore the rarity of these roles. Unlike the work of Salazar Parreñas ("The Care Crisis"), which saw little shifts in gender normativity around domesticity of fathers who stay behind and care for their children, the loss of both parents and their adult status means there are fewer extended family members willing and able to take on domestic roles for these Ecuadorian sons. Although young men's domesticity signals shifts in traditional gender ideologies, it is the evidence of emotionality and loss in their narratives that underscore challenges to dominant forms of masculinity.

MASCULINE VULNERABILITIES AND EMOTIONALITY

If a discursive analysis makes ideologies transparent, it can also reveal emotionality and vulnerabilities expressed through language and demeanor. My outsider-researcher role meant there was little interaction before and after the interviews that might suggest any connection outside the roles of interviewer and interviewee. Even with these rather distant dynamics, I left each interview with a great sense of sadness and astonishment that these young men would exhibit any form of emotionality during the interviews. Through the analysis, I came to understand that the tone and language with which the young men expressed the loss of a mother was the biggest shift in the gender order of the narratives.

The emotive discourse of each son surrounding his mother's absence was significant and pervasive. Breaking from the male-dominant order and showing vulnerability, according to Holling, "challenges hegemonic and hypermasculinity as well as the 'tough guise' image characterized by fearlessness, lack of emotion, and gaining respect through violence often associated with Chicano-Latinos" (105). Indeed, expressions of vulnerability minimize the stereotypical "macho" image. Considering that many men are socialized to evade emotionality, expressions of emotion to a stranger like myself fell outside hegemonic forms of masculinity (Connell and Messerschmidt; Noguera and Hurtado; Wester). Alberto, for example, voices repeatedly that the emotional turmoil he and his mother acknowledge is part of migration and the separation of families (Bohr and Whitfield; Scheib). Alberto states the following:

> Because it's also *ugly*, my mom also talked to me when I went to Spain and told me that Christmas is *horrible* sometimes, receive baskets and all that stuff and not have anyone to share it with, is the *most horrible*. And not have anyone to share those days with, that [mother's migration] was *the worst situation of our life* with my sister, it was *one of the worst*, how should we say, *traumas* that I was left with, that is, that *left me empty inside*.

Alberto's narrative speaks not only to his own sense of loss but also that which his mother experienced and transnationally communicated. The dialectical relationship of mother and son expressing loss and sacrifice is clearly felt in the narrative precisely because they speak to the lack of familial presence and relations during a special time of the year.

Samuel, twenty-three years old and married with children, expresses his loss of intimacy from the role of son and father:

Actually it didn't affect me a lot, my father's departure, but then *when my mother left, I did feel super bad* and I already have two kids…. Once it was empty [home] I felt *super bad* because my mom became father and mother. Sometimes, obviously *I've fallen under despair, I've fallen because of depression* and … my wife has been like my mother, because sometimes *one isn't well* and so when your parents call you on the phone *it is very different* and so she [wife] is like my mother.

The intersectional nature of men's numerous roles as sons, husbands, and fathers, like those of Samuel, intensifies their emotional response. As the only husband and father of the group, Samuel contended with many roles and responsibilities. He clearly admits that his fatherly role should assume an absence of sadness during his mother's departure; yet his mother's departure affected him not only as a son and father, but also as a husband.

Mothering from a distance, as Samuel suggests when speaking of phone conversations with his mother, does not replace or make-up for the loss that apparently led to his despair and depression (Parreñas "Long Distance Intimacy"; Salazar Parreñas "Mothering from a Distance"). Interestingly, his wife has now become that maternal figure that children and families who stay behind require (Bohr and Whifield; Salazar Parreñas, "The Care Crisis"; Trinidad Galván, "Global Restructuring").

This loss of intimacy was also expressed in Samuel's decision to never leave his wife and daughter behind. As in Salazar Parreñas' ("The Care Crisis") study, Samuel—as a parent—recognizes the tremendous loss that his absence would cause his daughter and wife.

Mateo, one of four brothers who stayed behind, had tears in his eyes when he spoke of the loss of his mother and father. As he reflects back to his behaviour towards his mother before her migration, he recognizes his lack of empathy and the manner in which his behaviour wounded her. The most significant part of Mateo's narrative and an important discursive shift is the emotion and vulnerability with which he expresses his transnational relationship with his mother:

And now I realize that I must learn to value those that I love the most in this life, because *when my mom was here I didn't obey her much*. I was very spoiled when my mom was here and well now I realize it and I myself am trying to avoid all the bad things I use to do; *make my mother suffer, make her cry*, because they say that *a son should never make a mother cry*.

Sometimes they call to ask what's happened or if there's anything new. Like when it was Mother's Day on a Sunday and you have to realize that my grandmother passed away on Saturday and it was a huge blow to my mom and we didn't even remember to call my mom to tell her, "*Happy Mother's Day mommy, we miss you*." We didn't communicate with her, our mom suffered a lot with the loss of her mother and *we felt awful*.

While distant mothers make efforts to foster a relationship by maintaining consistent communication with their children, sons still express a loss of intimacy (Parreñas "Long Distance Intimacy"). Without hesitation, sons in this study expressed the tremendous loss of affection and intimacy that migration, of mostly mothers, created. As Mateo so poignantly attests, transnationality has made him keenly aware of the mutually affective role he and his mother signify for each other. What is most significant in sons' discourses of vulnerability and loss is the awareness of the dialectic of these emotions. That is, because the absence of their parents was a matter of survival, they acknowledged it as a familial sacrifice and understood that both parents and sons feel the emotionality of loss and absence.

As Hurtado and Sinha posit in their research with Latino feminists, "Participants redefined masculinity in ways that allow men to experience the full range of the human experience (e.g., emotional expression, meaningful relationships with family, community, and others) unencumbered by the restrictions imposed by traditional masculine gender roles" (348). In effect, these expressions and changes were evident in these young men and, I argue, were a result of the intersectional nature of their social positioning and transnationality.

CONCLUDING THOUGHTS

As Salazar Parreñas suggests, "To say that children are perfectly capable of adjusting to nontraditional households is not to say that they don't suffer hardships" ("The Care Crisis" 53). In the absence of mothers or both parents, the narratives of sons who stay behind reveal varying transnational relations and vulnerabilities. These unequal relations underscore the intersectional nature of young working class Ecuadorian men's positionality and consequently the gender shifts in their narratives. As Collins suggests, "The notion of intersectionality describes micro-level processes—namely, how each individual and group occupies a social position within interlocking structures of oppressions," such as those created by the unequal conditions of migration (82).

An intersectional framework coupled with a critical discourse analysis revealed and facilitated an examination of the contradictory nature of sons' responses to domesticity, while challenging hegemonic forms of masculinity through the emotionality of their narratives. For instance, sons disclosed the added responsibilities and domestic chores that were required of them while also discursively insinuating these tasks were reserved for women. What was most significant was the "traditional" gender script of the dispassionate "tough guise" male did not overpower these young men's willingness to demonstrate emotion and vulnerability during the interviews.

ENDNOTES

[1]The qualitative interview study was part of a Fulbright Scholars Grant that I received in 2008 to research the migration phenomenon in Ecuador. Although the study also included husbands who stayed behind, I focus here on oral history interviews with three of four sons. Since two of the young men were brothers and reiterated their parents' migratory experience, I focus on only one of the brother's narrative.

[2]All names in this chapter have been changed to protect the participant's anonymity.

WORKS CITED

Battistella, Graziano and Maria Cecilia Conaco. "The Impact of Labour Migration on the Children Left Behind: A Study of Elementary Children in The Philippines." *Sojourn* 13.2 (1998): 220-241. Print.

Bohr, Yvonne and Natasha Whitfield. "Transnational Mothering in an Era of Globalization: Chinese-Canadian Immigrant Mothers' Decision-Making When Separating from Their Infants." *Journal of the Motherhood Initiative for Research and Community Involvement—Mothering and Migration: (Trans)nationalisms, Globalization and Displacement* 2.2 (2011): 161-174. Print.

Bonilla, Adrian and Mercedes Borrero. *Ecuador: La Migración Internacional en Cifras*. Ecuador: FLASCO/Fondo de Población de las Naciones Unidas, 2008. Print.

Collins, Patricia Hill. *Black Feminist Thought: Knowledge, Consciousness, and the Politics of Empowerment*. New York: Routledge, 1990. Print.

Connell, Robert. "A Whole New World: Remaking Masculinity in the Context of the Environmental Movement." *Gender and Society* 4.4 (1990): 452-478. Print.

Connell, R. W. and Messerschmidt, James. "Hegemonic Masculinity: Rethinking the Concept." *Gender and Society* 19.6 (2005): 829-859. Print.

Crenshaw, Kimberle. "Demarginalizing the Intersection of Race and Sex: A Black Feminist Critique of Antidiscrimination Doctrine, Feminist Theory, and Antiracist Politics." *University of Chicago Legal Forum* 140 (1989): 139-167. Print.

de la Torre, Carlos and Steve Striffler. *The Ecuador Reader: History, Culture, Politics*. Durham, NC: Duke University Press, 2009. Print.

Dillabough, Jo-Anne. "Gender Theory and Research in Education: Modernist Traditions and Emerging Contemporary Themes." *The Routledge Falmer Reader in Gender and Education*. Eds. Madeleine Arnot and Mairtin Mac an Ghaill. New York: Routledge, 2006. 17-32. Print.

Dreby, Joanna. "Children and Power in Mexican Transnational Families." *Journal of Marriage and Family* 69 (2007): 1050-1064. Print.

Fairclough, Norman. *Critical Discourse Analysis: The Critical Study of Language.* England: Longman Group Limited, 1995. Print.

Fairclough, Norman and Ruth Wodak. "Critical Discourse Analysis." *Discourse Studies: A Multidisciplinary Introduction: Vol. 2. Discourse as Social Interaction.* Ed. Teun. A. van Dijk. London: Allen Lane, 1997. 258-284. Print.

Haywood, Chris and Mairtin Mac an Ghaill. "Education and Gender Identity: Seeking Frameworks of Understanding." *The RoutledgeFalmer Reader in Gender and Education.* Eds. Madeleine Arnot and Mairtin Mac an Ghaill. New York: Routledge, 2006. 49-57. Print.

Haywood, Chris and Mairtin Mac an Ghaill. *Education and Masculinities: Social, Cultural and Global Transformations.* London: Routledge, 2013. Print.

Hernández Castillo, Rosario and Liliana Suárez Navaz. Introducción. *Descolonizando el Feminismo: Teorías y Practices Desde los Márgenes,* Eds. Liliana Suárez Navaz and Rosario Hernández. Madrid: Ediciones Cátedra—Grupo Anaya, S.A., 2008. 11-28. Print.

Hesse-Biber, Sharlene Nagy and Patricia Leavy. "Oral History: A Collaborative Method of (Auto)biography Interview." *The Practice of Qualitative Research.* Eds. Sharlene Nagy Hesse-Biber and Patricia L. Leavy. New York: Sage Publications, 2005. 149- 194. Print.

Holling, Michelle. A. "*El simpático* Boxer: Underpinning Chicano Masculinity with a Rhetoric of *Familia* in *Resurrection Blvd.*" *Western Journal of Communication* 70.2 (2006): 91-114. Print.

Hondagneu-Sotelo, Pierrette. *Gendered Transitions: Mexican Experiences of Immigration.* Berkeley: University of California Press, 1994. Print.

hooks, bell. *Writing Beyond Race: Living Theory and Practice.* New York: Routledge, 2013. Print.

Hurtado, Aída and Mrinal Sinha. "More than Men: Latino Feminist Masculinities and Intersectionality." *Sex Roles* 59 (2008): 337-349. Print.

Jokisch, Brad and David Kyle. "Ecuadorian International Migration." *The Ecuador Reader: History, Culture, Politics.* Eds. Carlos De la Torre and Steve Striffler. London: Duke University

Press, 2008. 350-358. Print.

López, Nancy. *Hopeful Girls, Troubled Boys: Race and Gender Disparity in Urban Education.* New York: Routledge, 2002. Print.

López, Nancy. "Racially Stigmatized Masculinities and Empowerment: Conceptualizing and Nurturing Latino Males' Schooling in the United States." *Invisible No More: Understanding the Disenfranchisement of Latino Men and Boys.* Eds. Pedro Noguera, Aída Hurtado, and Edward Fergus. New York: Routledge, 2012. 235-254. Print.

López de Lera, Diego and Laura Oso Casas. "La Inmigración latinoamericana en España: Tendencias y Estado de la Cuestion." *Nuevas Migraciones latinoamericanas a Europa: Balances y Desafios.* Eds. Isabel Yepez del Castillo and Gioconda Herrera. Ecuador: FLASCO, 2007. 31-68. Print.

Noguera, Pedro and Aída Hurtado. "Invisible No More: The Status and Experience of Latino Males from Multidisciplinary Perspectives." *Invisible No More: Understanding the Disenfranchisement of Latino Men and Boys.* Eds. Pedro Noguera, Aída Hurtado, and Edward Fergus. New York: Routledge, 2012. 1-15. Print.

Parreñas, Rhacel. "Long Distance Intimacy: Class, Gender and Intergenerational Relations between Mothers and Children in Filipino Transnational Families." *Global Networks* 5.4 (2005): 317-336. Print.

Reay, Diane. "Spice Girls, 'Nice Girls,' and 'Tomboys': Gender Discourses, Girls' Cultures and Femininities in the Primary Classroom." *The RoutledgeFalmer Reader in Gender and Education.* Eds. Madeleine Arnot and Mairtin Mac an Ghaill. New York: Routledge, 2006. 117-130. Print.

Salazar Parreñas, Rhacel. "The Care Crisis in the Philippines: Children and Transnational Families in the New Global Economy." *Global Woman: Nannies, Maids, and Sex Workers in the New Economy.* Eds. Barbara Ehrenreich and Arlie Russell Hochschild. New York: Metropolitan Books, 2003. 39-54. Print.

Salazar Parreñas, Rhacel. *Children of Global Migration: Transnational Families and Gendered Woes.* California: Stanford University Press, 2005. Print.

Salazar Parreñas, Rhacel. "Mothering from a Distance: Emotions, Gender, and Intergenerational Relations in Filipino Transnational

Families." *Feminist Studies* 27.2 (2001): 361-390. Print.

Savin-Baden, Maggi and Claire Howell Major. *Qualitative Research: The Essential Guide to Theory and Practice.* New York: Routledge, 2013. Print.

Scheib, Holly. "It's a Strange Truth: Experiences of Transnational Motherhood in Newly Arrived Migrants in Post-Katrina New Orleans." *Journal of the Motherhood Initiative for Research and Community Involvement—Mothering and Migration: (Trans) nationalisms, Globalization and Displacement* 2.2 (2011): 226-238. Print.

Trinidad Galván, Ruth. "Chicana/Latin American Feminist Epistemologies of the Global South (within and outside the North): Decolonizing *el Conocimiento* and Creating Global Alliances." *Journal of Latino/Latin American Studies* 6.2 (2014): 135-140. Print.

Trinidad Galván, Ruth. "Global Restructuring, Transmigration and Mexican Rural Women Who Stay Behind: Accommodating, Contesting and Transcending Ideologies." *Globalizations* 5.4 (2008): 523-540. Print.

Trinidad Galván, Ruth. "Renegotiating Masculinity in Transnational Relationships: An Innovative Research Perspective on Gender." *Innovación e Internacionalización de la Educación: Estudios de Caso y Propuestas.* Eds. Rosario Hernandez-Castañeda and Jocelyn Gacel-Avila. Guadalajara, Mexico: Editorial Universitaria, 2010. 303-332. Print.

Trinidad Galván, Ruth. *Women Who Stay Behind: Pedagogies of Survival in Rural Transmigrant Mexico.* Tucson: University of Arizona Press, 2015. Print.

Wester, Stephen. "Male Gender Role Conflict and Multiculturalism: Implications for Counseling Psychology." *The Counseling Pyschologist* 36.2 (2008): 294-324. Print.

Yepez de Castillo, Isabel and Gioconda Herrera. *Nuevas Migraciones latinoamericanas a Europa: Balances y Desafíos.* Ecuador: FLASCO, 2007. Print.

Zentgraf, Kristine and Norma Stoltz Chinchilla. "Transnational Family Separation: A Framework for Analysis." *Journal of Ethnic and Migration Studies* 38.2 (2012): 345-366. Print.

7.
TV's New Dads

Sensitive Fatherhood and the Return of Hegemonic Masculinity

DWAYNE AVERY

IN SEASON THREE of FX's *Sons of Anarchy*, Jax Teller—the show's menacing and melancholic biker outlaw—heads to Ireland in search of his son, who has been kidnaped by the Real IRA. While in Ireland, however, Teller undergoes an unexpected moral transformation: typically shown as a fierce leader of men who has no qualms about using torture and other violent atrocities to get his way, Teller slowly weakens in his resolve. Indeed, while the boy is eventually located, his rescue comes about not through the bold and daring iron will of Teller but by his mother, who uses her own remarkable propensity for violence to reclaim the boy. Holding a gun to the head of an orphan child, Jemma explains that she would rather have half of a dead grandson than let someone else raise him. Surprisingly, although Jax has made a career of engaging in the most heinous of crimes, he adamantly disapproves of his mother's outlaw version of the King Solomon story. Teller, the father, it seems, has a moral compass after all. Unlike his own mother, who is depicted as a monstrous maternal figure, Teller is shown to possess superior fatherly instincts; like the mother in the King Solomon story, Jax realizes that a truly loving father would rather sacrifice their child than subject them to a world brimming with cruelty, violence, and death. Subsequently, in order to rescue his son, Jax decides to give him up. Offering the boy a final loving glance, Teller sets off alone, comforted in the thought that his son will grow up never knowing the criminality and violence he inherited from his father.

What I wish to argue in this chapter is that the "King Solomon" episode not only encapsulates the overall tone and theme of the entire series but its twisted conjunction of domestic violence, parental redemption, and fatherly love gets at the heart of a notable trend in contemporary television. In its most rudimentary form, the story being told in so many post-network television narratives involves the reconstruction of the father figure as a postfeminist[1] champion of sensitivity, domestic care, and fatherly love. Unlike the idyllic, breadwinning father that formed a televisual archetype for the '50s and '60s or the bumbling dad that dominated the sitcom, the postfeminist father is imagined as having it all: he is a provider, a protector, a moral authority, and a caring nurturer—and he does all this without giving up his traditional masculinity. In short, the postfeminist father is an eclectic figure that derives its identity from a plethora of incompatible gender codes: soft and hard, sensitive and violent, rational and irrational. The fathers that appear in television shows like *Sons of Anarchy*, *Breaking Bad*, *Mad Men*, *The Shield*, *The Leftovers*, and *The Walking Dead* are notable for their attempt to exist along multiple fault lines. They are the split-personality parents of the postfeminist age, trying to fit together a cohesive parental identity that is always bursting at the seams. Like Teller, they can be pensive, sad, and melancholic fathers who try to do right by their children; yet they are just as likely to bring down the house, as their propensity to fits of asphyxiating rage creates precarious familial environments that threaten the lives of their children.

Undoubtedly, the postfeminist father represents a privileged parental identity in contemporary television; however it would be a mistake to think that this ubiquitous figure is constructed in isolation. Absent throughout much of the history of popular film and television, the attentive and loving father-figure emerges in contemporary media as a striking, albeit disingenuous, character who uses his sacrificial love and pensive ways to bolster his authority—all at the expense of women. Avoiding the obvious backlash against feminism that was pronounced throughout the 1980s and early '90s, contemporary television's reconstruction of fatherhood nonetheless reduces the power and visibility of its female characters, especially its maternal figures, which are, once again, treated as the villainous "bad mothers" that have adorned much of the history of popular media (Kaplan). Like Jemma, whose despicable assertion of motherly love is both sickening and unthinkable, contemporary television recasts motherhood as an institution that, as Monique Plaza observes, represents "the most prodigious and effective bastions of misogyny" (Ruddick, *Maternal Thinking* 34). Analysis of the media's representation of postfeminist fatherhood has been slowly gaining ground, as several theorists, such as Hamad and Lotz, have shown how fatherhood is bound up with the construction of contemporary masculinities. In this chapter, I take an alternative perspective. While I am also concerned with the construction of fatherhood as an ideal mode of masculinity, I use a maternal lens to determine how televisual images of postfeminist fatherhood relate to the institution of motherhood and maternal practices. Specifically, drawing on the maternal philosophy of Sara Ruddick, especially her contention that mothering is a social practice open to both men and women, I look at how care and protection are used to construct the meaning of TV's new dads. Some of the questions I investigate are: Is the model of fatherhood depicted in these shows significantly different from the dominant model of care associated with maternal thinking? Are there multiple models of fathering or do these images lead to a hegemonic form of "sensitive" fatherhood? How are traditional masculine characteristics—breadwinning, leadership, competitiveness, toughness—integrated into a fatherly model of care? How are women, especially mothers, depicted in these series? Are they featured as co-parents who assist fathers in the care of children? Or are they co-opted by the patriarchal father-head?

POSTFEMINIST FATHERHOOD

In the past few decades, postfeminism has emerged as a fraught and ambiguous term that can refer to any number of contradictory definitions. For some, it signals the jubilant end of second-wave feminism, especially its supposed restrictive hold on women, who are cast as victims in a misogynist, patriarchal social order. For others, postfeminism represents a time of immense equality and change, especially for the young career woman who uses the neo-liberal imperatives of contemporary capitalism to her advantage, choosing the products, services, and information that allow her to "have it all." It has been called a neo-conservative, backlash culture, which seeks to dismantle the real political strides made by previous feminists; a retro, sexist movement that mistakenly associates consumer choice with equality. Clearly, as a polarizing term that oscillates between the poles of freedom and regression, postfeminism, for better or worse, lacks any theoretical consistency. According to Stéphanie Genz, however, postfeminism's discordant nature holds the keys to understanding how gender is configured in contemporary cultures. Taking a liminal approach that avoids the either/or schematic of other postfeminist theorists, Genz invites us to think of postfeminism as a complex, multi-layered phenomena that maintains *both* the threat of backlash as well as the capacity for innovative change.

Genz's liminal understanding of postfeminism is, I feel, the most fruitful approach to accessing postfeminist masculinities, especially the hybrid construction of postfeminist fatherhood. According to Benjamin Brabon, for example, the postfeminist man can also be read as an incongruous and ambivalent subject position, which unsuccessfully blends together many different codes of manliness, from the sensitivity and domesticity promoted by second-wave feminists to the aggressive chauvinism associated with hegemonic masculinity. As he writes, the postfeminist man "is not a feature of a re-masculinization of contemporary Anglo-American culture—a forthright repudiator of second-wave feminism that can effortlessly be recognized as part of backlash—but, instead, an uneven and diffident subject position that is doubly coded" (122). For Brabon, the postfeminist man falls in line with postmodernism's emphasis on fragmentation and disunity, as he combines various irreconcilable "gender scripts" that maintain the potential for both innovation and regression. As Brabon continues, "Here, 'retro' and 'neo' forms of masculinity act as the strophe and antistrophe of postfeminist manhood, as progressive male subject positions are haunted by the threat of 'backlash' and invocations of older forms of masculinity are re-signified by pro-feminist interventions" (117).

But while the postfeminist man may be left adrift in a sea of conflicting codes about masculinity, he cannot avoid the gravitational force of fatherhood. As Hannah Hamad argues, the image of the sensitive father does not represent one code amongst an assortment of postfeminist markers of manliness; it is the *dominant* sign of postfeminist masculinity. She writes, "Notwithstanding its pluralities, its dualistic gender ideology, and its instabilities as a subject position, fatherhood has been consistently deployed in contemporary popular cinema as the paradigmatic formation of masculinity for postfeminist culture" (135). Rather than challenging hegemonic masculinity, postfeminist fatherhood employs the qualities of sensitivity, care, and domestic prowess to create a dominant model of masculinity that reinstates those "ghosts of hegemony" that have been supposedly eclipsed by the feminisation of culture. Hamad writes:

> Postfeminist fatherhood manifests in many guises.... However, dominant iterations tend toward a model of fatherhood that is (or becomes) emotionally articulate, domestically competent, skilled in managing the quotidian practicalities of parenthood and adept at negotiating a balance and/or discursive confluence of private sphere fatherhood and public sphere paternalism. Furthermore, hegemonic formations of postfeminist fatherhood configure this model at little cost to the legibility of fathers' more traditionally masculine traits. (2)

Hamad's detailed analysis of Hollywood fatherhood demonstrates succinctly the cinema's use of the father figure to ground its duplicitous version of contemporary masculinity. I would add that while the trope of the postfeminist father is featured heavily in other kinds of media, such as post-network television, its incompatible gender scripts resonates with a much larger social dynamic that envisions fatherhood as an institution riddled with social conflicts and contradictions, as the expectation and desire to become more than a breadwinner create new tensions and hopeful possibilities for men. For example, one of the demands advanced by second-wave feminists involved the need for a co-parenting family structure that minimized the domestic burdens placed upon women. Men were encouraged to rethink their reliance on a breadwinning model of parenting and accept responsibility for the nurturance and care of children.

In many ways, this call for a nurturing model of fatherhood has seen significant developments over the past few decades. In her in-depth study of stay-at-home dads, for instance, Andrea Doucet has found that while many contemporary men maintain their own "manly" ways of parenting, often emphasizing risk and play as essential aspects of the father-child relationship, men can still act as mothers. Subsequently, while caretaking is traditionally perceived as a distinctly female activity that has had great personal costs to women, the increased involvement of the men in Doucet's study points to a lessening of the gender disparity and imbalance involved in caretaking. Similarly, in her book *Superdads: How Fathers Balance Work and Family in the 21st Century*, Gayle Kaufman argues that the traditional breadwinning model of fatherhood has been broadened to include two other classes of fathers: "new dads" and "superdads." Whereas the "new dad" *attempts* to find a balance between the responsibilities of family and work, the "superdad" represents an entirely new model of fatherhood that is fully committed to replacing the breadwinning model with one that emphasizes the importance of domestic responsibilities, sensitivity, nurturance, and care. These fathers, Kaufman writes, deliberately alter their careers, often relying on flexible work schedules, in order to play an active role in the lives of their families.

On the other hand, while the emergence of the "superdad" is encouraging, it does not guarantee that postfeminist fatherhood remains committed to the aims of feminism. In his study of masculinity and fatherhood, sociologist Scott Coltrane has bemoaned the way the promotion of active fatherhood often leads to the re-establishment of hegemonic masculinity, as many come to see the return of the patriarchal, heterosexual family as the definitive answer to today's social ills. Coltrane writes, "As a researcher who studies how and why men get involved in raising children and maintaining households, I share the goal of making men more aware of the benefits of assuming domestic duties and getting involved in the details of raising children. What troubles me, however, is the narrow vision of family perpetrated by these moral entrepreneurs" (390). While Coltrane's observations pertain to the recent rise in various "father's rights" movements that seek to reestablish the father as the patriarchal head of household, such as the ultra-conservative Promise Keepers, other studies have shown that even when men attempt to construct a model of fatherhood that is in line with the demands of second-wave feminism, hegemonic practices still resurface. In their study of active and caring fathers, Brandth and Kvande conclude that even though many men have refashioned their sense of self by incorporating feminine traits, there has been little change to the gender dynamics of the home. Instead of undermining hegemony, the active father's sensitivity and nurturance is often used to sustain traditional masculinities, especially the father's authority over the household.

In the world of post-network television, it is easy to find examples of the hybrid and duplicitous postfeminist father. Whereas postfeminist television is typically associated with the adventures of the fashion-conscious, single, career-woman, in the past decade there has been no shortage of shows that feature hyper-masculine characters that are at home in a world enveloped in violence, chauvinism, and misogyny. As David Thier writes, "It's no coincidence that while the traditional masculine roles may be disappearing in reality, they've only become stronger on television. After all, the cowboy never became the pinnacle of American manhood until he was crushed by a freight train." However, it isn't the lone cowboy that has returned to re-masculinize contemporary television. At the center of these tough and gritty shows is not some lonesome, detached, action-hero but a broken, morally ambiguous father figure who attempts, at all costs, to keep his family intact. While this father-head bears some resemblance to the iconic "new man,"[2] his soft and nurturing ways are just as likely to be accompanied by extreme acts of violence and terror. More of a frontiersman than a conspicuous consumer, the postfeminist father demonstrates that, above everything else, violence is needed to care for and protect the home.

Here are just a few examples of the hyper-masculine, patriarchal worlds created by the top post-network brands, HBO, FX and AMC. In *The Walking Dead*, a southern cop is forced to battle an outbreak of dangerous zombies in order to keep his family alive; in the process he is transformed into the patriarchal leader of a small group that comes to rely on his "manly" instincts and gritty determination. *Hell on Wheels* follows the charming, post-bellum protagonist, Cullen Bohannon, on his quest to kill all the soldiers responsible for the deaths of his wife and children. In *The Shield*, Vic Mackey is a crooked cop who not only strives to be the "dad of the century" but also uses his police brutality to cleanse Los Angeles of its urban morass. In *Breaking Bad,* Walter White is a geeky science teacher who learns that he is dying and decides to start cooking meth in order to provide for his family. By the end of the series, however, White is transformed into a brutally sadistic drug lord, whose desire for money and power has a devastating effect on his family. Finally, *The Leftovers* follows the troubled life of Kevin Garvey, a single-father cop who is left in charge of his daughter after his wife decides to join a cult.

What do all these contradictory depictions of fathers say about the current televisual climate? Why has television invested so heavily in resurrecting the male hero only to have him crushed by the responsibilities of parenthood? According to Amanda Lotz, the rise in troubled TV dads is a testament to the tensions men face, as they confront the waning of patriarchal power and privilege. In essence, men no longer know how to act because the expectations involved in being a man and father differ fundamentally from the bread-winning model of years past. Here, I think, Lotz comes close to providing a televisual account of Susan Faludi's thesis on the betrayal of American men. In her book *Stiffed: The Betrayal of the American Man,* Faludi argues that men's identities were once secured through various institutions, from labour unions and church associations to community centers and veteran's groups. Centered on the value of hard work, these institutions gave men a real purpose and way to prove their identities. However, in recent times, the utilitarian function of men's identities has been replaced by an ornamental culture that teaches men to find meaning in various pre-packaged, consumer-oriented images of masculinity. Real men, for Faludi, are common and work with their hands; they do not cover themselves in a veneer of phony consumerism. Subsequently, without any real way to anchor themselves in a post-industrial world that no longer values men's utilitarianism, men are left without any significant social purpose and, as such, flounder within their roles as fathers, husbands, and workers.

While Lotz's analysis provides a good starting point for investigating the postfeminist father, I find her contention that images of fathers in crisis represent the struggles of some men who bravely try to become active, emotionally-engaged fathers somewhat troubling. For Lotz, problems in fatherhood have nothing to do with feminism and cannot be treated as a form of backlash; rather, "allocation of blame can be identified in the complicated relationships with and anger the men express toward their fathers. This blaming of the father . . . [maps] easily onto a blaming of patriarchy and the patriarchal masculinity the fathers are depicted to possess" (84). I agree that fathers in shows like *Sons of Anarchy*, *The Shield*, and *The Leftovers* are vastly different from the backlash-fathers featured in many films and television shows from the 1980s. The problem is that while women may not be explicitly *blamed* for these fathers' shortcomings, they are nonetheless caught up in a patriarchal system that continues to promote and value men's identities at the expense of women, especially mothers.

In her book *Feminism without Women*, Tania Modleski warns that when analyzing "men in crisis" it is important to remember that power is often consolidated by men through periodic moments of crisis. By focusing on the so-called plight of men, images of troubled masculinities often work to ensure that attention is drawn away from other, more marginalized subject-positions and placed back on men, who hope to retain their hegemonic importance. From this perspective, the recent interest in contemporary fathers may have little to do with the blaming of patriarchy; instead, it represents a final, desperate attempt to retain patriarchal privilege. As Lynne Segal writes:

> [The] growing stress on fathers has occurred at a time when men's actual power and control over women and children is declining. In the fifties the father was essential, but only, it seemed, for financial support, status and legitimacy.... [The] emphasis on the importance of fathering today would be to see it as a reassertion of the essential nature, significance and rights of fathers at a time when ...

[some] women are better placed to question any automatic assumption of paternal rights. Men's hold on their status as fathers is less firm and secure than ever before. (26)

By paying attention to the way postfeminist fatherhood is framed as a moment of crisis that is deeply tied to women's new self-governing powers and capacities as mothers, it becomes clear that, despite its evocation of progressive feminist values, postfeminist television nonetheless contains backlash characteristics. Just as Modleski (*Feminism*) argues that the "new man" operated through a manipulative veneer, which responded to the feminist demand for the equitable distribution of domestic labour by making women feel even more marginal, the troubled fathers I analyze take feminism into account only to, as McRobbie writes, repudiate it. That is, by accepting femininities into a hegemonic form of masculinity, the postfeminist father emerges as a sympathetic figure that uses the "ornament" of care to re-establish many of the violent tendencies associated with hyper-masculinity.

In the next section I explore two series—*The Walking Dead* and *Sons of Anarchy*—in order to demonstrate how this veneer of care is used to not only bolster the power of men but to blanket mothers, as many women are treated as ineffective, irresponsible, and manipulative mothers who prove inadequate and powerless.

MATERNAL THINKING

Sara Ruddick's philosophical understanding of maternal practice provides an effective starting point for determining the kinds of fatherly practices represented in recent television. Offering a normative account of the work of mothers, Ruddick outlines the different concepts, metaphysical attitudes, and cognitive capacities that mothers use to meet the demands of children. This collection of practices, Ruddick claims, represents a distinct mode of "maternal thinking." Importantly, for Ruddick, maternal thinking has little to do with biology or gender. Although, historically, more women carry out the work of maternal thinking, maternal practices are open to both men and women. The fundamental requirement for maternal thinking is a commitment to caring for children, a practice that involves meeting three fundamental demands: preservation, growth, and social acceptance. The lives of children need to be protected, their development nurtured, and their behaviour trained according to the values of society. "To be a mother," writes Ruddick, "is to be committed to meeting these demands by works of preservative love, nurturance, and training" ("Maternal Thinking" 17).

Although each of these demands could be used to provide a nu-anced account of the way postfeminist fatherhood is represented by television, I concentrate on the first demand—the protective care of children. This demand, I feel, is the most helpful in underscoring the way postfeminist fatherhood utilises a veneer of sensitivity to re-inscribe hegemonic masculinity, since the majority of shows focus on fathers who use violence and aggression to protect their children from some menacing threat. For example, in *The Walking Dead* the lives of children are constantly endangered by a zombie apocalypse, whereas in *Sons of Anarchy*, it is the dangerous crim-inality of Teller's motorcycle gang that puts his children at risk. Furthermore, according to Ruddick, the preservation of a child's life entails a mode of thinking that is deeply tied to the mother's capacity to feel. The commitment to protect cannot be done without acknowledging both the child's emotional capacities and the mul-tifarious feelings children instill in their mothers, especially as they are forced to deal with the uncertainties and dangers that regularly put the lives of children at risk. To deal with life's ambivalence, mothers adopt or reject what Ruddick identifies as four core values involved in the demand of preservative love: scrutinizing, holding, humility, and resilient cheerfulness ("Maternal Thinking").

Common to all of these concepts is a mother's universal need to *control*; preserving life entails a relentless and ongoing battle with nature that seeks to minimize risks and conserve the fragility of life. "To a mother," Ruddick writes, "life may well seem 'terrible, hostile, and quick to pounce on you if you give it a chance.' In response, she develops a metaphysical attitude toward 'Being as such,' an attitude which I call 'holding,' an attitude which is gov-erned by the priority of keeping over acquiring, of conserving the fragile, of maintaining whatever is at hand and necessary to the child's life" ("Maternal Thinking" 350). Not all mothers, however, are able to cope effectively with the world's hostility, as many resort to feelings of domination, melancholy, or denial. Instead of respecting the uncertainties of the world, the dominating or melancholic mother creates one that requires constant surveillance, often becoming consumed by an overwhelming sense of dread or a debilitating desire to control everything around the child. On the other hand, while "in the face of danger, disappointment, and unpredictability, mothers are liable to melancholy, they are also aware that a kind, resilient good humour is a virtue" ("Maternal Thinking" 350). In contrast to denial and melancholy, Ruddick envisions humility and cheerfulness not as the passive acceptance of powerlessness but a positive way to accept the fragility of life without giving in to despair. "Cheerfulness," she writes, "is a matter-of-fact willingness to accept having given birth, to start and start over again, to welcome a future despite conditions of one's self, one's children, one's society, and nature that may be reasons for despair" ("Maternal Thinking" 74).

As I have already mentioned, postfeminist cultures draw upon the emotional capacities of fathers, allowing sensitivity and care to take their place alongside the fatherly expectation to provide and protect. But what kinds of emotions and feelings are fathers depicted as possessing? Do they subscribe to Ruddick's criteria for preservative love? Or do postfeminist fathers possess an alternative mode of domestic care? On the surface, it does appear that TV's new dads have fully embraced a domesticated world of nurturance and care and, as such, remain in tune with the demands of second-wave feminists. The problem is that all too often this acceptance of maternal thinking is used to create a version of caretaking that extends, rather than challenges, hegemonic masculinity. This is not to say that all postfeminist models of fatherhood are the same. Quite the contrary, the version of preservative love depicted in *Sons of Anarchy* differs considerably from that found in *The Walking Dead*. Yet, despite these differing accounts of fatherly protection, both respond to feminism disingenuously, using care and sensitivity as an ornament to reinstate hegemonic power.

In *Sons of Anarchy*, postfeminist fatherhood is represented primarily through Teller's pensive and melancholic journey from a reckless life of self-centered debauchery to one dedicated to the responsibilities of family. When his junkie ex-wife goes into premature labour, Teller jumps into action, accepting fully his role as the boy's primary caretaker and the uncertainty and emotional vulnerability that comes from caring for children. Indeed, as a single father who wears his heart on his sleeve, Teller is, in no time, transformed into the poster boy for the nurturing sensitivity of postfeminist fatherhood. However, at no point along this journey does Teller subscribe to what Ruddick calls preservative love. In quiet moments, he may be shown to be enamoured by the fragility of his son; fatherhood may even be the catalyst for his desire to break free from his criminal ways. But these "nurturing" moments never amount to anything more than an ornamental façade. Even Teller knows better: in the series finale, Teller comes face to face with his failure as a father, telling his friend Nero, "I am not a good man and I want my children to know exactly what kind of man I am." Instead of embracing fatherhood with a spirit of humility and cheerfulness, Teller resumes his violent ways, denying the most fundamental requirement of maternal practice: the preservation of a child's fragile life. From the constant threats of the IRA to the reckless and murderous tendencies of the Sons of Anarchy motorcycle club, Teller's family is constantly on the verge of coming undone, a fate that owes everything to Teller's inability to shake off his dedication to the violence of toxic masculinity.

What is remarkable about a show like *Sons of Anarchy* is that despite its unadulterated display of gruesome violence, somehow a character like Teller continues to vie for the viewer's sympathies. In the morally ambiguous world of post-network television, *Sons of Anarchy* proves that the bad guys can win, giving birth to an entirely new breed of anti-heroes that, despite their moral bankruptcy and despicable criminality, try to model good parental behaviours. This parental defence, I contend, has everything to do with the way in which the show uses Teller's melancholic ways to strengthen his image as a "good father." As mentioned in the opening, in the "King Solomon" episode Teller is shown in a pensive spirit, attempting to reconcile his violent ways with his desire to be a good father. As a sorrowful song plays in the background, the viewer watches as Teller painfully hands over his son to another, more caring father. However, while this melodramatic display of sacrificial love may play at the audience's heartstrings, Teller hardly forms a transformative role model for sensitive fatherhood, as his melancholy is actually used to re-inscribe hegemonic masculinity.

In her analysis of postfeminism, Modleski ("Clint Eastwood") has shown how melancholy is used to bolster men's power. Using Juliana Schiesari's renaissance work on melancholia, especially her claim that melancholy has historically represented a privileged emotional response for men in power, Modleski examines how the "male weepie" uses the loss and sadness of men to elevate their position. A wonderful example of this re-inscription of male power can be seen in Clint Eastwood's recent transformation into a wounded and sombre figure whose melancholy not only glosses over Eastwood's iconic status as a champion of hyper-masculinity but it reveals just how easily men's suffering may be used to re-empower the wounded white man. Similarly, Hamad has established how the "male melodrama" uses the victim status of many postfeminist fathers to establish them as virtuous characters. Just as suffering and tragedy is used in the melodrama to elicit sympathy for women, in many postfeminist films, it is the melancholic father—especially the straight, able-bodied, single dad who endures some unimaginable loss—who is repositioned as a privileged parental identity.

Interestingly, while melancholy for Ruddick inhibits mothers from becoming optimal parents, in *Sons of Anarchy* it is used as an ornamental mode of sympathy that allows the viewer to excuse men of their continued reliance on toxic masculinity. This establishment of the male hero as emotional victim can be seen, for example, in the way Teller's pensive desire to break free from gang life positions him as a sympathetic father-figure whose exceptional acts of mourning and self-sacrifice grant him an everlasting "get out of jail free card." No matter what Teller does, no matter how many skulls he smashes in, he can be forgiven because everything he does is ultimately in the service of family. Even more astounding is the way this use of sympathy can even override the violent atrocities Teller inflicts upon women: when a porn star starts interfering with his domestic life, Teller shuts her up by beating her face in; to avoid a police investigation, he has a single mom executed because her son used one of his weapons to go on a shooting spree; and when his ex-wife attempts to gain custody of their son, he callously sends her back to rehab by forcing her to start shooting heroin again.

In *The Walking Dead*, a different strategy is used to depict the protectorate care of its protagonist, Rick—a rugged cop who is put in charge of keeping a small group of survivors safe from a zombie apocalypse. Whereas Teller is treated as a morally vacant father, Rick is, right from the beginning, positioned as the show's most loving and competent parent whose success owes everything to his ability to remain cheerful and optimistic. In the opening episode, Rick's caring ways become evident in the way he describes a recent fight he had with his wife: "The difference between men and women," Rick philosophizes, "is that I would never say something that cruel about her and never in front of our kid." Unlike many of the show's mothers, who are treated as ineffective and irresponsible, Rick is shown throughout as an exceptional practitioner of maternal thinking. When their son, Carl, is shot accidently and forced to fight for his life, it is Rick's wife, Laurie, who slowly succumbs to a melancholic denial, as she hopes that he will die in order to avoid life's ambivalence and cruelty: "Why do we even want Carl to live?" she pleads. "If he dies tonight, it all ends for him. Tell me why it would be better for him to live." A steadfast optimist, Rick replies by using the moral guidance of cheerfulness to set his wife straight. Commenting on how the first words Carl spoke after waking up from a coma involved the beautiful deer he spotted in the woods, Rick declares passionately, "He talked about something beautiful, not something uncertain and scary. There is a life here for us."

Although *Sons of Anarchy* and *The Walking Dead* use different strategies to make their father-heads sympathetic, both share in the media's continued degradation of mothers. As Kathleen Karlyn argues, inhospitable depictions of mothers have become a common strategy within contemporary media that works to reposition the father as an untainted pillar of virtue, usually by having the mothers extracted from the storyline. When Tara, Teller's second wife, decides to take the kids away from the gang violence, she is punished severely for acting outside her husband's patriarchal system of authority. Not only is she ejected from the story, but the way in which she leaves affirms the disingenuous and manipulative tendencies of postfeminist fatherhood: while it is Teller who ultimately prevents Tara from leaving by holding her hostage, in the end, it is his mother who does the unthinkable and has her killed. Here, not only is Teller absolved of any moral transgression but it is the show's maternal figures that are cast in an unwinnable situation, as Jemma becomes the villainous monster who must punish another mother for her maternal wrongdoings. Similarly, in *The Walking Dad*, matrophobia centers on the trope of absent mothers. Unlike the ever-present Rick, Laurie is cast as the misguided maternal figure that is unable to live up to her husband's paternal expectations. Not only is she shown as a mother prone to melancholy and despair, Laurie is also castigated for her pursuit of extra-marital sexuality and, like so many other bad mothers in popular media, punished for her wrongdoings by being killed off in the story—a feat that unsurprisingly strengthens our sympathy for the father-head. For even though Laurie dies horribly in childbirth, attaining a brief moment of sacrificial maternal power, in the end it is Rick who is celebrated as the mournful single parent whose loss allows him to dig deep and, once again, carry on as the ideal paternal figure: sensitive, nurturing, and tough as nails—patriarchy as the return of hegemonic fatherhood.

CONCLUSION

Raymond Williams once wrote that a time period's cultural productions often contain traces, however implicitly, of the major conflicts and tensions experienced within a given society. By noting changes to the narrative plot development, voice, and characterization, the cultural critic can reveal those submerged anxieties that often go unnoticed or remain invisible to the participants of a society. What, might we ask, do these televisual discourses reveal or teach us about the current state of men's identities, especially their social position as fathers? First, the very presence of so many media discourses on father figures is remarkable. Whereas mothers have been represented amply in the media (albeit in an often unfavourable light), little attention has been placed on the role of fathers, especially their desire to embrace an alternative model of fatherhood. The postfeminist father changes this, drawing attention to men's caretaking roles and emotional vulnerability to create a model of fatherhood that allows men to be seen as more than just breadwinners or figures of authority. Yet, at the same time, while the emergence of the televisual "superdad" is promising, the fathers on display are rarely portrayed as successful role models. Instead, they are depicted as fathers in crisis who are riddled by the expectation to straddle multiple subject positions. Perhaps, as Lotz contends, many of these tensions reveal the real struggles men face as they wrestle with the old patriarchal order. But I think there is something more disingenuous at play. As the shows discussed here demonstrate quite clearly, not only can sensitivity and caretaking be used to re-inscribe hegemonic masculine practices, they can just as easily be used to blanket the role mothers play in society. The arrival of the superdad is no doubt welcoming, but not if his arrival once again replays the matrophobic tendencies inscribed within the institution of motherhood.

ENDNOTES

[1]Postfeminism is a contentious term that is often used to designate the end of second-wave feminism. While for some theorists this means an optimistic time for women's rights, as women are now free to choose their destinies, for others, postfeminism represents a depoliticized, neo-conservative movement that forms a backlash against the strides made by second-wave feminists. These connotative inconsistencies have led some theorists, such as Amanda Lotz, to abandon the term altogether. I have chosen to stick with the term, despite its inconsistencies, since many of the ambivalences and contradictions found within postfeminist media cultures are applicable to images of televisual fathers, allowing parallels to be made between postfeminist men and women.

[2]The "new man" was an iconic figure from the '80s and early '90s that signified the incorporation of feminising traits into a "sensitive" model of masculinity. Perhaps the most iconic images of the "new man" involved various advertisements that showed men as nurturing fathers who openly embraced their capacity to

be caretakers. This model of masculinity, however, was short-lived and quickly replaced by a more egotistical model of masculinity that centered on the fashion-conscious, conspicuous consumer.

WORKS CITED

Brabon, Benjamin. "'Chuck Flick': A Genealogy of the Postfeminist Male Singleton." *Postfeminism and Contemporary Hollywood Cinema*. Eds. Joel Gwynne and Nadine Muller. New York: Palgrave, 2013. 116-130. Print.

Brandth, Berit and Elin Kvande. "Masculinity and Child Care: The Reconstruction of Fathering." *The Sociological Review* 46.2 (1998): 293-313. Print.

Coltrane, Scott. "Marketing the Marriage 'Solution': Misplaced Simplicity in the Politics of Fatherhood: 2001 Presidential Address to the Pacific Sociological Association." *Sociological Perspectives* 44.4 (2001): 387-418. Print.

Doucet, Andrea. *Do Men Mother?: Fathering, Care, and Domestic Responsibility*. Toronto: University of Toronto Press, 2006. Print.

Faludi, Susan. *Stiffed: The Betrayal of the American Man*. New York: Harper, 2000. Print.

Genz, Stéphanie. *Postfemininities in Popular Culture*. New York: Palgrave, 2009. Print.

Hamad, Hannah. *Postfeminism and Paternity in Contemporary U.S. Film: Framing Fatherhood*. New York: Routledge, 2013. Print.

Kaplan, E. Ann. *Motherhood and Representation*. New York: Routledge, 1992. Print.

Karlyn, Kathleen Rowe. *Unruly Girls, Unrepentant Mothers: Redefining Feminism on Screen*. Texas: University of Texas Press, 2011. Print.

Kaufman, Gayle. *Superdads: How Fathers Balance Work and Family in the 21st Century*. New York: New York University Press, 2013. Print.

Lotz, Amanda D. *Cable Guys: Television and Masculinities in the 21st Century*. New York: New York University Press, 2014. Print.

McRobbie, Angel. "Post Feminism and Popular Culture: Bridget Jones and the New Gender Regime." *Feminist Media Studies* 4.3 (2003): 255-264. Print.

Modleski, Tania. "Clint Eastwood and Male Weepies." *American Literary History* 22 (2010): 136-58. Print.

Modleski, Tania. *Feminism without Women: Culture and Criticism in a Postfeminist Age*. New York: Routledge, 1991. Print.

Ruddick, Sara. "Maternal Thinking." *Feminist Studies* 6.2 (1980): 342-367. Print.

Ruddick, Sara. *Maternal Thinking: Toward a Politics of Peace*. Boston: Beacon Press, 1995. Print.

Segal, Lynne. *Slow Motion: Changing Masculinities, Changing Men*. New Brunswick, NJ: Rutgers University Press, 1990. Print.

Thier, David. "FX: Television for Men That Men Actually Want to Watch." *The Atlantic* 28 Sept. 2010. Web. July 1, 2015.

Williams, Raymond. "The Analysis of Culture." *The Long Revolution*. Peterborough, ON: Broadview Press, 2001. 57-88. Print.

8.
What's So Funny About Childbirth?

The Projection of Patriarchal Masculinity in
Popular Comedic Childbirth Guides

JEFFREY NALL

IN 2008, MY PARTNER, April, birthed our daughter Mimi Lucille in our then West Palm Beach home. My attitude toward childbirth was transformed by witnessing this dramatic expression of feminine agency and creativity through the often denigrated and mistrusted female body. This experience also spurred a critical reconsideration of the relationship between childbirth, cultural representations of childbirth, and patriarchal sexism. Influenced by my engagement with feminist theory in graduate school, I was encouraged by my mentor, cultural theorist Jane Caputi, to pursue this inquiry, yielding a dissertation and later a book: *Feminism and the Mastery of Women and Childbirth: An Ecofeminist Examination of the Cultural Maiming and Reclaiming of Maternal Agency during Childbirth*. During my research I discovered a pregnancy and childbirth guide marketed as "by and for everyday men": Ian Davis' *My Boys Can Swim! The Official Guy's Guide to Pregnancy*. Despite low expectations, I was surprised by the book's profoundly disrespectful attitude toward women's birth projects, as well as its thinly veiled misogyny and shallow portrayal of "true" manhood. I was further surprised that the book, written in 1999, continued to be popular, as indicated in sales rankings and reader praise. I soon learned that the work was not alone, but was part of a sub-genre of pregnancy and childbirth guide literature: comedic birth guides by and for so-called regular and real men.

This discovery prompted me to contemplate what these works and readers' reactions had to teach us about (1) the function of sexism in the disguise of "ironic" humour—how is dehumanizing discourse hidden in the plain sight of normalized humour about women; (2) the continued presence and function of deeply embedded patriarchal concepts, including androcentrism, gender polarization, and gender stratification; (3) how misguided conceptualizations and interpretations of childbirth perpetuate patriarchy's vision of female inferiority.

My findings are that the mainstream of the comedic "by and for men" birth guides' genre extends salient presuppositions of the patriarchal worldview, including the hyper-separation of men and women and the superiority of men and masculinity over women and femininity. Particularly significant, these birth guides generally deny and/or undermine respect for the agency, creativity, and value of women's birth projects. These guides do not understand pregnancy and childbirth as indication of the power, potency, and perhaps even "divinity" of women's capacity to make and birth new life. Instead, they use pregnancy and childbirth as props to bolster familiar stereotypes wherein women are viewed as irrational, victims, unworthy of mention, or in need of rescue. The works' (mis)representation of women's childbirth as "disgusting," "horrific," and/or requiring paternalistic, medicalized management, perpetuates women's alienation from their bodies. Against the contention that "humorous" works such as these are not meant to be serious, these comedic birth guides, and the readers who enjoy them, teach us that hegemonic masculine men's humour showcases quite serious values, attitudes, concerns, and beliefs. These works provide a window into the contemporary patriarchal worldview where sexism is thinly disguised as ironic or playful humour. A final important objective of this chapter is to show how these birth guides dehumanize not only women but also men. They do so by endorsing and propagating an exclusionary, if not impossible, model of masculine selfhood that marginalizes alternative conceptions of manhood. Yet the authors of the six guides reviewed here do not have the last word. While many men conform to and perpetuate the hegemonic mode of masculinity amplified in these birth guides, some men, as represented in critical reader responses, vocalize resistance and even denunciation of this vision of manhood.

SOCIAL CONSTRUCTION OF MASCULINITY

Gender and feminist theorists contend that the essentialist theory of gender, that gender is a product of biology, is incorrect and that such a model of masculinity is normative rather than merely descriptive. Put differently, gender is socially constructed. An entity is socially constructed insofar as it is the way it is largely due to conformity to dominant social classifications and not merely biological forces (Haslanger 19). Men who act out the part of patriarchal masculinity are socially constructed entities insofar as they are the way they are largely in response to social ideals about what constitutes appropriate male selfhood. Despite a growing cultural belief in the primacy of biology over socialization in the shaping of human selfhood, masculinities scholar R. W. Connell contends that the human species uniquely "produces and lives in history, replacing organic evolution with radically new determinants of change" (81). To view gender as a social construction is to accept that the way we conceptualize men and women "is a matter of historical and social reality" (Warren, "The Power and Promise" 331) and that our conceptualizations have the power to shape our experiences.

The socially constructed masculine ideal, dominant in contemporary Western society, has its origins in the long-standing but ever evolving institution of patriarchy. Feminist historian Gerda Lerner writes that patriarchy "means the manifestation and institutionalization of male dominance over women and children in the family and the extension of male dominance over women in society in general. It implies that men hold power in all the important institutions of society and that women are deprived of access to such power" (239).

A direct consequence of increased feminist studies of masculinity, theorists are increasingly taking the position that the patriarchal model of masculine selfhood is not only problematic for the women and children who suffer from its enactment but that it often also deprives men of quality lives. According to hooks, while most men rarely think about the ways in which patriarchy works, it is nevertheless "the single most life-threatening social disease assaulting the male body and the spirit in our nation" (*The Will to Change*

17). Today, the dominant form of masculinity promoted throughout society urges men to see themselves in opposition to all things feminine (Adams and Coltrane); valorizes "acts and attitudes of independence, aggression, and sexuality" (Reed, *Birthing Fathers* 232); and "teaches men that their sense of self and identity, their reason for being, resides in their capacity to dominate others" (hooks, *Feminism Is for Everybody* 70). A key concern of this work is the exploration of how comedic birth guides directed at men contribute to this harmful construction of masculinity.

MEN ATTENDING BIRTH

Just as masculinity is a social construction, so too is fatherhood, and like many constructions it has and continues to undergo significant change. While men were deemed irrelevant to childbirth a century ago, the present popular belief is that men are an integral part of the process (Odent, *The Farmer* 96). Today, fathers are not only permitted but also expected to attend the hospital birth of their child (Reed, "Birth Fathers"). Whatever their importance to birthing women, men's role in birth is individually and socially significant. Reed writes, "American father's assistance in birth is a rite of passage to fatherhood" (*Birthing Fathers* 14). This rite of passage begins before the birth of the infant, taking place during birth classes, in interactions with family and friends, and during the delivery and afterward (Reed, *Birthing Fathers* 18). Reed compares fathers' role in birth to that of initiates in boot camp and fraternity initiation. He explains that "birth ritual separates men from society, imposes its symbolic process on them, and finally reintegrates them into conventional society as changed beings" (*Birthing Fathers* 14). Reed's contention echoes that of pioneering American traditional midwife Ina May Gaskin: "birthing is an occasion that may radically change the father's outlook on things" (327). Birth provides men an opportunity to "alter their old social identities by establishing their new roles and relations as fathers" (Reed, *Birthing Fathers* 19).

Childbirth has the power to transform not only mothers engaging in this creative act but also those in attendance. Yet the kind of transformation that occurs will significantly depend upon the conceptualization of childbirth shaping one's experience. A conceptual framework functions "as a finite lens, a 'field of vision,' in and through which information and experiences are filtered" (Warren, "Critical Thinking" 156). Gender norms are significant components of most people's conceptual frameworks. With this in mind, the present work seeks to critically explore the way concepts of patriarchal gender function to shape interpretations of women, men, and childbirth in the specified birth guides.

SIX BIRTH GUIDES BY AND FOR "REAL" MEN

I chose the herein analyzed texts for their comedic tone,[1] for their presentation as "by and for real and/or everyday men" and dealing "realistically" with pregnancy and birth in comparison to feminine-geared works, and for their topical emphasis on discussing not only pregnancy but also childbirth. My initial search and selection of birth guides took place in 2011. In 2014, a sixth text (Pfeiffer) was selected in order to increase the size and timeliness of the sample of examined works. The books include *Dude, You're Gonna Be a Dad!* (John Pfeiffer), *Pacify Me: A Handbook for the Freaked-Out New Dad* (Chris Mancini), *The Dudes' Guide to Pregnancy: Dealing with Your Expecting Wife, Coming Baby, and the End of Life as You Knew It* (Bill Lloyd and Scott Finch), *The Guy's Guide to Surviving Pregnancy, Childbirth, and the First Year of Fatherhood* (Michael Crider), *My Boys Can Swim! The Official Guy's Guide to Pregnancy* (Ian Davis), and *She's Having a Baby—and I'm Having a Breakdown* (James Douglas Barron). The men who authored these titles make no claim to medical or sociological expertise. Instead, they draw from personal beliefs and experiences to offer kernels of wisdom to both help other "everyday" men chart a course in the new territory of fatherhood and help them understand and/or "deal" with their pregnant partner.

I found the books chosen for examination through a thorough search for birth related guides on Amazon.com. The website was chosen because it offers what is probably the most extensive listing of popularly available book titles. Amazon also provides a real-time and ever changing sales ranking for all merchandise. Amazon's considerable number of costumer reviews also allowed for a fuller understanding of how the works in question were understood and assessed. To gain an accurate understanding of the thinking exemplified in these books, the analysis that follows reflects not only the books but also thorough consideration of reviews available during the time of analysis (2011-2014).

TAKING HEGEMONIC MEN'S HUMOUR SERIOUSLY

Some might argue that books so clearly identified as humorous are not meant as a means for dispensing meaningful information and, thus, are not meant to be seriously analyzed for meaningful discussion of masculinity and childbirth. Theorists including Shira Tarrant, however, contend that humour can be utilized to "mask aggression" (22). Another clear reason why humorous works deserve serious attention is indicated in reader responses to the six comedic birth guides under examination. Many readers indicated that they found the works both entertaining and *informative*. Consider the example of *My Boys Can Swim* (Davis), a title with more than two hundred reader comments. In 2011, a total of forty-eight readers (1) gave the book three to five stars, out of a total of five; (2) discussed the book's merits in terms of being, according to readers, "factual," "accurate," "truthful," "honest," "insightful and/or informative." Just seven readers noted that the book was *strictly* funny, with another seven noting that, while humorous and helpful, the book lacked information. A clear majority of such readers, thirty-four, indicated that the book was both humorous and informative in some way or another. One reader, self-identifying as a physician, described his efforts to remedy father disengagement from women's pregnancy, which he describes as a regular problem, by giving out the book to males whose partners are pregnant. Another reader notes that as a Lamaze instructor, she suggests the work to her male students. This survey indicates that while some will claim it is obvious that such a book is not to be taken seriously, many others contend that the book offers keen insight into pregnancy and childbirth.

Positive reader responses of works such as *The Guy's Guide to Surviving Pregnancy, Childbirth, and the First Year of Fatherhood* also claim that humour and insight coincide. One reader wrote

that Crider's book both offers an escape from "other overly serious pregnancy books" and provides "an honest and entertaining
account of what most of us expectant fathers are going through"
(Michael Rustici). Similarly, readers of *The Dude's Guide to Pregnancy* indicated that the work's humorously irreverent tone was
an important aspect of its honesty: "FreshD" wrote, "Very true
and not sugarcoated"; Macystike1 wrote that she recommends the
books to friends because "it's funny and well, honest." A father
named "David L. Lengel" wrote, "The bottom line is this, without
the book, I would have been up that creek with no paddle." Several
other readers responded with similar comments indicating that
the work was a "must read for any expectant father" or that the
book provided critical insight into the pregnancy and birth process. Over one hundred of more than two hundred reviewers gave
Dude, You're Gonna Be a Dad! five of five stars. (An additional
forty-eight reviewers gave it a four of five stars.)

The most consistent theme in positive reviews was that the
book balanced humour and pertinent information. In all, these
comments indicate that while such works utilize humour and are
said to be free of a serious tone, they are nevertheless believed
to, at least at times, provide sincere, accurate information about
pregnancy and childbirth. Such reader reactions dispel the notion
that humour should necessarily be interpreted dismissively, as
mere mindless word-play.

The patriarchal masculine ideal promotes the notion that "real
men" do not engage in serious, in-depth personal and emotional
discussion. Indeed, Mancini equates poor communication skills
with being a man (4). In *She's Having a Baby—and I'm Having a
Breakdown,* James Douglas Barron encourages men to put their
feelings on paper since other men have no interest in discussing
such things: "Men truly don't want to hear that you're hurting"
(22). Barron bases this conclusion, in part, on his experience attempting to share his feelings with a friend over beer. His friend
"listened, a helpless, empty expression crossing his face like a
cold shadow. Finally his eyes glazed over, he lifted a finger for
the waiter: 'Check please.' End of conversation" (22).

In this context, humour provides an important safe haven for men
to openly address personal, emotionally charged subjects without

jeopardizing the fragile hegemonic masculine selfhood. Humour allows men a transitory space to withhold emotional commitment while seeking validation and/or connection. Indeed, the very aim of the texts herein examined is to supplement the lack of a male-to-male discussion about pregnancy and birth. Mancini makes this explicit when he writes that his work seeks to fill a void in communication between men. After attributing men's silence to their being "men," he explains his hope to address the male communication void without transgressing appropriate gender boundaries: "So I'm hoping if I write [my thoughts about becoming a father] down, it will sound less ... girly" than verbally sharing them (4-5). Humour protects those who cast a proverbial "line" in the water in the hopes of catching receptivity to thoughts and feelings that may be quite serious. If a counterpart reacts with ridicule, the speaker simply reels in his feelings, insisting that they were not meant to be taken seriously. Thus it would be a mistake to presume that male humour is necessarily void of individual significance.

Since men who are deemed too emotional or too serious about personal matters outside of more supposedly "abstract" duties are open to ridicule, the authors of these works are able to utilize humour to safely convey their personal feelings on such a dramatic, personal experience as childbirth. Yet in using humour the authors also benefit from a "fail-safe" switch, allowing the author to discount ideas they wish to examine or share without, we are told, laying claim to them. This leads to contradictory assertions such as the comment by a reader of Crider's work. One reader writes that *The Guy's Guide* is "not intended to be a serious guide on how to deal with pregnancy" and that it "has some very real insight into pregnancy from a guy's perspective" (Bullock). At first these two statements appear to be logically contradictory. Upon further examination, however, the implication of such a statement is perhaps not that the book lacks serious insight but that such insights are packaged in a humorous, protective tone.

BY MEN FOR MEN

Most of the birth guides under review implement and perpetuate gender polarization and essentialist visions of gender by purporting to give a "male" perspective on pregnancy and childbirth, one that may prove to be disconcerting or even offensive to females. Lloyd and Finch write that their book is "intended for *male reading only*" and "explicitly not intended for a female audience" (xi). Their book, they claim, offers "The Dudes' point of view, something sorely lacking in all the other pregnancy primers out there, almost all of which are aimed at your wife" (1). Similarly, Crider writes that his book is "a guy's guide to fatherhood" (xv) and warns female readers "a male's point of view on this subject is one that may be difficult for you to swallow" (xv-xvi). Crider validates the essentialist notion of gender by linking his gendered perspective with not having a "vagina" (xvi). Describing himself as "your everyday Joe" (xiv), Davis writes that his book fills the existing void for a pregnancy and birth book that "a typical guy could relate to" (xii). Pfeiffer indicates his intended audience members are those who have not "dreamed about" parenthood in the way women have: men (3).

These authors employ the supposition that males and females occupy bifurcated, nearly mutually exclusive, realms. The error of such gender polarization is not in identifying differences between different groups of people but rather overemphasizing such differences at the expense of recognizing the far greater commonality. Moreover, the differences are falsely attributed to biological determinism or essentialism—the idea that our sex dictates a gender identity—rather than the more likely culprit of social influences and expectations. Indeed, these works participate in the maintenance of precisely such gendered social scripts that feminist theorists contend have long upheld a worldview that undermines respect for women.[2]

SPOKESMEN FOR "AUTHENTIC" MANHOOD

The comedic birth guides in question marginalize not only femininity but also the multiplicity of masculinities. This is done by rendering patriarchal masculinity as "authentic" or "real" masculinity. In the foreword of *The Dudes' Guide to Pregnancy,* Lloyd and Finch explain that they are writing for men who like themselves "enjoy fried foods, electronic gadgets, professional sports, and 'your mom' jokes" (vii). The last of these showcases a prevalent use of femininity as the poll of "otherness" used for ridicule. Crider writes that he "loves gadgets" and assorted "electronic devices ... like most other men" (47). Mancini endorses the conception of true manhood as defined by detachment. He writes that men are "in our own little world and we like it there. We'll come in and visit reality periodically, but it's not where we live. Think of reality as a man's summer home" (52). Such definitions are cornerstone features of the dominant model of masculinity that, as Tarrant explains, identifies masculinity with strength, the ability to provide, protect, and fix things (6) as well as with detachment more generally.

To his credit, Pfeiffer is more nuanced in his discussion of "men," implicitly acknowledging that his tone may not be fitting for all male readers. This is clear when he writes, "I hate to stereotype, but it requires so much less thought. So if the following description doesn't jive with your experience, I apologize in advance" (26). This and other exceptions aside, Pfeiffer equates being a "man" with hegemonic masculinity throughout his text. No man gets excited about "choosing the color of the [baby] car seat cover" (xiii); "Most men" do not think through their family plan (19) nor do they scrub toilets and do the laundry (31); and "guys" are poor communicators when it comes to discussing feelings and fears (18).[3]

MEN FEAR FATHERHOOD

A common thread knitting the six birth guides together is the contention that men enter fatherhood with reluctance and fear. For example, in two of the books, news of their partners' pregnancy was greeted as an indication that life as the authors knew it was over (Davis xii; Mancini 1). The realization was thoroughly frightening: "If the idea of becoming a parent scares the hell out of you, you're not alone" (Davis 2). Mancini writes that "*most guys are terrified of having a child*" and "*It's perfectly normal to be freaked out about having a child*" (5). Mancini goes so far as to agree with a piece of "wisdom" offered by his doctor: "No man wants a child until it's in his arms" (Mancini 10). The interpretations and explanations offered in these birth guides must be placed in the context of the dilemma domestic, familial life presents men with. As sociologists Michele Adams and Scott Coltrane point out, most boys in the United States are reared to be served and nurtured and are inducted into a form of masculine self-hood that is mostly alien to "domestic settings" (230). Yet men are increasingly called upon to be more engaged as fathers, even in the realm of pregnancy and childbirth. Consequently, by the time men join contemporary families and their evolving expectations, they have "little ideological precedent for living harmoniously in a family environment, especially one that is increasingly predicated on ideals of democratic sharing" (Adams and Coltrane 233). Thus, it is of little wonder that pregnancy, childbirth, and becoming a father provoke such fear in males who identify with hegemonic masculinity.

REAL MEN HATE BABY SHOWERS

As the authors of the birth guides in question enter into conventionally defined "feminine" terrain, they seek to reaffirm their commitment to hegemonic masculinity and its distinction from femininity. The guides generally agree that self-respecting men loath joint baby showers. Lloyd and Finch joke, "Each heterosexual male at a couples shower will contemplate suicide at least once during said couples' shower" (120). They advise fathers-to-be "to do anything in your power to prevent the couples' baby shower" (121). Pfeiffer describes the "couple's shower" as "a lame attempt to include the father in the pregnancy experience" (72), one that ranks below events such as "professional sports, scantily clad women, great food, or, ideally, all three" (73).

For Crider, the male and female baby showers represent the continued demoralization of authentic American manhood. In agreeing that men and baby showers are antithetical, Crider explains the supposedly natural differences between men and women: "I'm sorry, but certain gatherings should involve solely men *or* women, but not both. Bachelor parties: men. Bachelorette parties: women. Poker night: guys. Lingerie party: gals…. Getting together for wings and football at Hooters: men. Baby showers: women" (71-72).[4] Crider attributes men's participation in baby showers, or "pussification" parties (74), to the "Pussification Period" in America (72). He protests the merging of once polarized gendered spheres, contending that the "pussification period" began "during the Clinton administration," which was marked by men being encouraged "to get in touch with their feminine side and embrace the diversities of men and women" (72).

"Pussification" is clearly implemented as a feminine-identified pejorative, used to mark out the violation of patriarchy's conceptualization of masculinity as both antithetical and superior to femininity. Masculinity, as such, is a form of ontological purity, much as Western culture has conceptualized whiteness, and this purity stands in contrast to femininity, like blackness, as comparatively impure. Philosopher Anna Camaiti Hostert writes that "the one-drop rule" held that "in order to be white all of one's ancestors must be white" (13). In contrast, blackness lacked such stringent requirements for group entry, requiring members only to "have a single drop of black blood in one's ancestry" (13). While women carefully embracing aspects of "male" culture—attending football games, attempting to be as athletic or as bold as a man, or perhaps being one of the "guys"—*can* be met with tolerance or at least temporary approval, the reverse is less likely. As such, to embrace the baby shower, often a celebration of conventionally defined femininity, is to embrace not merely that which is different but that which is inferior to one's identity and, thus, is denigrating.

One way to interpret the reason for the authors' embrace and deployment of patriarchal concepts is that they act as a defense to protect the fragile and evolving, yet socially significant, construct of hegemonic masculine selfhood. While these "real" men lay claim to their masculinity, rejecting the "femininity" of baby showers, birth classes, and the color pink, they nevertheless are, by virtue of writing or reading pregnancy and childbirth guides, wading into waters that have long been demarcated as explicitly and exclusively "feminine." So while these men navigate or perhaps even embrace the shifting social expectations of fathers—namely to play a more significant, direct role in the care of pregnant women and children—they are, at the same time, attempting to reinforce their status as "real" men through two time-tested methods: (1)

differentiating themselves from women; (2) asserting their superiority over women.

Some of the birth guide authors also "comically" implement homophobia to establish a boundary between "real" men and those false men who may be drawn to the feminine. Crider writes that he "hated going to these baby showers, as would any red-blooded heterosexual man" (72). The clear message is that real men are heterosexual and that real men hate so-called "female" events. What, precisely, is so non-masculine about the event? Crider writes that the parties are "boring" and "feature a lot of giggling women eating dainty little snacks" and admiring baby clothes (72-73). Men who dare to transgress such dominant gender-based social prohibitions run the risk of being emasculated by being labelled "homosexual." The use of homosexuality as a threat against violating dominant masculine selfhood perpetuates the ritual shunning of gay people (Schulman 10). Thus the authors police not only dominant gender norms but also discriminatory sexual norms.

PREFERRING BOYS

The birth guides reflect dominant gender norms related to sports and toys. They further implement androcentrism—conceptualizing elite male identity, interests, experiences, and beliefs/thinking as the "norm," "standard," or "the mythical norm" (Lorde 293) against which all other perspectives should be judged—in identifying maleness as a unique, laudable attribute and femaleness as either not noteworthy or explicitly a *lack*.[5] Lloyd and Finch indicate that fathers who have boys will have opportunities to get involved in sports such as "baseball, basketball, football, hockey, wrestling, lacrosse, etc."; but if the child is a girl fathers can look forward to her playing "softball" (99). The authors imagine ways in which fathers can vicariously live through their sons, such as being "a fighter pilot" or "rock star" and "win[ing] a poker tournament" or "bang[ing] his hot high school history teacher" (99). A daughter, however, offers comparatively fewer opportunities: "hook you up with a continual, free supply of Girl Scout cookies" and "other important girl stuff that we can't think of right now" (99). The devaluation of the feminine is explicit.

Such a conceptualization of women is unsurprising given that in the patriarchal imagination, women do not play starring roles. Instead, they are often props used by men to establish their own value as, for example, sex objects.

The authors' exaltation of the *meaning* of the penis and/or testicles further perpetrates patriarchal devaluation of women and qualities associated with femininity. Their works present the possession of male genitalia as an attribute worthy of acknowledgement and even praise and enthusiasm. Lloyd and Finch go into detail over the pride a father may experience in seeing that their new child has testicles or, as the authors put it, a "nutsack" (202). Crider spends even more time discussing the event of witnessing his son's penis: "There, in all its glory was ... a *penis!* Even I could tell. The stem was on the apple! We were going to have a boy! 'Ryan' was on the way" (51). Indicative of the androcentric perspective, the authors understand possession of male genitalia (testicles, penis) as an attribute, one worthy of praise and enthusiasm. The authors do not comment on or celebrate the presence of female genitalia, indicative of the conceptualization of female genitalia as an absence of a noteworthy attribute: an apple with no stem.

Such thinking is not new but rather an extension of patriarchal thought and culture's efforts to uphold male superiority by inscribing ontological primacy onto the penis. As Nancy Tuana explains, early Western thinkers including Aristotle, Galen, and Aquinas proffered variations of a lasting and influential thesis: that women were misbegotten men (18-25). The Greek physician Galen identified woman's genitals as malformed male genitalia (Tuana 22). Outside of an androcentric worldview, such thinking is absurd given that without mothers there would be no males. Yet, patriarchal thinkers have long reversed such intuitively obvious truisms to ensconce male supremacy. As ecofeminist philosopher Val Plumwood explains, Aristotle awarded agency to men's contributions in reproduction while casting women's role to the background: "Aristotle's age erased women as social and political agents, enabling Aristotle to disappear women's reproductive agency in his award of the reproductive ownership of the child of the father" (*Environmental Culture* 30). This is done even more vividly in the *New Testament* where we read that men should not cover their heads, as women do, since they are "the image and glory of God ... for the man is not of the woman; but the woman of the man. Neither was the man created for the woman but the woman for the man" (1 Corinthians 11:7-9). Pertaining to the birth guides, Crider and Lloyd and Finch praise the penis but are silent about the vagina even amidst the context of women's birth projects. The authors are praising the glory of the penis while ignoring the woman and the female body responsible for literally *making* and *birthing* the male infant. The denial of women's reproductive agency is a pillar of patriarchal power. For if the obvious—that "man" begins in and depends upon "woman"—were not so profoundly obscured, fictions of "self-made men" and ideologies of male supremacy would collapse under the weight of their absurdity.

THE DAMSELS AND KNIGHTS OF CHILDBIRTH

The birth guides in question construct childbirth as an event wherein women are damsels in distress, subjected to a pathological pregnancy and birth that makes them susceptible to mindlessness. Crider describes imagining having to "save the day" when his wife water breaks: "So you get home, rush into the house, boil some water, roll up your sleeves, and catch the baby as it flies out of your wife's crotch. You're a hero" (84). In an alternative scenario intended to be funny, Crider imagines that he becomes a hero for having the skills to "steam clean the carpeting" after his wife has "made a mess" giving birth "on the living room floor" (84).

Such distortions are fundamental to the patriarchal worldview, for patriarchy cannot be sustained unless male dependency on female life-givers is denied (Rich 11). In *Of Woman Born*, Adrienne Rich explains that the dominant institution of "motherhood" aims to keep women, their reproductive powers, and their children "under male control" to maintain the social and political systems dependent upon their unrewarded or inadequately rewarded maternal labour (13). The "most fundamental and bewildering of contradictions" within the patriarchal worldview and social life is that women are both alienated from and incarcerated within their bodies (13).

DENYING MATERNAL BIRTHING AGENCY

All of the birth guides under examination contribute to the foundational patriarchal practice of alienating women from their bodies. This alienation is fomented by backgrounding their unique labour and, implicitly, exploiting their creative maternal agency in their birth projects. Backgrounding or denying dependency entails denying one's dependence upon the contributions of the other, often precisely the individual or group upon whom one and one's group is most reliant (Plumwood, *Feminism* 48). Rather than encouraging fathers to embrace the incredible opportunity to witness a woman birth a new life into the world, Pfeiffer encourages fathers to "realize how amazing the whole thing is," the "thing" is seeing one's "child enter the world" (148) or, as he puts it elsewhere, witnessing "another human emerge" (150). Even as Pfeiffer describes the post-birth environment, mother and father are presented as equally amazed at the birth (148); there is no discussion of pride, reverence, or honour felt toward the person foremost responsible not only for forging nascent life into infancy but also birthing this new life into the external world.

Pfeiffer leaves no doubt about his conceptualization of childbirth by defining birth as "the event of being born," adding that it is an event that happens "to you and your woman" (137).[6] The false equivalency between the contributions of the biological mother and biological father is repeated when Pfeiffer explains "push" gifts—presents given to women after their births—as a means for "men" to "acknowledge the pain and sacrifice women go through to carry and birth a child into the world" (113).[7] Jim Gaffigan undermines this false equivalency by utilizing comedic overstatement:

> Think about it this way: a woman can grow a baby inside her body. Then a woman can deliver the baby through her body. Then, by some miracle, a woman can feed a baby with her body. When you compare that to the male's contribution to life, it's kind of embarrassing, really. (48-49)

In truth, biological fathers need not be embarrassed for making an essential contribution to pregnancy through conception. It should be recognized, however, that from the point of conception, the mother is clearly the direct agent over the creative project that is gestation and childbirth.

Authors of each of these works participate in removing mothers as the subjects doing the work of birthing babies. In describing the act of his partner birthing their child, Crider explains how his son "began to appear," how his "head made its debut," and that their "son was born" (102-103). In discussing the birth of his child, Davis also neutralizes maternal agency. He writes that men should take a photo when their "baby begins to emerge" (76): "Once the baby's body fully emerges and the doctor clamps the umbilical cord, you may be asked to cut the cord" (77). Note how the mother's agency is dismissed but the doctor's is acknowledged; the baby "miraculously" emerges while the *doctor* "clamps."

In their discussion of "the birth" of the child, Lloyd and Davis write, "With one final push, your scary-as-hell-looking child has emerged" (196). Maternal agency is similarly pushed to the background in Finch's retelling of his post-birth question and answer session with friends and family. He reported that his daughter was "born via vaginal delivery" and had "descended into the birth canal" (205). However unintentional, such descriptions of women's birth projects diminish or altogether deny appropriate acknowledgement of the mother's will as the agent of the child's "appearance," "emergence," "debut," and "birth." Sports writers do not write that "a winning touchdown was thrown" or "a game-winning homerun was hit." They recognize the agent behind such actions, explaining that *Payton Manning* threw the winning touchdown or that *Sammy Sosa* hit the game-winning homerun. The discourse about childbirth in these guides, however, trivializes or effectively *disappears* maternal agency. Consequently, the authors fail to recognize what I call "maternal magnificence": the sheer awesomeness of birthing a new life one has forged within one's own body.

Even when women are described as actively participating in birthing their infant(s), their efforts are often trivialized: "It takes some women longer, and some women squirt out their kid in as little as two hours" (Crider 92). Whereas men save the day (Crider 84), women merely "squirt out" a baby. Similarly, Lloyd and

Finch limit acknowledging maternal agency to sentences describing women as "crapping out" kids or babies (190, 201). Pfeiffer, too, participates in discussing birth without acknowledging maternal agency. For example he writes, "Toward the end of the pregnancy, your exhausted partner will be hoping for the birth, and the sweet relief that follows, to mercifully come" (98). Here birth is something that simply happens to the mother. Her expression of autonomy is limited to awaiting merciful relief. Even in cases where medical intervention is limited Pfeiffer identifies childbirth as something that "Mother Nature" "does" to women, the outcome of which is that "when the baby is ready, it comes out" (138). Throughout his work, Pfeiffer denies maternal agency in birthing new life. Consequently, one is little surprised that he attributes the "miracle" of birth to the natural "process" and to the exclusion of the birthing woman (148).

THE HORROR OF BIRTH

The "horror" of childbirth is a prominent theme in the selected comedic birth guides. In *My Boys Can Swim*, Davis discusses his reaction to seeing video of an actual birth in a childbirth class. He describes the video as a "horror show" and a "film from hell," and likens viewing it to getting "root canal surgery" (53). Davis further writes that "no guy in his right mind would be interested in viewing multiple scenes of a woman in deep labor moving from shower, back to bed, sitting doggy style—all the while groaning in agony" (52). The author of *Pacify Me* concurs, writing that the "mind-numbing boredom" resulting from birth class "suddenly and unexpectedly turned into mind-numbing horror" when he watched a birth video. He describes a video "close-up of a woman giving birth" as a "horror fest" (37), noting "I swear, it was like if Stephen King made a porno. Like *Debbie Does Carrie*. It resembled one of those scary movies that frighten you into not committing crimes or driving drunk" (Mancini 37-38). Davis also relays a segment on National Public Radio in which a new father "described his wife's vaginal birth as the 'Saturday Night Massacre'" (74). Lloyd and Finch mock the so-called miracle of childbirth, describing it as "horrific" (193). They also liken the birth video shown in birth classes to the snuff genre of pornography: "Yes, if you haven't seen one before, you will see your first snuff film in a prenatal education class. You will also discover that there are some things you simply can't un-see, no matter how hard you try" (134).

This sentiment is shared by Pfeiffer, who describes "birthing class" as a mentally "scarring" event that "no man can ever be properly prepared for" (90). The most terrifying aspect of the class he attended was the video depicting a woman's vaginal birth, which he compares to a CIA "black-ops" mission (91). Pfeiffer jokes that such videos are potentially "hazardous to [men's] sex life" and ultimately recommends that fathers to "close" their "eyes when the main event comes on" (91). His rational for avoiding such an experience is that most men's partners will "probably be floating on painkillers" and "won't look anything like that monster you just saw [on the video]" (91). The clear message is that a woman engaged in actively birthing a new life vaginally is interpreted as monstrous, whereas one in a comparatively sedated state is, in Pfeiffer's words, a "sweet bride" (91).

Such attitudes are likely due to the way in which childbirth highlights the impossible demands of hegemonic masculinity. The culturally dominant model of manhood emphasizes men's responsibility to take care of and protect those in their family. Yet male partners are largely unable to take charge of childbirth: it is not something men can "do" for women, nor is it something that they can "save" them from. This gender-consternating circumstance is compounded by the preconception that women are ill equipped to endure and persevere in the face of intense adversity but rather are dependent upon masculine heroism.

The belief that birth is a "horror" women are oppressively burdened by fosters an attitude that normalizes the routine medical control of women's labour and births. Mancini claims that his wife's response to the film was to express her desire for a Cesarean section (38). In the event their partners have a Cesarean section and feel "disappointed about missing on the experience of labor," Mancini suggests that men show their partners the "horror video from class" (62). He also reassures his readers that they will not suffer any "horror-inducing" movies at the hospital (73), despite the fact that low-risk women who have a homebirth generally experience fewer complications and recover more quickly than those who choose hospital birth (Nall, "Mother Beware" 42). Of course these authors are not the first, nor are they alone, in envisioning childbirth as inherently terrifying.[8]

Despite attempts to help men retain an element of masculine control via the popular labour "coach" role, when men are confronted with the difficulty many women experience during hospital birth, medical authority and accompanying rituals are "a most welcome and reassuring intervention" (Mardorossian 48). Even when their demands are at odds with their birthing partners' desires, "fathers find great comfort in being able to relinquish their power" to the medical authorities (Reed, *Birthing Fathers* 218), for in doing so men become alleviated of a responsibility they were unlikely capable of (*Birthing Fathers* 214-216). Crider alternates between describing medical interventions such as induction as "ideal" and "civilized" and complaining about frequent medical intrusions, including checking vitals and blood pressure, changing IV bags, and checking baby's heart rate (94). In addressing the rhetorical question of how a man is supposed to support his partner in such an intrusive environment, Crider writes, "Unfortunately, I'm here to tell you that there's no use fighting it, man. These things have been going on since before you and I were born and the procedures aren't likely to change in this lifetime" (94).

The authors' discomfort with viewing natural childbirth videos is likely due in part to the transgression of dominant feminine gender norms. In patriarchal culture, women's worth is primarily based upon her sex-object status (Gilligan 60). This is clear from the way in which dominant culture polices and stigmatizes women for engaging in sexual activity that is tolerated, if not expected and encouraged, in men. In the discussed natural childbirth videos, women's sex-object status is confounded, as they are seen engaging in a physically challenging labour that many men find terrifying. Moreover, the symbol of women's sex-object status, the vagina, is seen outside of a sexual context, as a source of feminine potency and creation. This stands in stark contrast to conventional gender polarization, what cultural theorist Jane

Caputi calls "gender-porn," wherein "females are positioned to suggest vulnerability, stasis, and service," while males are depicted as "active, incipiently violent, and in control" (85). Thus it could be argued that what men find disconcerting about women birthing is that such displays of potency shake the pillars of dominant gender norms.[9] For, as Rich puts it:

> The power of the mother is, first of all, to give or withhold nourishment and warmth, to give or withhold survival itself. Nowhere else . . . does a woman possess such literal power over life and death.... In de Beauvoir's words, "It was as Mother that woman was fearsome; it is in maternity that she must be transfigured and enslaved." The idea of maternal power has been domesticated. In transfiguring and enslaving woman, the womb—the ultimate source of this power—has historically been turned against us and itself made into a source of powerlessness. (67-68)

READERS' RESISTANCE TO HEGEMONIC MASCULINITY

Davis, Mancini, Lloyd and Finch, Crider, and, to a lesser extent, Pfeiffer fortify the patriarchal masculine standard of manhood. Many supportive readers reinforce this conception of authentic manhood. Yet, despite such homogenized portrayals of masculinity, many readers actively resist the depiction of a naturalized form of masculinity presented by the birth guide authors. Readers challenged Davis' work, with one father complaining, "As a man who is interested in his wife and in learning about his yet unborn child, this all too common outlook about men and pregnancy is exactly what we do not need on our bookshelves" (Scribbler at Heart). Another commenter wrote of her husband's reaction to Davis' book: as someone who "actually likes being a father," he was insulted by the book (ny mom). Another reader wrote, "If men are this disinterested in the gestation of their own DNA, they should reconsider procreating" (Hamilton).

Judith Kegan Gardiner writes that masculinity has numerous forms that "are contingent, fluid, socially and historically constructed, changeable and constantly changing, variously institutionalized, and recreated through media representations and individual and collective performances" (11). This is evidenced in many readers' rejection of the vision of masculinity and manhood proffered in these birth guides. Reader Chad Oberholtzer describes Crider's work as "sophomoric, arrogant, crude, juvenile, uninspiring, condescending, and brutally honest. He appears to be mostly annoyed, disinterested, disengaged, and immature about his entry into the world of fatherhood." Oberholtzer contends that Crider's work does not represent "the guy's" perspective on fatherhood and childbirth. Another reader, whose gender is not indicated, characterizes Crider's work as "macho and insensitive" and "strongly" advises against reading the book for "tips on how to deal with your new role and responsibilities as a father" (Demirdjian). Yet another wrote that her husband "was disgusted with the tone of the author immediately and the 'humor' throughout the book" (Mike P). "Baglia" complained that the book reminded him of men he encounters in his day to day life: men "totally hung up on themselves, avoiding their wives and children, drinking Budweiser and getting away with it. Of all the ignorance; who prints this crap?"

To his credit, Pfeiffer encourages fathers to respect dads who are not primary breadwinners, including stay-at-home dads. A consistent theme throughout his book is that contemporary demands on men have positively shifted to expect more from fathers in terms of meaningful participation in parenting and caregiving. He also criticizes men who uphold hegemonic masculine roles, including behaviours such as leaving a crying baby for the mother to tend to, failing to communicate their feelings, and demanding mother to play the idealized domestic role of cooking dinner and taking care of household chores (170-171).

Such critiques of dominant masculinity were not enough to dissuade several reviewers identified as men from criticizing the book's use of stereotypes and shallowness. William Reardon describes the book as "awful" and suggests that instead of reading the work to "find a drunken frat buddy—ideally one who is a failed comic." Beyond lobbing invectives, Reardon criticizes the book for making "every stupid cliché joke you can think of." Clayton Campbell complains the book assumes "men are idiots and then proceeds to speak to them like they are bros at a frat party." Another reviewer writes he is offended by the book's stereotyping of men as incompetent and insensitive: "I'm a 'dude' who grew up with two older sisters who practically raised me. Father was a social worker who cleaned the house and cooked better than my mother.... No, I did not read the entire book. I'd have no hair left if I had because it would be all pulled out" (Traveler).

A reviewer who planned to be a stay-at-home-father complained that the book "coaches everything as if you're a Neanderthal with a frat-boy mentality and your wife is a shrieking frilly fru fru harpy" (Quite Wanderer). He sums up Pfeiffer's advice to fathers as, "Put your beer down and stop watching football long enough to help your crazy wife paint your man-cave baby colors." So while Pfeiffer's advice may sound novel to men who have long embraced patriarchal gender norms, Quite Wanderer and other critical men found such advice lacking. This is clear from "Traveler," who says the author "seems to think he speaks for all other men. He doesn't. He's an idiot writing for other idiots. Unless you're one of those guys, stay away." Articulating a similar sentiment without the personal attack, G. Hopping writes that "as a man who regularly cooks and cleans and respects his wife as an equal," he found the text "awkward" and unamusing.

Taken together, such critiques indicate that while these six popular comedic birth guides uphold patriarchal masculinity, it is not the case that all men applaud or identify with their vision. Indeed, it is clear from the examples given above that many men reject such definitions of manhood and vocally express their resistance. In so doing these men forge an alternative vision of male selfhood that is more closely aligned with feminist masculinity (Nall, "Exhuming").

CONCLUSION

Childbirth is an important prop for hegemonic patriarchal masculinity (Nall, *Feminism*). As has been shown, authors of six popular comedic birth guides use birth as an occasion to reinforce patriarchal masculine norms such as the rejection of femininity and exaltation of hegemonic masculinity. These birth guides also reinforce patriarchal definitions of women as being restricted to hyperemotionality and as generally inferior to men. The authors tend to ignore or trivialize women's agency in childbirth instead of interpreting women's births as creative projects that entitle the mother to honour, praise, or awe. Moreover, the authors of these works have anointed themselves spokesmen for authentic masculinity, thereby marginalizing alternative masculinities and the men who might well object to such views of women. Against the thrust of these hegemonic men, "other" men are "talking back." By posting critical and even condemnatory reviews, these men quietly and significantly contest the homogenization of masculinity and the normalization of hegemonic patriarchal definitions of manhood.

The dominant trend of male socialization fosters antipathy toward domesticity. This provokes fear in males who later are confronted with fatherhood and growing expectations for fatherly domestic responsibilities. Given this fear, it may well be the case that the authors of the comedic birth guides have deployed gender polarization and stratification in order to protect an inadequate and increasingly antiquated model of masculinity. For as much energy as the authors put into disparaging "feminine" activities such as baby showers, birth classes, and dollhouses, they may be consciously or unconsciously seeking to obscure the basic fact that pregnancy, childbirth, and babies, the subjects of their books, have long been deemed to belong to "woman's" realm and not "man's." Perhaps reaffirming male difference from and supremacy over females allows the authors to more securely adapt to domestic aspects of life conventionally identified as belonging to women. On the one hand, this indicates that even males who identify with conventional masculinity are embracing duties that have long been left to women. On the other hand, it reminds us that patriarchy is capable of adapting to changing demands in ways that maintain sexist social norms. Perhaps most significantly, pregnancy and childbirth continue to be "ground zero" for the misogynistic denial of respect for one of the most deeply entrenched domains identified with femininity, mother-hood. As such, pregnancy and childbirth must also be viewed as a crucial front for a revolutionary re-evaluation of the value of female personhood.

ENDNOTES

[1]All but one (Pfeiffer) of these works were featured on the bestseller lists of both a humour-oriented category and a non-humour, parenting category. At the time of my search, the guides were ranked in the top one hundred books in several categories, including "Parenting and Families, Fatherhood," 34 (Crider), 73 (Barron), 61 (Mancini), 3 (Pfeiffer); and "Pregnancy and Childbirth," 29 (Davis), 82 (Lloyd and Finch); 4 (Pfeiffer). These works were also highly ranked in the category of "Parenting and Families Humor," 31 (Lloyd and Finch), 79 (Mancini), 97 (Barron), and 46 (Crider). Another work (Davis) was ranked as the ninety-fifth bestseller of all humour books and 3,177 of all books on Amazon. When Barron's work was first published, it was praised by Michael J. Fox and awarded "best parenting book of 1998" by *A Child Magazine*. All of the books examined in this work with the exception of *Dude, You're Gonna Be a Dad* (Pfeiffer) were selected for analysis on March 3, 2011. The relevant sales rankings correspond to that date. Pfeiffer's sales ranking is based on an October 14, 2014, search. Most of the texts chosen in 2011 remain high-ranking sellers in the given categories in 2015.

[2]The guides in question further implement gender polarization to distinguish birth guides for men as compared to birth guides crafted for women. According to Lloyd and Finch, "every sentence of every women's pregnancy book is complete bunk" (3). Their work, in contrast, sets out to show men the "fountain" of awfulness and insanity their "wives" become during pregnancy. A reader identified as Ronald D. Bruner Jr. found the book not only humorous but also accurate. He wrote that *The Dudes' Guide* "seemed different than the usual moronic broads' point of view books" and was nothing like the "stupid" works likely to be discussed on "Oprah or The View." Whereas "skeezers" (women) "tend to go off on 5 paragraphs when one sentence is sufficient," Bruner promises that Lloyd and Finch get the job done in a succinct manner. Thus some readers not only interpret such birth guides as accurately representing the polarity between men and women but as also endorsing misogynistic derision of women.

[3]Pfeiffer imagines that some men might be good emotional commu-

nicators, but mainly in order to highlight its unlikeliness as a very peculiar exception (14). Summing up masculinity, Pfeiffer writes, "Men, you and I are simply men: the stereotypical man.... Our role upon entering manhood initiation was to carry all burdens that were given to us and never discuss our feelings" (14). It could be the case that Pfeiffer embraces essentialist notions of manhood in order to critique them, drawing in readers who identify with hegemonic masculinity. In doing so, however, he reinforces the "normality" and "naturalness" of this disposition.

[4]Along the same lines, Pfeiffer equates bonding with mature male children with "beers and wings at the local Hooters" and bonding with mature female children with giving them "our credit card and point them to the nearest mall" (163).

[5]Mancini writes that, like "most men," he wanted a boy so that there would be a family member in the house "we kind of understand" and there would be "an heir to the throne if you will" (49). Fathers of boys, explains Mancini, will "be able to play with cooler toys," such as "pirate ships" rather than "tea parties" (51), and also play with superior toys such as GI Joe figurines and baseball mitts rather than dollhouses and Barbie (50). The obvious presumption here is that genitalia determine gender roles and girls will not be interested in playing with the supposedly "cooler" toys. Only Barron dares to transgress such gender polarities and the presumed superiority that so often accompanies them, noting that boys and girls alike can play catch in the front yard and play with dolls (66).

[6]Reinforcing the deep denial of maternal agency is the fact that Pfeiffer includes a father's personal account of attending his partner's birth for the specific purpose of addressing his book's failure to meaningfully discuss the actual childbirth "event." Yet the supplied story, written by John Mueller, similarly disappears maternal agency: "The baby's head was already starting to show..."; "All of a sudden, 'WHOOSH!' the baby was out..."; "As quickly as it had started, it was over" (196). There is no achievement, no triumph; the birthing woman becomes a passive landscape upon which childbirth occurs.

[7]He goes on to complain that there is no gift for men for enduring the challenges of dealing with a pregnant partner. Indeed Pfeiffer

attributes less agency to the birthing woman than he does to the fetus she is primarily responsible for creating. Criticizing a couple's baby shower, he wrote that the décor and games were "intended for the pregnant lady and her *birth-canal storming offspring* [emphasis added] to enjoy" (72). Lloyd and Finch also attribute agency to the baby when they contend that the parents will have decided, prior to the mother's labour, who will be witnessing the "child emerge triumphantly" (176). The authors are clearly joking. What makes the jokes worthy of serious consideration, however, is that the authors' works limit birthing agency to these comedic absurdities.

[8]Popular film propounds similar themes of both the trivialization of women's birthing agency and the "horror" of birth (Nall, "Fade to White"), while popular news media and scholarly discourse around childbirth present homebirth as a perilous option compared to the safety of medicalized birth (Nall, "Mother Beware").

[9]Some ask, How else is a man or anyone else to react to witnessing a woman enduring the pain that so often accompanies childbirth but to feel fear or even pity for the mother? The answer is best expressed in a comparison: male athletes are regularly revered for their virility even as they are carted off the field of "battle"—in football for instance. The experience of pain does not necessarily indicate that one is not powerful or to be pitied. Particularly in athletes, the capacity to play through pain is regarded as a mark of supreme masculine potency.

WORKS CITED

Adams, Michele and Scott Coltrane. "Boys and Men in Families: The Domestic Production of Gender, Power, and Privilege." *Handbook of Studies on Men and Masculinities*. Ed. M.S. Kimmel, J. Hearn, and R.W. Connell. Thousand Oaks, CA: Sage, 2005. 230-248. Print.

Baglia, Joel B. "Do Not Buy This Book." *Amazon.com*. Web. 28 Mar. 2006.

Barron, James Douglas. *She's Having a Baby—and I'm Having a Breakdown*. New York: William Morrow and Company, Inc., 1998. Print.

Bruner Jr., Ronald D. "Actually worth reading." *Amazon.com.* Web. 6 Feb. 2010.

Bullock, Warren P. "Great Book, But You Have to Be Smart to Enjoy It!" *Amazon.com.* Web. 16 Sept. 2009.

Campbell, Clayton. "written for imbeciles." *Amazon.com.* Web. 29 Dec. 2012.

Caputi, Jane. *Goddesses and Monsters: Women, Myth, Power, and Popular Culture.* Madison, Wisconsin: University of Wisconsin Press, 2004. Print.

Connell, Raewyn. *Masculinities.* Cambridge: Polity Press, 2005. Print.

Crider, Michael. *The Guy's Guide to Surviving Pregnancy, Childbirth, and the First Year of Fatherhood.* Cambridge: Da Capo Press, 2005. Print.

Davis, Ian. *My Boys Can Swim! The Official Guy's Guide to Pregnancy.* New York: Three Rivers Press, 1999. Print.

Demirdjian, A. "Poor, uninspiring and a waste of money." *Amazon. com.* Web. 8 Mar. 2007.

FreshD. "Best." *Amazon.com.* Web. 22 Oct. 2009.

Gaffigan, Jim. *Dad is Fat.* New York: Crown Archetype, 2013. Print.

Gardiner, Judith Kegan. *Masculinity Studies and Feminist Theory, New Directions.* New York: Columbia University Press, 2002. Print.

Gaskin, Ina May. *Spiritual Midwifery.* Summertown, Tenn.: The Book Publishing Company, 1977. Print.

Gilligan, James. *Preventing Violence.* New York: Thames & Hudson, 2001. Print

Hamilton, J. "You've Already Read the Best Part … The Title." *Amazon.com.* Web. 9 Feb. 2007.

Haslanger, Sally. "Gender and Social Construction: Who? What? When? Where? How?" *Theorizing Feminisms: A Reader.* Ed. Elizabeth Hackett and Sally Haslanger. New York: Oxford University Press, 2006. 16-23. Print.

hooks, bell. *Feminism Is for Everybody.* Cambridge, MAA: South End Press, 2000. Print.

hooks, bell. *The Will to Change: Men, Masculinity, and Love.* New York: Atria Books, 2004. Print.

Hopping, G. "Did I seriously buy a book with "Dude" in the

title?" *Amazon.com*. Web. 3 Apr. 2014.

Hostert, Anna Camaiti. *Passing: A Strategy to Dissolve Identities and Remap Differences*. Madison, New Jersey: Fairleigh Dickenson University. 2007. Print.

Lengel, David. L. "Must Have." *Amazon.com*. Web. 28 Aug. 2009.

Lerner, Gerda. *The Creation of Patriarchy*. New York: Oxford University Press, 1986. Print.

Lloyd, Bill and Scott Finch. *The Dudes' Guide to Pregnancy: Dealing with Your Expecting Wife, Coming Baby, and the End of Life as You Knew It*. New York: Wellness Central, 2008. Print.

Lorde, Audre. "Age, Race, Class, and Sex: Women Redefining Difference." *Theorizing Feminisms: A Reader*. Ed. Elizabeth Hackett and Sally Haslanger. New York: Oxford University Press, 2006. 292-297. Print.

Macystike1. "Funny if your [sic] into comedy." *Amazon.com*. Web. 25 Sept. 2009.

Mancini, Chris. *A Handbook for the Freaked-Out New Dad*. New York: Simon Spotlight Entertainment, 2009. Print.

Mardorossian, C. M., "Laboring Women, Coaching Men." *Gendered Bodies, Feminist Perspectives*. Eds. J. Lorber, L. J. Moore. Los Angeles: Roxbury Publishing Company, 2007. 45-49. Print.

Mike P. "As the Title says, He is Merely Trying to Survive." *Amazon.com*. Web. 26 Jun. 2009.

Nall, Jeffrey. "Exhuming the History of Feminist Masculinity: Condorcet, 18th Century Radical Male Feminist." *Culture, Society and Masculinities* 2.1 (2010): 42-61. Print.

Nall, Jeffrey. "Fade to White or Stereotype: Patriarchal Policing of Gender Norms in Television and Filmic Representations of Childbirth." *Gender Questions* 2.1 (2014): 12-34. Print.

Nall, Jeffrey. *Feminism and the Mastery of Women and Childbirth: An Ecofeminist Examination of the Cultural Maiming and Reclaiming of Maternal Agency During Childbirth*. Palo Alto, CA: Academica Press LLC., 2014. Print.

Nall, Jeffrey. "Mother Beware: Perilous Scholarly and News Media Discourse around Homebirth." *Communication and Health*. 2 (2013): 37-48. Web. 31 Oct. 2014.

New Testament of Our Lord and Saviour Jesus Christ. The Church of Jesus Christ of Latter Day Saints. n.d. Web. 18 Feb. 2015.

ny mom. "For dumb dads." *Amazon.com*. Web. 12 Sept. 2007.

Oberholtzer, Chad. "Basically, a waste..." *Amazon.com*. Web. 9 Sept. 2009.

Odent, Michel. *The Farmer and the Obstetrician*. New York: Free Association Books, 2001. Print.

Pfeiffer, John. *Dude, You're Gonna Be a Dad!: How to Get (Both of You) Through the Next 9 Months*. Avon, Mass.: Adams Media, 2011. Print.

Plumwood, Val. *Environmental Culture: The Ecological Crisis of Reason*. New York: Routledge, 2002. Print.

Plumwood, Val. *Feminism and the Mastery of Nature*. New York: Routledge, 1993. Print.

Quite Wanderer "Book Fan 80." "Condescending garbage fit only for idiots." *Amazon.com*. Web. 7 Jul. 2014.

Reardon, William. "I *HATED* This Book." *Amazon.com*. Web. 27 May 2013.

Reed, Richard. "Birth Fathers or Knaves-in-Waiting?" *Midwifery Today with International Midwife* (1999): 12-14. Print.

Reed, Richard. *Birthing Fathers: The Transformation of Men in American Rites of Birth*. New Brunswick, New Jersey: Rutgers University Press, 2005. Print.

Rich, Adrienne. *Of Woman Born: Motherhood as Experience and Institution*. New York: W.W. Norton & Company, 1976. Print.

Rustici, Michael. "Rolling on the floor." *Amazon.com*. Web. 7 Jul. 2005.

Schulman, Sarah. *Ties that Bind: Familial Homophobia and Its Consequences*. New York: New Press, 2009. Print.

Scribbler at Heart. "Don't waste your time—this book is worthless!!!." *Amazon.com*. Web. 30 Jun. 2006.

Tarrant, Shira. *Men and Feminism*. Berkeley: Seal Press, 2009. Print.

Traveler. "Insulting and idiotic." *Amazon.com*. Web. 15 Jul. 2013.

Tuana, Nancy. *The Less Noble Sex: Scientific, Religious, and Philosophical Conceptions of Woman's Nature*. Bloomington: Indiana University Press, 1993. Print.

Warren, Karen J. "Critical Thinking and Feminism." *Re-Thinking Reason: New Perspectives in Critical Thinking*. Ed. Kerry S. Walters. Albany: SUNY Press, 1994. 155-176. Print.

Warren, Karen J. "The Power and the Promise of Ecological

Feminism." *Environmental Philosophy: From Animal Rights to Radical Ecology.* Ed. M.E. Zimmerman, J. B. Callicott, G. Sessions, K. J. Warren, J. Clark. Upper Saddle River, New Jersey: Prentice Hall, 1998. 325-344. Print.

9.
Just Along for the Ride?

A Father-to-be Searching for His Role

C. WESLEY BUERKLE

Begetting a child doesn't mean that the woman or the man must fall ineluctably into patterns nor must recharge the circuit of reproduction. —Hélène Cixous

THE EXPRESSION "WE'RE PREGNANT" seems wrong coming from a man; he will not deal with the many physical and emotional changes and challenges that can accompany pregnancy. But a male partner saying, "She's pregnant" sounds like a subtle declaration that this is her "problem" to handle on her own.[1] Certainly many a man has said, "She's pregnant" while being fully invested in my partner and her experience of pregnancy; I'm sure I used that very phrase more than once during my partner's pregnancy—though I preferred the communal, "We're having a baby." Those word choices ultimately matter less to me than what the debate in my head signified about my experience and identity as a partner, father-to-be, and a feminist: what was *my* role in *her* pregnancy of *our* child? After all, this was not my body enduring the strains of pregnancy; I was not anticipating the discomfort and medical interventions of childbirth; I also would not know any of the excitement that might attend carrying a growing life.

At the same time, my love for Dawn,[2] who would experience a high-risk pregnancy, my concern for the baby we were expecting, and my tendency to be a caretaker ruled out the possibility I would sit idly by and just wait for a request for assistance. As Hélène Cixous indicates in the epigraph above, heterosexual couples (or any couple, for that matter) entering into parenthood need not blindly fall back into well-worn patterns of masculinity and femininity. Critiques of childbirth and women's health in industrialized nations reveal a pattern of women, especially during pregnancy and birth, being treated as medical objects with directives for their care dictated by an androcentric medical tradition and the men with whom women have their children (Martin; Reed). As a feminist, I struggled to understand how to respect Dawn's pregnancy as her own experience and yet help her manage the complications of her pregnancy. More than a travelogue or confession, this essay examines my eight-month journey from an expectant to a new father and the tension I felt in trying to balance and understand what constituted caring for my partner and what became taking charge.

HELPER

If Rickey Ricardo (of *I Love Lucy*) was any indication, my only job during Dawn's pregnancy would be midnight runs for sardines, pistachio ice cream, and hot fudge (thankfully Dawn just wanted chocolate milk—but more on that later). Other than the likes of Ricky, men have few images of being an expectant father to go by.[3] Consequently, much of the tension I felt during Dawn's pregnancy came from not knowing where I fit in the process of expectant parenthood, as I was neither the one pregnant nor responsible for the care of a child. My feelings were like the experience of at least one father who likened his role to that of a hitchhiker, passively riding along with somebody else to a new destination (Draper). By extension, participating in expectant parenthood as a man meant sitting back and getting up when called on. I mean, right? I was excited—eager, even—to be a father, so, predictably, I was eager to support and encourage Dawn during pregnancy (Adamsons; Habib and Lancaster). That said, I had read Judith Butler on the conscription of men and women to worn cultural ideals, Cixous and her call for rebellion against the presumption to use women's bodies and lives for men's goals, and Emily Martin's accounting of the subjugation of women's bodies through medical practices. Women and their bodies have long been subjected to the interventions of men, many times in the name of obstetric—and thus industrial—advancement: I was not going to fall into that old trap; no thank you. What, then, was my role?

The positive sign on the pregnancy test stick took Dawn by surprise, to say the least. She found herself overwhelmed by what pregnancy entailed and asked me for help. "My job!" I thought. This is what I could do; she would explain what she needed and I could arrange it. I did whatever she needed, from locating an obstetrician to keeping fresh emesis bags handy and discarding used ones; I went from sharing household work to doing most all of the grocery shopping, dinner cooking, and cleaning up so she could literally put her feet up and sometimes nap. I also took the liberty of finding a good pregnancy book that I could reference to answer questions and allay concerns, even if Dawn decided not to read it. Aha, yes, I had found a good helper role, and I was going to fill it—even when Dawn did not think or know she wanted the help.

Just helping was not always so easy. I admit, not being the one carrying the growing baby created tension in terms of agency. I found myself in the same position that Richard Reed notes men experience across cultures: I began to feel I had the duties of father to my unborn child. I wanted to do what I could to ensure the wellbeing of the baby but, of course, I was not carrying the baby, which meant my interventions to care for the child would be interventions into my partner's agency. *Helping*, then, meant having to invoke the platinum rule: do for others as they would have done for themselves.

I truly struggled to only help when asked, as when Dawn had to stay hydrated. Generally Dawn does not care or feel the need to drink much, but the OB warned Dawn she needed more fluids for her own sake. Seeing how little Dawn drank made me nervous. Dawn told me to remind her to drink, so I did. My gentle reminders were often met with a groan or complaint and then a few small sips. When she found she liked Jell-O—congealed water, as far as I was concerned—I made individual serving containers of the sugar-free, lime-flavoured stuff every night before going to bed. There! I was helping, doing as she thought she needed. When the OB diagnosed Dawn as dehydrated around week eighteen, she sent her for IV fluids. Having been tasked with helping Dawn keep herself hydrated, I felt I had failed. I believed that as the helper my job was to make sure Dawn had as smooth a pregnancy as possible. Being unable to fully give the agency of her pregnancy to her, I took this hiccup as a sign that I was not doing enough. This moment did not directly affect the way I thought about or responded to Dawn's pregnancy, but it occurred at a time when my intention to hold back and wait for Dawn to call on me as she needed began to wane.

CARETAKER

I have been a caretaker nearly all my life, I am told. My mother recounted to me that when she was confined to bed for days with migraine headaches I, as a toddler, played in the space outside her bedroom door, refusing to leave my post even to eat. Years later, in my mid-teens, my mother would have a brief bout with cancer that would tax her most during the weeks of recovery and post-surgical radiation treatment. Coming after my parents' separation and my siblings' departure for marriage or college, it was just me in the house to care for her. My job was more than doing the marketing while she sat in the parking lot. I was the marshal in the house: I screened phone calls and decided who would be allowed to interrupt her sleep and who would have to call back; I made sure she ate something regularly, even if just coaxing her with peanut butter on toast. She was my mother, but I had the responsibility to keep her healthy.

As the minor complications of Dawn's pregnancy set in I felt myself again becoming a caretaker. Much like the findings of men who provide care for their wives with cancer, caretaking became the embodiment of love and enabled me to feel the connection of our relationship (Wagner et al.). The primary risks and concerns during Dawn's pregnancy stemmed from her Type II diabetes. Dawn had her diabetes under control when we found out we would be parents, but pregnancy and diabetes have a tendency to complicate one another.

Near her second trimester, Dawn experienced her blood sugar dropping unexpectedly and precipitously, leaving her weak and dizzy. Dawn has never wanted to burden anyone; I had long seen her denying a problem until the situation had gotten a bit worse. Once during pregnancy I found her in the kitchen grasping the double doors of our refrigerator with both hands. "Dawn," I asked in a paternalistic voice and knowing good and well that her blood sugar was dropping faster than she could fix it, "what's wrong?"

"Nothing," she replied in our dance around the truth. "I just need a glass of chocolate milk."

"Honey, why didn't you just call me?" I whined.

"I'm fine," she implored.

Challenging her, I then suggested that she let go of the refrigerator handles that she held on to with a white-knuckle grip. She grinned in the way two people who can be vulnerable with each other do; the jig was up. I helped her to a chair and made the chocolate milk that got her feet back under her in a few minutes.

This incident and others like it created an internal crisis for me. On the one hand I wanted to be there for Dawn as she asked for help, recognizing this as her pregnancy and her body. On the other hand I felt it difficult to be merely a helper, the one who supports the will and work of another person, when I see that person—my partner, no less—having difficulties. Whether it stems from my deep concern for those I love or my inability to resist taking over—what can be called a feminine desire to care and tend for another or the masculine propensity to control others—I began taking charge of Dawn's health in a way similar to my response to my mother's cancer recovery.

Immediately after the refrigerator standoff, Dawn explained that she checked her blood sugar and it was little low; she thought she could beat the decline. I then made her promise me that if her blood sugar was below seventy she would eat a glucose tablet (which provides immediate but short-lasting relief from hypoglycemia) before getting up to eat something more and that she would eat two tablets if her meter read below sixty; she agreed. Sometimes I would get a text from Dawn that she had checked her blood sugar, found it was low, and was waiting for her glucose tablets to kick in; subtle suggestions that she wanted me to be part of her management. Other times, I would apologize if it seemed like I was too demanding but, I would explain, I was genuinely worried about her wellbeing. Dawn always assured me that she knew I was just concerned about her health. Despite Dawn's kind reassurance, I continued to feel torn, as a feminist who teaches about our culture's control of women's bodies and my own attempt to manage my partner's health. The tension and my behaviour would only escalate when complications did as well.

Changes in Dawn's diabetic medication created more complications in regulating blood sugar. The first episode of middle-of-the-night hypoglycemia occurred, as most of them would, around 3:00 a.m. Dawn woke me, asking me to check her blood sugar, which I had only seen her do but never performed myself. We already knew Dawn's blood sugar was low by the fact that she could barely move her arm to wake me and because she was soaked with perspiration. When the meter read forty-seven, I panicked (the ideal is to not fall below seventy during pregnancy; much lower than forty-five, I am told, and diabetics are likely to lose consciousness). As I brought the glass of chocolate milk to Dawn, I asked her the day. After a pause she answered correctly; if she had not answered with any day of the week I was calling 911. I pulled Dawn up to a semi-reclining position and raised the glass to her lips. After a short time her blood sugar moved to a normal range, and we went back to sleep. When the new medications brought about regular, repeat performances of that night's act, I made a rule: until the numbers stayed in the good range through the night, we would wake every three hours for a blood-glucose check.

After a couple of nights of having to wake twice to check her blood sugar, Dawn suggested that the checks seemed extreme. "So far you have been hypoglycemic three out of four checks," I retorted. "When that changes, we'll talk." Of course, my word choices and tone suggested pretty clearly that our "talking" would be about me deciding if I would concede to what she wanted. Even now, with Dawn and our child safe and well, I think about my actions. I can never fully reconcile my choices with my feminism, yet I cannot bring myself to consider handling the situation differently. I was terrified of a condition I did not fully understand and that Dawn seemed unable to fully control, so I intervened. I suspect I will carry the guilt and the righteousness for a long time.

BYSTANDER

One Tuesday morning, with Dawn on leave from work, she and I sat on the couch watching a rerun of *Saturday Night Live* with no real plans for the day other than an OB appointment that afternoon. That was some of our last moments together as a child-free couple. With a sharp kick from the baby, Dawn's water broke and we were off to the hospital. A brief ultrasound revealed feet where shoulders should be, so a C-section was scheduled for the next hour. As we sat in the triage room, a string of nurses and other medical staff went in and out asking questions, previewing what would happen, and presenting forms to be signed; I felt strangely relieved. Concerns about how Dawn would handle hours of labour and what I would need to do to help her through the process became moot. Instead, a team of professionals formed with their focus on my partner and giving her the best care they could. Thus, in the tradition of the medicalization of childbirth, I handed the responsibility for my partner's care into the hands of professionals (Reed 85). Sitting there in the room, I noticed that the group forming included only women. As the lone male in the room I felt like I was the visitor (only there on good behaviour) allowed into the women's space, where women care for one another: it was beautiful and I was glad to just be there.

Admittedly, the relief itself came because I was handing the worry and care of Dawn off to someone else. In reflection, I recognize that women have been treated as objects in institutionalized birth, and thus my relief came at the expense of Dawn's agency to industrialized medicine (Young), even though Dawn has said she had a very positive experience with her Cesarean section. Though she regretted not feeling the sensation of a new life emerging from her body and missing out on immediate skin-to-skin contact with our daughter, Dawn found that the process and the people were quite lovely and made for a smooth birthing experience.[4] That she had a pleasant birthing experience does assuage some of my guilt, but my own relationship to the experience only goes to highlight the sense of ownership that had crept into my care for Dawn.

After only an hour or so with us, Lucy, our new daughter, was taken to NICU for low blood sugar and a dropping body temperature.

Dawn and I were deeply saddened, but my attention soon turned back to Dawn, whose blood pressure spiked despite medications. The elevated blood pressure made Dawn vomit constantly (a problem that would not be resolved for hours). After an hour or so, with Dawn's blood pressure still spiking and her still retching uncontrollably, we agreed I would dart up to NICU to check on our baby for the both of us, not wanting Lucy to be "alone." Walking down the corridor to NICU, I felt the anxiety of the moment weigh down on me, but I pushed it back to remain composed for my child. Once buzzed into NICU and scrubbed to the elbow, I was taken to Lucy's isolette, a box made of Plexiglas I had only seen on TV when a baby is made to seem pitiable and frail.

As I sat in front of my six-pound seven-ounce child with an IV in her arm sleeping in a little incubator, I broke down. Placing my hand on the rail of her cart, I dropped my head and wept heavily. In the height of melodrama, I muttered, "What have I wrought?" I felt responsible for my child in the plastic box and my ill partner in another wing: I had wanted a baby from the time I was a small child and I now had my wish at the expense of others. Feeling genuinely responsible for Dawn's and Lucy's health reveals both my own narcissism—that their wellbeing is about me somehow—and the sum of a caregiver's potential for guilt, because once you identify someone else's health with your own abilities, their decline is your failure.

A kind nurse came along and suggested I just take Lucy out of her isolette and hold her. As I took Lucy into my arms, just as I had after she was born that afternoon, I realized she was not so fragile and I not so in charge. We—Lucy, her mom, and I—were going to have to learn to make do together. Once home, that was a lesson Dawn would have to help me learn.

PARENT

The most repeated motto I had heard of newborn parenting was to "sleep when your baby sleeps." It took me a solid week to understand that recommendation was more than a practical survival tip; it was permission. Just as I easily adopted rules like, "We will wake every three hours to check your blood sugar," I assumed unspoken rules of social decency from my childhood: every hour slept past 8:00 a.m. is an increasing degree of sloth.

In our household, Dawn and I took shifts caring for Lucy. The general pattern that organically emerged had each parent on for two feedings and then off for two. I ended up covering the early morning swing from about midnight to 5:00 a.m., with bits of sleep between feedings, sleeping until about 11:00 a.m., and then covering for Dawn while she slept for several hours. The hours of sleep and feeding were predictably erratic. We three were only awake together in the evenings, so we would take a walk at a near-by park around 8:00 p.m. (our daughter having been born when daylight does not cease until nearly 10:00 p.m.), maybe driving to a large but empty book store for everyone's visual stimulation. Some nights we ate our common meal together as late as 10:00 p.m. before going to bed together until Lucy woke for a bottle.

Dawn and I both found those early weeks of fragmented sleep, unusual hours, infrequent meals, and social isolation from our friends and family to be some of the most blissful times of our relationship. The hours and work were exhausting, of course, but I have never known a time when I felt more free than then. Our home was a sanctuary from the strain of the world outside. I used to joke there were only three rules in the house: if you're tired, sleep; if you're hungry, eat; and always wipe Lucy from front to back. To Dawn this all seemed natural but for me it was a learned release. My orientation to time and order that I believed to have been so beneficial during Dawn's pregnancy had to go away for us to be happy as a family.

During Lucy's first weeks at home, I thought often of Adrienne Rich's reflections on the masculine disciplining of motherhood vividly captured in a recollection of a summer spent with her children while her husband was away: "Without a male adult in the house, without any reason for schedules, naps, regular mealtimes or early bedtimes … we fell into what I felt to be a delicious and sinful rhythm.…We were conspirators, outlaws from the institution of motherhood; I felt enormously in charge of my life" (194-5). Rich's story gave voice to my experience as Dawn's expectant partner and subsequent co-parent: I had spent months crafting and enforcing rules, trying to plan a safe and proper course for Dawn's pregnancy, but following Dawn's lead to let go of the demand for discipline created the opportunity for an intimate and happy time as a family. Rich's account pointedly critiqued my tendency toward a masculinist need for order that would have crushed the easy breathing of a liberated lifestyle.[5] My lack of broad agency—my lack of imposition of order onto myself and others—allowed Dawn and me to be equal partners and parents caring for each other and Lucy.

FEMINIST

In writing about motherhood and feminism, Amber Kinser emphasizes that there is no clear feminist way, no good and true means of mothering—or parenting, I would add—that is *feminist*. The whole matter is messy, and we are left to make the choices we believe bring the most good for ourselves and those we love. Having written my doctoral dissertation about Margaret Sanger's rhetoric of birth control, I spent two years thinking and writing about discourses that either facilitate or inhibit women's control of their bodies; the ironies of my behaviour of caretaking during Dawn's pregnancy were not lost on me.

In reflection, I think also about Dawn's complicity. When—for I really do not know when—did she want me to be the one who made the decision she did not want to make? For instance, when sometime in her eighth month of pregnancy her belly began to brush up against her steering wheel, I suggested she hand over driving duties to me until the baby came. Dawn groused some and then relented. She would protest in a light-hearted way to my sister (herself a mother of three) as well as her OB; both would sort of smile and offer words of conciliation, such as, "Oh, that happens."

Were these women who were avoiding entering into a domestic squabble? Did Dawn, who loves to drive, need me to take away her keys so that she could say, "Wesley won't let me drive" rather than admit defeat of her own freedom behind the wheel to pregnancy? Was I a culprit or an assistant? Even after Lucy came, Dawn said she probably should not have driven any longer than when I suggested she stop but would have happily kept driving until the baby came. Were some of the decisions I made the dirty work of being a caretaker, the consequence of my inability to remain quiet, or some amalgamation of both?

Cixous opined that women cannot be worried about men's psychic struggles until men own their relationship to women and women's bodies: "It's up to him to say where his masculinity and femininity are at: this will concern us once men have opened their eyes and seen themselves clearly" (877). I cannot say how clearly I have seen myself. When I have asked Dawn how she felt about my efforts to support her in her pregnancy and if I went too far, she would dismiss my concern with, "You're fine. I know you always meant well." Rather than belabor the point and place upon her the burden of counsellor and confessor or push us into an argument about matters of her health already resolved, I have kept much of my worry off her. This essay, however, provides the opportunity for an accounting of my choices, for better or for worse.

Remembering David Terry's warning that confessional tales often serve the purpose of catharsis without the intent or potential for broader structural change, I offer this essay as neither confession nor apologia but as a critical reflection. Even now, with mother healthy and child toddling, I consider if my behaviour during Dawn's pregnancy was feminist and, if not, how I could have behaved otherwise. On the one hand, core goals of feminism, such as the liberation of women's bodies and the defense of women's agency, may conflict with my propensity to make choices for Dawn in her pregnancy. On the other hand, who, feminist or not, would think it better to remain a quiet bystander when someone needs assistance for health's sake? The challenge for me always returned to wanting to help Dawn out of my love for her and also step back out of my respect for her. For all my reflection and angst, my true energy and focus now points toward building and nurturing my relationship with Dawn and how together—in genuine collaboration—we can raise a happy and healthy daughter who can make a fulfilling life for herself.

ENDNOTES

[1] A pair of articles written by two different men provides a nice

point-counterpoint on this matter, with Patrick Quinn concerned that the phrase "We're pregnant" sounds presumptuous and Michael Carley arguing that the expression emphasizes the bonding between two people who will share a lifetime as parents to the same person (see Quinn; Carley).

[2]I have changed the name of my partner and child to protect the innocent; I have used my own name to reveal the guilty.

[3]My experience was similar to that of contemporary fathers interviewed by Kerry Daly who express that they have no clear role models for an engaged fatherhood.

[4]Laura June writes of her quiet satisfaction with having a child by C-section, which runs up against notions about an idealized "natural" birth experience.

[5]Andrea Doucet's *Do Men Mother?* broadly explores whether fathering and mothering can be the same thing; she falls toward the conclusion that the different experience of men and women, as gendered beings, makes talking about equivalence a tricky matter.

WORKS CITED

Adamsons, Kari. "Possible Selves and Prenatal Father Involvement." *Fathering* 11.3 (2013): 245-55. Print.

Butler, Judith. *Gender Trouble: Feminism and the Subversion of Identity*. New York: Routledge, 1990. Print.

Carley, Michael. "You Heard that Right. WE Are Pregnant." *The Good Men Project*. 29 Jul. 2014. Web. 29 Jul. 2014.

Cixous, Hélène. "The Laugh of the Medusa." Trans. Keith Cohen and Paula Cohen. *Journal of Women in Culture and Society* 1.4 (1976): 875-93. Print.

Daly, Kerry J. "Reshaping Fatherhood: Finding the Models." *Fatherhood: Contemporary Theory, Research, and Social Policy*. Ed. William Marsiglio. Thousand Oaks, CA: Sage, 1995. 21-40. Print.

Doucet, Andrea. *Do Men Mother? Fathering, Care, and Domestic Responsibility*. Toronto: University of Toronto Press, 2006. Print.

Draper, Janet. "Men's Passage to Fatherhood: An Analysis of the Contemporary Relevance of Transition Theory." *Nursing Inquiry* 10.1 (2003): 66-78. Print.

Habib, Cherine, and Sandra Lancaster. "The Transition to Father-hood: Identity and Bonding in Early Pregnancy." *Fathering* 4.3 (2006): 235-53. Print.

June, Laura. "An Unnatural Birth: In Praise of the Caesarean Section." *Jezebel*. 9 Oct. 2014. Web. 9 Oct. 2014

Kinser, Amber E. "Introduction: Thinking About and Going About Mothering in the Third Wave." *Mothering in the Third Wave*. Ed. Amber E. Kinser. Toronto: Demeter, 2008. 1-16. Print.

Martin, Emily. *The Woman in the Body: A Cultural Analysis of Reproduction*. Boston: Beacon, 2001. Print.

Quinn, Patrick. "We Are Pregnant." *The Good Men Project*. 22 Feb. 2012. Web. 1 Oct. 2014.

Reed, Richard K. *Birthing Fathers: The Transformation of Men in American Rites of Birth*. New Brunswick, NJ: Rutgers University Press, 2005. Print.

Rich, Adrienne. *Of Woman Born: Motherhood as Experience and Institution*. New York: Norton, 1976. Print.

Terry, David P. "Once Blind, Now Seeing: Problematics of Con-fessional Performance." *Text and Performance Quarterly* 26.3 (2006): 209-28. Print

Wagner, Christina, Lala Tanmoy Das, Silvia M. Bigatti, and Anna Marioa Storniolo. "Characterizing Burden, Caregiving Benefits, and Psychological Distress of Husbands of Breast Cancer Patients During Treatment and Beyond." *Cancer Nursing* 34.4 (2011): 21-30. Print.

Young, I. M. "Pregnant Embodiment: Subjectivity and Alienation." *Journal of Medicine and Philosophy* 9 (1984): 45-62. Print.

10.
Mommie Dearest

Undoing a Gay Identity Through Pregnancy

JACK HIXSON-VULPE

CTS OF REPRODUCTION can be understood in a multitude
of ways: reproducing texts, reproducing identities, reproducing people. Queerness and reproduction have often
been thought of, and theorized, as having a fraught relationship.
In queer theory, discussions of reproduction and queerness often
pertain to the (re)production of identities, exploring conversations around how queerness is reproduced through cultural and
social norms. At the same time, these conversations posit that
queerness has a unique quality due to an inability to reproduce
through sexual acts. In the early 2000s, as a response to the rise
of social acceptance of certain factions of LGBT communities (e.g.,
winning the right to marry in Canada and cascading acceptance
in the United States, as well as the right to serve openly in the
military), a resurgence of conversations around how queer identities play into normative social structures occurred. Two voices
that contributed to this discussion around this time were Lee
Edelman and José Muñoz. Both scholars take up the theoretical
position of "the Child" within contemporary social structures.
Where Edelman condemns any investment in "the Child" and
any sense of the future, Muñoz invests in futurity, while still
citing queerness as a response to heteronormative expectations
of reproduction.

The notion of "reproduction" as outlined by Edelman and Muñoz
primarily relates to non-bodily forms of reproduction. Edelman
postulates "reproduction" to mean the (re)production of identity
markers in social and political worlds. As he explains, our worlds

are created through fantasy, "an order, an organization [that] as-sures the stability of our identities as subjects and the coherence of the Imaginary totalizations through which those identities ap-pear to us in recognizable forms" (7). In his view, fantasy creates these worlds by which we are able to form intelligible identities. It is through self-perpetuating processes that political and social worlds are created and evolved, thereby generating recognizable identities, which in turn continually (re)produce these worlds. For Edelman, "the Child" comes to represent the *how* and *why* of this cyclical process.

Edelman draws on the "cult of the child" as the problematic signature of futurity, believing that any investment in futurity will continue to leave those in the present "savagely beaten and left to die" (154). While Muñoz agrees with Edelman in his critique of the "cult of the child," he takes a more redemptive stance, believing that a sense of potentiality can exist within futurity. Instead, Muñoz critiques the investment in the temporal and teleological construction of futurity. He questions the under-standing of futurity as moments that belong to the "future," thus relegating futurity to that which is ultimately never attainable. He pushes for a collapse of this teleological understanding of time, arguing that "we must vacate the here and now for a then and there" (185).

For Muñoz, queerness represents the "then and there" and exists as "not yet here but it approaches like a crashing wave of potenti-ality" (185), whereas Edelman believes that queerness represents, almost an answer to the problem of investing in futurity. It is here, in the conceptual gap between Muñoz and Edelman where I pose my fundamental question, where both Edelman's and Muñoz's arguments slide in and out of naturalizing homosexuality as an-ti-reproductive. For me, this logic provokes the following queries: What happens when a homosexual interaction results in the re-production of the child? And to Muñoz, whose focus rests on the political and aesthetic realm of futurity, how can an embodiment of futurity be situated?

I have never configured my sex life with my partner as anything but gay, actually queer more precisely. We were just two queer

*boys. We never held hands walking down the street and we never
kissed on street corners. But behind closed doors, we knew how to
queer up our space: me on my knees with his cock in my mouth,
me bent over with my hands on the bathroom mirror for support
and him inside me with his hand on my clit. Our sex was inco-
herent to many and disturbed the ossified beliefs of what gay sex
was; our gay relationship was complicated and not always read
as such. As two gay boys living in a world where so much came
before us, our relationship and sex challenged these temporal and
teleological definitions of what made gay sex gay.*

*While we understood ourselves to be gay, my ability to pass was
precarious and thus our gayness was often partially translated.
Often we were read as a boy and a girl, or even on the rare occasion, two girls. We straddled worlds of coherence, being read as
one thing but comprehending ourselves as another. This comprehension of our gayness existed in relation to our sexual lives with
one another, yet was a considerable point of rupture for many.
The question of what type of sex we did have was often open for
interpretation. These interpretations remained fluid and outside
of my own conception of self; I just always thought of myself
as having gay sex with my partner. This solidified perception of
sex remained untroubled until the evidence of our sex began to
exist past the reminiscences on the sheets or between my legs, the
ephemera of our sex became a concrete, tangible, yet temporary
addition to my life.*

Muñoz presents queerness as that which has yet to arrive, an
excitement that rests within anticipation—continual waves of potential that remain indefinable. He contends that utopian realities
are achievable through a collapse of the heteronormative ordering
of time. No longer is the future defined by a linear understanding
of "growing up" and reproducing the next generation, but instead
life invests in anticipation. For the future, a matter of "becoming"
must tear itself from the normative order, as set up by heteronormative structures, and begin to align itself to the "ephemeral," the
trace evidence that queerness leaves behind.

Borrowing from Derrida, Muñoz evokes the notion of "ephemeral" (65) as a trace which was never meant to continue yet re-

mains "hanging in the air just like a rumour" (65). For Muñoz, ephemera act as the evidence of queer lives. Through ephemeral trace evidence, queerness is allotted space and becomes memorable. It disturbs heteronormative lineages and creates a space for itself in our historical and contemporary narratives. For Muñoz, the traces linger within the looks cast as queers cruise the streets, the bars, the bath houses, within the stories that are passed from queer lips giving away hints or blatant exposure. The traces and gestures, much like rumours that are impossible to evade, bring about queer thoughts while remaining visible yet hard to detect under the harsh light of normativity and mainstreamability.

As Elizabeth Freeman points out by in "Times Binds, or, Erotohistoriography," events considered worthy of documentation are hugely influenced by the development of discourses of race, gender, class, and sexuality (57). In similar fashion to Muñoz, Freeman believes it is important to work against heteronormative constructions of time. She argues for "erotohistoriography," as an investment in a politic of embodied pleasure (59) and an important tool to trouble linear narratives of normative growth and development. For both Freeman and Muñoz, queerness and queer acts create space that is otherwise never allotted to queerness; they unbecome the straight path walked by heteronormative time.

In his bachelor apartment, it was my first time in Winnipeg; his bed was right next to the kitchen. It was a kid's bed with lots of storage underneath. He had finally gotten rid of the sheets that saw us through two cities. The blood stains from getting his wisdom teeth removed or from me forgetting to take my T-shots during my month-long trips to him.

I looked out over Princess Street at the Metis flag in the distance and the Dim Sum restaurant. We pretended I was never going to leave; he came inside me again and again. I straddled him, rocking back and forth. Each time he came he would laugh and hug me. He always smiled and held me when it was all over. We played out our future as something that may perhaps pass; our life together existing outside the visible realm. We never held hands or exchanged visible affection; our fleeting existence seemed only visible to queers and homophobes.

In the Princess Street apartment I made dinner for when he came home from work. We played out a perverted version of a heterosexual relationship.

As I boarded the plane from Winnipeg to Toronto, I assumed the ephemera and evidence of our relationship, once again, would exist encased over copper cables and wireless radio waves. I was proven wrong; further evidence existed but remained unnamable.

Edelman's critique of reproductive futurism assumes queer sexuality as non-reproductive and thus calls on queerness to acknowledge its significance as anti-social. According to Edelman, queerness must "accept its figural status as resistance to the viability of the social" (3). The figural status of resistance comes from queerness and its relationship to the death drive (3). For Edelman, the attachment between queerness and the death drive is explained as the queer standing in, as the sinthome, the Lacanian figure which exists free from the language of the Other. For Lacan, it is through the creation of the Other that one becomes a subject, recognizable through a fiction of political and social intelligibility. The sinthome exists to work against the signifiers of the subject.

Edelman takes the sinothome, a non-translatable concept, and imagines "sinthomosexuality" (34). For him, the homosexual carries "the burden of sexuality's demeaning relation to the sinthome" (39), an assumption that is entrenched in the notion of queerness as always already non-reproductive. Henceforth, the queer and the sinthome become bedfellows; queerness "inhabit[s] the place of meaningless associated with the sinthome; to figure and unregenerate, and unregenerating sexuality whose singular insistence . . . reject[s] every constraint imposed by sentimental futurism" (47-49). The connection of queerness to the sinthome requires queerness to reject the concept of generational succession through the act of reproduction.

For Edelman, the character of the sinthomosexual rejects social coherence and therefore rejects the Child, which shapes the logic of political worlds (2). This rejection of political coherence relies not only upon the disavowal of the Child. Standing outside of reproductive futurism, it then becomes the place of queerness to mark the side of not fighting for the Child.

I had been nauseous all day and every day for at least a week. I hadn't bled since getting home, but that didn't seem out of the ordinary—I took testosterone, so I wasn't meant to bleed. Each day that passed brought an underlying level of exhaustion; each day my sense of smell fluctuated. I craved chicken, potatoes, and spinach. But if you put anything else in front of me, I was liable to spend my night in the restroom. My colon was so backed up that my doctor's face registered surprise. Her hands pressed into my abdomen, she followed the maze of my colon, "Yup, it even goes around the corner!"

These words didn't fill me with joy.

I had told her all my symptoms. She had no explanation. Eat more fiber, get more sleep, be more active and it should all figure itself out; the ambiguous words of a physician who is confounded and over-worked.

I tried all these things. It got worse. I couldn't eat anything and I was barely sleeping. I had no words, mechanisms, thoughts, or feelings to understand what was going on in my body. My symptoms evaded translation. Each time I typed my symptoms into a search engine, I scrolled past the first six pages to get past the "EARLY SIGNS OF PREGNANCY" section. I had visited multiple doctors, multiple times and the thought of me being pregnant didn't make sense. My symptoms couldn't be read and the cause remained undefined until June 29th when a translation of sorts was provided by a double blue strip.

To be queer is to critique and denaturalize the normative narrative of "straight time" (Muñoz 22); it is to challenge the ossification of neoliberal ideologies that represent queerness solely as an identity category within contemporary mass culture. Instead, queerness should be held "in a sort of ontological humble state" (22) where we reject a coherent identity and understanding. Queerness becomes a matter of "stepping out of line" (25), forging a path that may not ever finish; it will turn back, go around, swerving left and right, to and fro, and all directions at once.

Week 1 and 2 conception occurs.
Week 3 fertilization occurs; egg and sperm unite in the fallopian

tube to form a zygote.

Week 4 implantation, zygote implants into the uterus and placenta begins to grow.

Week 5 embryonic period begins; brain, spinal cord, heart, and other organs begin to form.

Each week the changes going on inside my body were explicable by an outward narrative; a common narrative shared through pregnancy.

Each week demarcated according to the zygote and cells moving through my body, beyond my control and understanding. Yet externally these changes did not translate. I stood in front of multiple doctors listing the same symptoms: "Nausea, fatigue, constipation, sensitivity to food and smells." And each time they had no explanation. I had no explanation.

My narrative when disconnected from a trans body read clearly, becoming a matter of "straight time," yet when sutured to me became unreadable. It is always already only women who can become pregnant. And it is always already queers who cannot become pregnant.

Stepping away from linear time is a fundamental aspect of potentiality within queerness, according to Muñoz (25). He believes this stepping out of line is the project of ecstasy, which leaves behind traces that are faintly discernible within a heterosexist context. These traces, or ephemeral evidence of queerness, destabilize heterosexualized concepts of time and space. This destabilized narrative of time paves the way for a utopian future. This utopia will bring about the collective, turning to the fringe of political and cultural production to counteract hegemonic normativity and the violence that follows. For Muñoz, "queerness is utopia, and there is something queer about the utopian" (26).

The narrative throughout this piece addresses what becomes of queer identities when this temporal confusion becomes embodied. As described by Muñoz, this temporal confusion and collapse is a matter of ecstasy, but what about the complications when this temporal chaos is sutured to embodied experiences?

I had refused to take a pregnancy test, I couldn't be pregnant;

Google search was often wrong in my attempts to self-diagnose and I refused to give into my usual panic. I was a boy; I couldn't get pregnant.

This experience, removed from a trans person, according to many would be normal. A well-off twenty-four-year-old with a long-term steady partner gets pregnant through safe and loving means. I was a poster child for a young parent in so many ways; yet no one thought of me that way, not even myself. Even my pregnant body could not be understood by the medical community that had created me.

I had been on testosterone for five years, prescribed and moni-tored by the same doctor. I was one of the more privileged trans people. I had a medical clinic that supported me in many ways. Yet, the narrative of the pregnant trans body only existed in the realm of choice. Some trans men chose to get pregnant, they chose to go off testosterone, they had discussions with their partners, they were expecting it and it came as good news.

When my time came, I hadn't done any family planning; I was 2,227 kilometers away from the other half of the mass of cells inside me. We had never had discussions of what would happen if I got pregnant. I never went off testosterone, we weren't expecting it and nor did it come as good news. The double blue strip on the stick seemed to me like a jump, it couldn't be happening, this wasn't the time nor was I the body.

What are the implications for Edelman to perpetuate such a polemic understanding of how queerness should be defined in a context that perpetually requires a future? Edelman's critique of futurity denies the bodies that have already been erased by the very discourse that he critiques. In taking up the understanding of queerness as antithetical to reproduction, he works to further solidify what defines queer as queer. And while he does not speak out against any real child, what is lost when condemning repro-duction within queered bodies?

While Muñoz offers an embodied notion of futurity, he doesn't fully address issues embodying temporal chaos and how it can affect the body and psyche. Muñoz's redemptive reading of the embodied chaos does not attempt to engage some of the more traumatic experiences, which Heather Love believes is an integral aspect of disturbing normative narratives of progression. Muñoz's reading of queer ephemera works to document only the positive evidence, which leaves me wondering: where can we place the ambivalent, or potentially negative, experiences of queerness? How can a "turn to the negative in queer studies" (Love 2) allow us to more holistically queer utopia?

Queerness is taken up as a site of disturbance that represents critiques to straight narratives of time. Yet this assumption is steeped in a history of queerness, which is understood as non-reproductive. With this in mind, what does it mean that both Edelman and Muñoz move towards queerness as a solution to heteronormative narratives steeped in generational succession? Queerness is conceptually anti-linear and thus can collapse and reconfigure heteronormative structures. This reading of queerness remains embedded in the culturally signified, intelligible, and assumed composition of what defines queer sex as queer.

To equate the homosexual to the sinthome or to understand queer utopia through the creation of temporal chaos work to perpetuate the queer body as ultimately non-reproductive. While the queer body was created as non-reproductive, it has become a self-fulfilling construction.

I scheduled an appointment at a "women's clinic." The clinic talked about the busy lives of women who might need to schedule abortions and all the help they were willing to provide for women. To go through this process, I knew I would have to be a woman. Without any option, I made an appointment booked under my legal name. A boy couldn't walk into a women's clinic. So, what is a boy like me to do?

It was here that a sense of chaos enveloped me. I had been thrust simultaneously into a "straight sense of time" (Muñoz 22) and my pregnant body was relatable on through narratives of heterosexual families, yet this narrative remained incomprehensible to me. Of course, I could still count the hours and knew that I had booked my appointment for July 6th. My comprehension of time became scattered each time I looked in the mirror or thought about what was going on inside me. The symptoms of my reality had created a being that was unidentifiable to those around me, and the diagnosis had solidified my undoing. In these moments, I resisted a coherent notion of self-conception and remained untranslatable to many around me. I existed beyond my intelligible identity, yet remained entwined in the world around me.

The answer was to become a woman for a two-hour stretch. I entered the clinic. They referred to me by legal name and used female pronouns to a point that just seemed redundant to me; they asked when I conceived, how I knew I was pregnant, and gave me a quick breakdown of the entire procedure. I sat in the waiting room littered with fashion and gossip magazines. A woman sat down next to me and flipped through a magazine. I started a conversation. My hairy legs and short hair made me feel conspicuous. I needed to get out of my head. She talked to me about how she had done this before. I am pretty sure she could tell how nervous I was; she told me that everything was going to be okay.

While this story has taken time to settle and (re)work itself, it remains unfinished within me. As I reread this work, I have begun to notice a strong thread of irony intertwined within this narrative. The irony that, as a man, I could get pregnant in a gay relationship. And how it took homosexuality for me to get pregnant. The irony that the doctors who created me could not read me. The irony that I had to go back to being a woman in order to rid myself of the evidence of my homosexuality. There are times when this irony evokes laughter and times when it evokes tears, and it is in these contrary reactions that I have begun to tie the importance of irony into understanding the impact of this narrative.

Edelman understands irony to represent a "syntactical violence of anacoluthon" (24), which severs syntax from the "very logic of making sense" (24). Edelman takes queer theory to represent a form of irony thus presenting a radical threat to the heteronormative. Queerness becomes about *not* making sense, about embodying the figural lack of identity (24), about disavowing the very value of identity, which attempts to straight queer bodies into a heteronormative narrative.

I have attempted to weave the ways in which a transmasculine body sexually reproducing through a gay relationship can begin to question the assumption of queerness as antithetical to reproduction, but to also understand the ramifications of the embodied chaos and ecstasy that Muñoz speaks of in his understanding of queerness. In drawing these lines, I am not attempting to imply that trans pregnancy holds any specific potential to re-signify (or remove signifiers) from societies and bodies, thus altering the significance given to intelligibility and teleological temporality. Instead, I wish to examine my pregnancy to highlight the potentiality in queer reproduction. The reality produced inside me left me unravelled and unidentifiable, evidence of the fragility and undoablility of self-conceptions. Not only was my identity undone but my body was unreadable, not only to me but also to many around me. I could not be pregnant because I was supposed to be a man, but when I was a man I had to become a woman in order to "deal" with the situation. These chaotic embodied temporalities created a liminal space in which I was simultaneously intelligible yet rendered unintelligible.

Prior to my pregnancy, my interactions with the world had been through a male identity and the relationship that had made me pregnant was understood to me as gay—this equation did not add up to pregnancy and I wondered at the outcome. I wondered at my symptoms. Doctors wondered at my symptoms. Friends wondered at my symptoms. I wondered how I would get through my pregnancy. I wondered how I could obtain an abortion. I wondered at how I could be gay and pregnant. All my assumptions dissolved in my experiences, re-routed and re-opened based on wonder. I had written and been written into a new story.

Wonder exists as a verb (I wonder why) and as a noun (with the wonder of a child) and as the prefix to an adjective (wonderful). It has three sites: one consisting of the desire or curiosity to know; another of the mingling feelings of surprise and admiration; and, lastly, one of inspiring delight that I believe we should inhabit. It is here at the crossing of these three that I wish to consider the potentiality of wonder—not solely as one or the other but as a matter of perpetual intermingling.

As Phillip Fisher outlines in *Wonder, the Rainbow and the*

Aesthetic of the Rare Experience, wonder is "one of the most neglected of primary aesthetic experiences within modernity" (2). Fisher understands wonder as the drive behind discovery, as the "step-by-step practice of thought" (32). Yet he recognizes that this process is not a simple passage from wonder to explanation (136). He explains the process as "an unfurling of knowing and curiosity that finds itself at every moment in mixed conditions" (136). Wonder then becomes a continual process that is not necessarily stabilized.

For Fisher, wonder is a driving force in the world. He understands it as the aesthetics of surprise, drawing on the emotions of witnessing the creation of the first skyscraper as a moment of feeling that one is "seeing the impossible happen" (4). Wonder rests on the edge of recognition, acting as a map of thinking that guides us to a feeling of intelligibility. It is a moment of recognizing the impossible and knowing one's ignorance or, as Fisher states, "knowing that one does not know" (10).

Fisher considers wonder as a primary passion and thus only the "beginning of philosophy" (10). He takes the concept of wonder as a primary passion from René Descartes, for whom wonder becomes the driving force from which knowledge is sought; "it appears to me that wonder is the first of all the passions" (Descartes qtd in Irigaray 106). In a similar reading to Fisher, Irigaray takes up Descartes' "meaning of wonder," believing that it is "the motivating force behind mobility in all dimensions" (106). For both Fisher and Irigaray, wonder becomes the precursor to intelligibility, the emotion and aesthetic that exists prior to an understanding.

Standing at the edge of intelligibility, I wondered. I was able to re-write my ignorance of what it meant to be queer, of what it meant to be a man, of what it meant to be a woman, of what it meant to be. This wondering experience exposed the ways in which queerness has become a more solidified identity and not necessarily one that continues to evade definition and understanding. I wonder if it might be time for us to reframe relationships to queerness through a sense of never-ending curiosity. Is it time for us to bring wonderful and wonder back into our lives? Wonder pushes us to a brink while, hopefully, taking the edge off existing on the edge.

Through wonder as a verb, noun, and adjective, we can begin to understand the everyday as magical, as becoming utopian, as becoming that which is outside the realm of the known. What would it mean for us to wonder at each other's actions and lives as opposed to defining and solidifying their meaning? What would it mean for us to wonder at how to change the world as opposed to definitively saying that one method is right and one is wrong? As Irigaray says, wonder is about "remaining impossible to delimit, impose, identify (which is not to say lacking identity or borders)" (112). Wonder is not space where boundaries are created, but it also does not deny the existence of boundaries. Wonder does not define but instead continues to open up spaces for whatever might come next.

WORKS CITED

Edelman, Lee. *No Future: Queer Theory and the Death Drive.* North Carolina: Duke University Press Books, 2004. Print.

Freeman, Elizabeth. "Time Binds, or, Erotohistoriography." *Social Text* 5.7 (2007): 57-68. Print.

Fisher, Philip. *Wonder, the Rainbow, and the Aesthetics of Rare Experiences.* Cambridge: Harvard University Press, 2003. Print.

Irigaray, Luce. "Wonder: A Reading of Descartes *The Passions of the Soul.*" *Feminist Interpretations of René Descartes.* Ed. Susan Bordo. Pennsylvania: The Pennsylvania State University Press, 1999. 105-114. Print.

Lacan, Jacques. *Book 1: Freud's Papers on Technique* Trans. Jacques-Alain Miller. New York: Morton, 1988. Print.

Love, Heather. *Feeling Backward: Loss and the Politics of Queer History.* Cambridge: Harvard University Press. 2007. Print.

Muñoz, José E. *Cruising Utopia: The Then and There of Queer Futurity.* New York: New York University Press, 2009. Print.

11.
The Ties that Bind Are Broken

Trans* Breastfeeding Practices, Ungendering Body Parts, and Unsexing Parenting Roles

A.J. LOWIK

THE DECISION WHETHER to breast- or bottle-feed one's child is rarely a simple one. It is structured by economic conditions, is laden with sociocultural meaning (Schmied and Lupton 236), and is made within a context of moral and health-oriented pressure to feed infants in particular ways (Smyth 85). Beyond providing nourishment, breastfeeding is seen as crucial to developing a healthy and bonded relationship with one's child (Schmied and Lupton 238). Not all people who engage in breastfeeding are mothers, for example the hired wet nurses of the early twentieth century (Rosenblum 70). Men and non-lactating women have also acted as dry-nurses, both within and outside of parental roles (Giles 306). Further, not all people who are capable of lactation are cisgender[1] women, as many are trans*[2] and may identify as a variety of things, including as men. The complex entanglement of bodies, behaviours, and identities is the crux of the investigation of this chapter—how the physiological process of lactation is linked to moral constructions of "good" mothers (and fathers) and how this is played out for, and challenged by, trans* parenting practices.

In particular, this chapter considers the case of Winnipeg-based, transgender dad Trevor MacDonald. MacDonald's struggle to become a lactation support worker with the La Leche League of Canada (LLLC) exemplifies the issue at hand: in order for institutional policies and practices to be truly trans* inclusive, work must be done to untangle the web that ties having a particular body with identifying as a particular gender and with taking on a particular parental role (e.g., people with breasts are women and if parents, they are mothers). This untangling can begin with two important shifts: a move to "ungender" body parts (Spade) as well as one to "unsex" acts of parenting (Downing; Karaian; Rosenblum). Each will be considered in turn, along with a brief discussion of trans* breastfeeding within the law.

When Trevor MacDonald and his partner Ian[3] decided to start a family, they got advice from their doctor. MacDonald stopped his hormone therapy for six months before trying to get pregnant, which he did in July 2011. He birthed his son Jacob in April 2012. Initially, the MacDonalds assumed they would formula-feed and even sent away for free samples (MacDonald). Having learned about the benefits of even a small amount of breast milk, Mac-Donald decided to investigate his own breastfeeding potential. The question was whether he could breastfeed without breasts, having had a mastectomy. He attended his first LLLC support meeting and was delighted at the support he received; in fact, it was MacDon-ald's LLLC lactation coach who helped Jacob latch on for the first time, just moments after he was born (MacDonald). Committed to breastfeeding, MacDonald began using a supplemental feeding system when it became clear that he was not producing enough milk to support Jacob's growing nutritional needs. The couple engaged a global milk-sharing network called Human Milk 4 Human Babies, and they received donated breast milk from a total of thirty women, which fed Jacob for the first year of his life (McMahon, "The Dad" 9).[4]

Wanting to pass along his knowledge and provide support to other parents on their path to breastfeeding, MacDonald applied to be a lactation support worker with the LLLC. In his application, he acknowledged that his role as a breastfeeding father might be new but that he could provide advice and support to other trans* parents, as well as those women and trans* parents struggling to produce milk (Tapper, "La Leche League"). Seven weeks later, the LLLC rejected his application. MacDonald published the rejection letter on his blog, MilkJunkies.net, and the media got hold of the story ("Breastfeeding Group"; Tapper, "La Leche League"). The LLLC's decision was based on an eighteen-year-old policy and they reasoned that since "the roles of mothers and fathers are not interchangeable" (Tapper, "La Leche League"), as a father, MacDonald would not be able to represent the LLLC philosophy of mothers supporting mothers in the pursuit of breastfeeding. According to the LLLC, a leader is "a mother who has breastfed a baby," so despite MacDonald's experience with breastfeeding, his identity as a father (and by extension, as a man) was why his application was rejected—he lacked "mothering knowledge" (Tapper, "La Leche League"). MacDonald was dismayed by the response of an organization that had been so crucial in helping him attain his own breastfeeding goals. Nearly two years later, after almost a year of internal review, the La Leche League International (LLLI) quietly removed the gendered language from their lactation coach requirements (Tapper, "Transgender Man"). National branches, including the Canadian branch, quickly followed suit. Now anyone with nine months of breastfeeding experience, regardless of gender, can apply to be a lactation support coach with the LLLI (Tapper, "Transgender Man"). However, the organization still identifies itself as a "mother-to-mother" support group and gendered language is pervasive in their various publications and websites. MacDonald, who recently gave birth to his second child, is thrilled with this decision; he had been critical of the policy, as opposed to the organization itself, which he still values and credits for his breastfeeding success. Throughout the ordeal, MacDonald has continued to work with the LLLC, even developing a tip sheet for lactation coaches who are supporting trans* parents (Tapper, "Transgender Man."). Diane West, a spokesperson for the international body, said that the LLLI is "just trying to be on the right side of history" and that "it was thought that only women could breastfeed. Once it became clear it wasn't as straightforward as that, the policy had to change (Tapper, "Transgender Man")." This shift in policy is one among many, as fertility clinics, abortion clinics, and various other body-based service providers have begun to reconcile their policies and practices with the lived realities of their trans* clients.[5]

The LLLI is a maternalist organization that has historically focused on women's "natural mothering" ability vis-à-vis breastfeeding advocacy. At stake for them in this negotiation over trans* inclusion are the very principles on which the organization is based—that "breastfeeding focuses our attention on the aspects of maternal experience that are not amenable to assimilation to a male norm of embodiment" (Hausman 276). That is, lactation (as well as pregnancy, menstruation, childbirth, and menopause) are all uniquely female experiences (Grosz), so it is important to theorize motherhood in a way that recognizes "the reproductive burden women experience through their bodies" (Hausman 278). Breastfeeding as an embodied practice centralizes the female body, and breastfeeding has been a paradigmatic, if not vexed, feminist issue (Schmied and Lupton 246). Rarely questioned however, has been this underlying constant that only women lactate and that breastfeeding is, by extension, an act of mothering that precludes male experiential knowledge.

For MacDonald and other trans* men who have breastfed their children, the practice is one of utility rather than being gender specific (Riggs 67)—it is an act of parenting. MacDonald has called the labels *mother* and *father* trite, and he says that he uses *father* or *dad* for lack of a better term; first and foremost, MacDonald identifies as a parent (Tapper, "La Leche League"). For MacDonald, "breastfeeding is not about sex—it is about feeding a baby. It doesn't make me feel feminine or female to feed Jacob" (Riggs 67). Indeed, some trans* men have indicated that nursing their children is the only time that their breasts are not unwanted; instead, nursing is a utilitarian and pragmatic use of one's breasts and, as such, the breasts are serving their purpose (Riggs 65). Breastfeeding is seen as practical or a duty performed for the sake of the child's health even if it is perceived by some as not particularly enjoyable (More 326).

MacDonald's decision to breastfeed, as with any other parent, was made because it was what he felt was right, healthiest, and best. He wanted to do "what is right for my child" (MacDonald qtd. in McMahon, "The Dad" 9). Throughout MacDonald's blog, and within the various newspaper and press articles written about him, MacDonald sings the praises of breastfeeding. He persevered in breastfeeding Jacob with a supplementary feeding system, despite a mix of public reactions, because of his belief in the benefits of breast milk and the caring and nurturing power of nursing (MacDonald; McMahon "The Dad").

By breastfeeding despite all the obstacles, MacDonald's stance on breastfeeding may be contributing to a moral construction of "good trans* parenthood." A trans*-inclusive pro-breastfeeding discourse might very well include the notion that because a trans* man has the ability to breastfeed he should do so. MacDonald indicates that "responding to my baby appropriately also means ignoring everyone else" (MacDonald qtd. McMahon, "The Dad" 9). That includes ignoring stares, whispers, giggles, and accusations of abuse (McMahon, "The Dad" 9). Americans for Truth about Homosexuality called MacDonald a "freak show," a "pretend man" and "a confused woman" in desperate need of God's help (LaBarbera). Just as pregnant and lactating women are at increased risk of abuse (Van Esterik 49), it follows that pregnant and lactating trans* people are at a similarly increased risk. Arguably, their risk of violence is significantly higher because they are seen as violating natural parental relationships and gender norms. A good trans* dad, then, is one who breastfeeds. He does it in spite of any gender dissonance he might feel and in spite of his surgical history. He must ignore questions about whether he is a "real man." Everyone from right-wing, Christian bloggers to medical professionals to other trans* people may question the legitimacy of a trans* person's "new" gender identity if they engage in behaviour historically understood as quintessentially and uniquely associated with their "former" one (LaBarbera; Ware; Califia-Rice; More 324). The fact that a person is pregnant or breastfeeding renders that person female in the eyes of many.

Describing the differences between breastfeeding alone versus with others in view, one participant in a 1998 study said, "When I was alone I had no problems breastfeeding, it was very natural, animal-like. But when company was present they related to me as female, even when they didn't say it. It was extremely uncomfortable" (Matt qtd. in More 325). This accusation of being "inauthentic," this fear of being rendered female, has been noted as one of the prominent stress factors during pregnancy and thereafter for trans* parents (More 325). This negative attitude reflects a particular understanding of being trans*; using the reproductive capacities associated with one's natal sex is seen as being in contradiction with a diagnosis of "transsexuality" (More 325). The reasoning is that someone who was truly "suffering" from gender dysphoria would not use their genitals, especially their reproductive system, in accordance with the gender they renounced. A persistent discomfort with one's natal sex is a symptom of gender dysphoria. Trans* people seeking access to hormones or surgery may be discouraged by therapists and other medical professionals from using their bodies in ways that seem to run counter to their new gender. Jason Cromwell, author of the first in-depth examination of what it means to be a female-bodied trans* person, states that "most clinicians have been dumbfounded by learning of trans people using their genitalia for sexual reproduction.... Many would be even more astounded by those who derive pleasure from genitalia, including vaginal penetration" (131). To be pregnant or to breast-feed is a woman's role, and someone transitioning from female to male would presumably be a father and he should therefore restrict himself to "appropriate" fatherly tasks and behaviours.

This oversimplified and binary understanding of sex, gender, and parental role is similarly apparent in various laws relating to trans* gender identity. That is, many countries allow trans* people legal recognition of their chosen gender if and only if they conform to certain prescriptions regarding their behaviour (Karaian; Rosenblum; Cruz; More). For instance, the 1995 New Zealand case of *Attorney General v. Otahuhu Family Court* held that a post-operative transsexual person could marry someone of the now "opposite sex" if they "no longer operate in his or her original sex" (Cruz 1168-1169). That is, a female-to-male transsexual person can be legally recognized as male and eligible to marry a woman if he "never appear[s] unclothed as a woman, or enter[s] into a sexual relationship as a woman, or procreate[s]" (Cruz 1168-1169). For some countries, this extends to mandating genital surgery as a condition of legal gender recognition, ostensibly sterilizing the trans* person.

The Ontario Human Rights Tribunal recently decided that requiring trans* people to undergo surgery is discriminatory and does not take into account all of the various reasons (financial, medical, etc.) that a person may choose to forego surgery (Karaian 221). To be a trans* man who has birthed his children, or who breastfeeds them, would bring one into direct violation of these laws and put one's legal status as male in jeopardy. The proverbial miner's canary of gender, trans* people "expos[e] the extent to which the law's disparate treatment based on sex and gender is arbitrary" (Rosenblum 91). Other provinces in Canada have followed suit, although this change does not undo the sterilization of all those trans* people who would have made different decisions about their reproduction had this requirement never been in place. Different countries across the world continue to have diverse requirements for trans* people regarding how they can have their gender legally recognized.

Two important shifts need to take place in order to keep pace with the lived experiences of trans* people: the "ungendering" of body parts (Spade) and the "unsexing" of acts of parenting and embodied experiences like pregnancy and breastfeeding (Downing; Karaian; Rosenblum). These changes could have immeasurable impact on how we theorize and understand notions of mothering and fathering and on how trans* people are framed within the law as well as within institutions like the LLLC.

In a brief, unpublished piece, trans* theorist Dean Spade called upon us all to "dismantle gendered language about bodies that enforces harmful norms" by avoiding the compulsory gender assignment of body parts and their functions. Strategies for this include speaking with specificity about penises, vaginas, ovaries, etc., without labelling them as a female or male body part; using "pregnant person" or "person who menstruates" instead of identifying the pregnant or menstruation person as a woman; and substituting references to "female bodies" with references to "bodies with vaginas" (Spade): "In this way we get rid of the assumptions that all people who identify as a particular gender have the same kind of body or do the same things with their bodies, as well as the mistaken belief that if your body has/does that thing, it is a particular gender" (Spade).

This process of unlearning and untying the binary linkages between bodies, identities, and behaviours is well-suited to discussions of trans* breastfeeding behaviour. Breasts become just that—simply another part of the body[6]—and lactation part of their function, as opposed to a part of the female body whose function is intrinsically interconnected to a woman's natural role as a mother. This is in line with the few first-hand accounts of trans* breastfeeding available where lactation and nursing are a functional aspect of their embodiment rather than a gendered one (MacDonald; Tapper; More). Breasts, which may have caused the trans* person some discomfort or distress, may no longer do so when used according to their purpose (Riggs 63). MacDonald is clear: breastfeeding does not compromise his masculinity; in fact, the act of breastfeeding renders his breasts gender neutral (Riggs 67). However, MacDonald's experience is not generalizable, and the few first-hand accounts are just that—a few accounts. It is likely that there are trans* men who would never choose breastfeeding because it does contradict their male identity.

Alongside an undertaking to "ungender" body parts, trans* reproductive and family practices prompt an "unsexing" of parenting (Downing 106). More specifically, there are two "unsexing" projects, one to unsex mothering as the primary parental relationship and another to unsex fathering as breadwinner (Rosenblum 60). These projects recognize that "legal and social norms configure parenting as a sexed endeavour" (Rosenblum 61) and that an alternative is required to the binary and gendered discourse of parenting insofar as it fails to capture the diversity and fluidity of parents and families.

There is considerable consensus that responsibility for children is the essence of motherhood (Fox and Worts 330; McMahon, *Engendering Motherhood* 273; Ruddick 40) and that "ultimate responsibility for children ... transforms women into mothers" (Doucet, "Gender, Equality" 105). By virtue of their sexed bodies and the reproductive burden of pregnancy, women are constructed as natural primary caregivers. More than that, the ways that "childcare is handled in modern, Western, capitalist societies with articulate divisions between private and the public spheres, and the consequent division of labour ... [has] generated a view of childcare and nurture as single-gendered" (Chopra 446), specifically female gendered. Gender, as well as factors like race, age, ability, and sexuality "play out in men's and women's identities and practices related to caring and earning" (Doucet, "Gender, Equality" 106) and have informed how we conceptualize gendered parenting roles.

Men who mother challenge the feminine image of mothering and there is "a large body of research attesting to how fathers can be nurturing, affectionate and responsive to their children" (Doucet, "Gender, Equality" 110). Some of these men experience scrutiny when providing care to children, and their movements are surveyed and society appears suspicious of their intentions (Doucet, "Gender, Equality" 115). Mother-dominated social settings hinder fathers' ability to engage in community networking, which is considered one of three major maternal responsibilities, along with caring for children's emotional and moral needs (Doucet, "Gender, Equality" 109-112). Labelling all nurturing behaviour performed by men as "acts of mothering" may contribute to the invisibility of nurturing fathers—men may "mother," but if they identify as fathers are not all of their acts of parenting acts of fathering? Fathers who are primary care-providers in their families risk being deemed "Mr. Mom." This may, on the one hand, "legitimate domesticity and nurturance as appropriately masculine" (Douglas Vavrus 352).

On the other hand, the binary, gendered, and role-based foundations of parenting discourse is, at best, minimally challenged when this male nurturing is labelled as "motherly." Unsexing parenting will undoubtedly foster an environment where fathers, men, and by extension masculinity can be linked to care-taking and nurturing without it being framed as feminine, womanly, or motherly (Chopra 446).

The broader unsexing project also includes untying the knot that connects sex to particular parental roles and acts. Insofar as there are gender-related styles of parenting, they have been unnecessarily fused to particular bodies and body parts. The embodied quality of some parental narratives aside, there are contexts and acts within parenting where embodiment is either negligible or inconsequential (Doucet, *Do Men Mother?*). The weight that embodiment has been given in naming and differentiating the roles of differently sexed parents seems to far outweigh the role one's body truly plays in parenting (Doucet, *Do Men Mother?*).

Beyond parental acts, "mother" and "father" serve as the identity labels for differently sexed parents. "Mother," on the one hand, is laden with connotations of embodied parental responsibility and "father," on the other, is protector, provider, and disciplinarian. The terms invoke the tasks and responsibilities assigned to each. These terms are often inadequate for queer and trans* parents and for those in polyamorous families who have created new terms to more accurately capture their parenting role, such as "zaza" and "nini," and have reclaimed Old English terms like "cennend."[7] Polly Pagenhart is a proud lesbian dad (35) and uses the title "baba," a term from "many cultures denoting a warm, loving caregiver or protector" (Dorsey). Matt Rice and ex-partner Pat Califia have a son, Blake. Matt, who was pregnant with and birthed Blake, identifies simultaneously as a mother, father, and a trans* man (Califia-Rice). The terms mother and father, and derivations thereof, all similarly overemphasize the various tasks, roles, and responsibilities of parenting, just as embodied elements of parenting are overemphasized. This is not to say that parents should not be able to choose "mother" or "father" as terms to refer to themselves. Rather, it is the reduction of parents to just mothers and fathers that is over simplistic for cisgender and trans* parents alike.

Unsexing parenting has legal applications and ramifications as well. In 2012, a controversial law was proposed in France. If it had passed, the law would have removed the gendered terms *mère* and *père* (French for "mother" and "father") from the Civil Code (Wells). The law would have not only defined marriage as a union between two people of different or of the same gender but would have also removed the prohibition on gay and lesbian people accessing fertility treatments and other assistive reproductive technologies. In using "parent" in place of "mother" and "father," every law in the French Civil Code referencing parental rights and responsibilities would have been made neutral (Wells). Although the proposed law in France did not pass, Sweden's parental leave policy does manage to promote balanced and unsexed parenting (Rosenblum 95), and there are an ever-increasing number of policies and laws that do the same. An unsexed parenting would see any law concerning the right of women and "mothers" to breastfeed in public, for example, to be redrafted to refer to breastfeeding "parents," thus including trans* parents who may or may not identify as mothers, as well as cisgender men who engage in dry nursing.

Returning now to the La Leche League International, its founding principles and philosophies, and its shift towards trans* inclusion. At its core, the LLLI believes that breast is best—that along with providing sustenance, breastfeeding is a bonding experience, an act of caring. This embodied experience has long been understood as uniquely a woman's (for some, a part of her reproductive burden). It is therefore of little surprise that pro-breastfeeding discourse understood women as having sole access to this experience and that there is something special, singular, and perhaps superior about that. However, welcoming men and others into the club of people who can share this bond of sustenance and nurturing with their children should not threaten those who already experience this connection. If breast is best, it simply should not matter whether that breast is attached to someone who identifies as a mother, father, *baba*, or by some other parental identity. The LLLI and other body-based service providers will need to reconcile the sexed and gendered philosophies on which their organizations are founded with the projects of ungendering body parts and unsexing parenting.

More trans* people are choosing to form their families using their bodies in ways not traditionally associated with their genders. This is often in opposition to how many think trans* people should relate to their "wrong" body and its functions, as well as to the roles and identity labels associated with their "wrong" gender. Fundamentally, trans* people's reproductive practices, including breastfeeding, urge us to question some of the fundamental principles on which society and law are based: that there are two distinct and separate sexes attached to two corresponding and aligned genders, and that one's biology should determine one's parental role within a two-opposite-sexed-parents family. Discourses of mothering and fathering, whatever their strengths, fall short when it comes to trans* people and families. It is insufficient to attribute "fatherhood" status to all male-identified parents and "motherhood" status to all female-identified parents, whether they are cisgender or trans*. When maternal practice is understood as having gender flexibility, this is nevertheless a cis-focused flexibility, where male experiential knowledge is reduced to include only these experiences of cisgender men. It is also problematic to frame all acts of parenting as either acts of mothering or fathering; this binary approach to parenting discourse does not reflect the queer ways in which trans* people parent, from the names they choose to be called by their kids to the ways they ungender the embodied aspects of parenting, like breastfeeding. In some ways, the neutral noun and verb *parent* does not seem to capture the *mushy* aspects of parenting; however, the gendered discourse of parenting currently attributes all of these aspects to motherhood, to women.

Cisgender men who identify as fathers and engage in the *mush* of parenting are essentially muted when these behaviours are framed as "acts of mothering." Trans* men who engage in these behaviours have their male identities challenged, and their acts of care and nurturing can be misconstrued as abusive insofar as they run counter to how men are "supposed" to, and allowed to, engage with children. Challenging the already tenuous connection between bodies, identities, and behaviours when it comes to parenting benefits not only trans* parents but will better reflect the complex ways in which parents of all sexes and genders relate to their children, engage in parenting tasks, divide labour in their households, etc.

When breasts are ungendered and when breastfeeding as a parenting practice is unsexed, trans* and cisgender parents alike will be freed from the ties that bind: breast-having with womanhood, lactation with motherhood, breastfeeding with parenting (as opposed to, for example, lactation "play" as part of a consensual, adult sexual and/or kinky relationship; see Giles). Breasts, ungendered, are no longer "private" and public breastfeeding, consequently, is no longer understood as a potentially obscene act of public nudity. In keeping with various topless equity laws wherein all people can (or cannot) appear topless in the same places, an ungendered and unsexed breastfeeding would not shame public breastfeeding. Instead, breasts are body parts that serve various functions, including but not limited to providing sustenance and comfort to infants. Gender-neutral parenting terms would allow trans* and cisgender parents alike to choose from an array of terms that suit their personality, rather than terms that describe and define their role in their family. Unsexing parenting and ungendering bodies would removes acts, roles, and (un)embodied experiences from the holds of the binary-sex/gendered parental subject positions around which parenting discourse is currently framed.

ENDNOTES

[1]From the Latin prefix *cis* meaning "on the same side," cisgender replaces "non-transgender." It refers to individuals who have a match between their sexed-body, the gender "assigned" to that sexed-body, and their personal identity (Schilt and Westbrook 461).
[2]Trans* is a term used to denote inclusivity. Its origins are reportedly in computer search terms, where an asterisk is used to stand in for any number of possible endings to a word. In this case, the asterisk signifies all of the numerous and varied non-cisgender identities and expressions, including, but not limited to, transgender, transsexual, genderqueer, gender neutral, bigender, polygender, androgyne, agender, third gender, two-spirit, transmen and transwomen. See "What Does."
[3]The surname MacDonald and the first names Ian and Jacob are pseudonyms.
[4]It is interesting to note that these donors are identified by Mac-Donald, as well as by those writing about MacDonald, as women, and specifically as mothers. It is unclear whether the donors actively identified as mothers or whether the donors' ability to donate breast milk meant that they were assumed to be women and mothers, perhaps wrongly.
[5]Unfortunately, inclusion is often considered only on the basis of gender identity. That is, women's organizations are engaged in discussion over when/how to include trans* women because they identify as women and share a gender identity with the individuals for whom the service/space was originally designed. This means that trans* men and other non-woman-identified trans* people are automatically excluded on the basis of their having a "different" gender identity than the women for whom the service was envisioned. When the potential inclusion of trans* men is discussed, inclusion is argued for on the basis of history—that the trans* man *was once* a woman and as such isn't "knocking

on the door of the feminist movement asking to be let in" (Noble 21). Rather, trans* men with a long history as women, feminists, and lesbians argue that they should not be ejected from feminism and women's spaces and communities simply because they now identify as male. This discussion of inclusion does not take into account the bodies of the trans* people. When service is provided based on a particular bodily function, part, or ability, inclusion should take the bodies of their potential clients into account and reflect that diversity in their staff. Further, since bodies, genders, and roles are often unnecessarily tied, services for "mothers," for example, will undoubtedly encounter male mothers and will need to reconcile reality with their understanding of "motherhood."

[6]This project to "ungender" body parts, particularly breasts, is also well-suited to discussions of non-normative men's bodies, specifically gynecomastia. At present, one third of the people we understand to be men experience gynecomastia or breast-tissue growth (Yost). Having breasts, then, is not a uniquely female experience even among cisgender people.

[7]No scholarly articles could be found to support this. However the Gender Queeries blog includes a list of gender-neutral parenting terms, and this author has friends and peers who use such terms to refer to themselves.

WORKS CITED

"Breastfeeding Group Rejects Transgender Dad's Leadership Bid." *CBC News*. Canadian Broadcasting Corporation. 21 Aug. 2012. Web. 27 Oct. 2014

Califia-Rice, Patrick. "Family Values: Two Dads With a Difference—Neither of Us Was Born Male." *The Village Voice*. The Village Voice. 20 Jun. 2000. Web. 9 Dec. 2014

Chopra, Radhika. "Retrieving the Father: Gender Studies, 'Father Love' and the Discourse of Mothering." *Women's Studies International Forum* 24.3/4 (2001): 445-455. Print.

Cromwell, Jason. *Transmen and FTMs: Identities, Bodies, Genders and Sexualities*. Chicago: University of Illinois Press, 1999. Print.

Cruz, David. "Heterosexual Reproductive Imperatives." *Emory Law Journal* 56 (2007): 1157-1172. Print

Dorsey, Abby. "The New Lesbian Dad: How Women are Reinventing What it Means to Be a Parent." *The Advocate*. Here Media Inc. 8 Apr. 2013. Web. 9 Dec. 2014

Downing, Jordan. "Transgender-Parent Families." *LGBT-Parent Families: Innovations in Research and Implications for Practice*. Eds. Abbie E. Goldberg and Katherine R. Allen. New York: Springer. 2013. 105-114. Print.

Doucet, Andrea. *Do Men Mother?: Fathering, Care, and Domestic Responsibility*. Toronto: University of Toronto Press, 2006. Print.

Doucet, Andrea. "Gender, Equality and Gender Differences: Parenting, Habitus and Embodiment (The 2008 Porter Lecture)." *Canadian Review of Sociology* 46.2 (2009): 103-121. Print.

Douglas Vavrus, Mary. "Domesticating Patriarchy: Hegemonic Masculinity and Television's 'Mr. Mom.'" *Critical Studies in Media Communication* 19.3 (2002): 352-375. Print.

Fox, Bonnie and Diana Worts. "Revisiting the Critique of Medicalized Childbirth: A Contribution to the Sociology of Birth." *Gender and Society* 13.3 (1999): 326-346. Print.

Giles, Fiona. "Relational and Strange: A Preliminary Foray into a Project to Queer Breastfeeding." *Australian Feminist Studies* 19.45 (2004): 301-314. Print.

Grosz, Elizabeth. *Volatile Bodies: Toward a Corporeal Feminism*. Bloomington: Indiana University Press, 1994. Print.

Hausman, Bernice. "The Feminist Politics of Breastfeeding." *Australian Feminist Studies* 19.45 (2004): 273-285. Print.

Karaian, Lara. "Pregnant Men: Repronormativity, Critical Trans Theory and the Re(conceive)ing of Sex and Pregnancy in Law." *Social and Legal Studies* 22.2 (2013): 211-230. Print.

LaBarbera, Peter. "Trevor MacDonald, 'Breastfeeding Dad'—Latest Freak Show in our Politically Correct, Confused Culture." *Americans for Truth about Homosexuality*. Americans for Truth about Homosexuality. 29 Aug. 2012. Web. 28 Oct. 2014.

MacDonald, Trevor. "How I Learned to Be a Breastfeeding Dad." *The Huffington Post*. The Huffington Post. 29 Apr. 2012. Web. 27 Sept. 2014.

McMahon, Barbara. "The Dad Who Breastfeeds." *The Times*. Times Newspapers Limited. 8 Dec. 2012. Web. 26 Sept. 2014.

McMahon, Barbara. *Engendering Motherhood: Identity and*

Self-Transformation in Women's Lives. New York: Guilford, 1995. Print.

More, Sam Dylan. "The Pregnant Man—An Oxymoron?" *Journal of Gender Studies* 7.3 (1998): 319-328. Print.

Noble, Jean Bobby. *Sons of the Movement: FtMs Risking Incoherence on a Post-queer Cultural Landscape*. Toronto: Women's Press, 2006. Print.

Pagenhart, Polly. "Confessions of a Lesbian Dad." *Confessions of the Other Mother: Nonbiological Lesbian Moms Tell All!* Ed. Harlyn Aizley. Boston: Beacon Press, 2006. 35-58. Print.

Riggs, Damien W. "Transgender Men's Self-Representations of Bearing Children Post-Transition." *Chasing Rainbows: Exploring Gender Fluid Parenting Practices*. Eds. Fiona Joy Green and May Friedman. Toronto: Demeter Press, 2013. 62-71. Print.

Rosenblum, Darren. "Unsex Mothering: Toward a New Culture of Parenting." *Harvard Journal of Law and Gender* 35 (2012): 58-116. Print.

Ruddick, Sara. *Maternal Thinking: Toward a Politics of Peace*. Boston: Beacon, 1995. Print.

Schilt, Kristen and Laurel Westbrook. "Doing Gender, Doing Heteronormativity: 'Gender Normals,' Transgender People and the Social Maintenance of Heterosexuality." *Gender and Society* 23.4 (2009): 440-464. Print.

Schmied, Virginia and Deborah Lupton. "Blurring the Boundaries: Breastfeeding and Maternal Subjectivity." *Sociology of Health and Illness* 23.2 (2001): 234-250. Print.

Smyth, Lisa. "Gendered Spaces and Intimate Citizenship: The Case of Breastfeeding." *European Journal of Women's Studies* 15 (2008): 83-99. Print.

Spade, Dean. "About Purportedly Gendered Body Parts." *DeanSpade.net*. Dean Spade. 3 Feb. 2011. Web. 5 Apr. 2014.

Tapper, Josh. "La Leche League of Canada Rejects Breastfeeding Dad's Bid to Become Lactation Coach." *The Toronto Star*. Toronto Star Newspapers Limited. 19 Aug. 2012. Web. 27 Oct. 2014.

Tapper, Josh. "Transgender Man Can Be Breastfeeding Coach." *The Toronto Star*. Toronto Star Newspapers Limited. 25 Apr. 2014. Web. 27 Oct. 2014.

Van Esterik, Penny. "Breastfeeding and Feminism." *International*

Journal of Gynecology and Obstetrics 47 Supplement (1994): 41-54. Print.

Ware, Syrus Marcus. "Going Boldly Where Few Men Have Gone Before: One Trans Man's Experience of a Fertility Clinic and Insemination." *Who's Your Daddy? And Other Writings on Queer Parenting.* Ed. Rachel Epstein. Toronto: Sumach Press, 2009. 65-72. Print.

Wells, Charlie. "French Lawmakers May Ban 'Mother' and 'Father' From Official Documents." NY *Daily News.* 25 Sept. 2012. Web. 7 Dec. 2014.

"What Does the Asterisk in Trans* Stand For." *It's Pronounced Metrosexual.* n.d. Web. 27 Oct. 2014.

Yost, Merle James. *Demystifying Gynecomastia: Men with Breasts.* Novato: Gynecomastic.org, 2006. Print.

12.
Becoming Mother's Nature

A Queer Son's Perspective on Mothering in an Era of Ecological Decline

MICHAEL YOUNG

I have the looming sense that I am becoming Mother—

I AM A THIRTY-YEAR-OLD queer, feminist, cisgendered, Caucasian, male environmentalist and writer, three years shy of the age my mother was when she conceived me. I am not married, not monogamous (by mainstream definitions of the word), and not gainfully employed (by mainstream conceptions of career). I live with my partner, four cats, a dog, a lot of houseplants, and my ninety-two-year-old grandmother (the partner, dog, cats, and houseplants are all my doing). I wrestle with the reality that, short of growing a surprise womb, having a child will be difficult for me. And despite all of this, I feel like I am becoming a mother—my mother, to be exact.

"Becoming Mother" means two things to me. First, it means that I am becoming a version of the woman who raised me (in fact, there were three, as I will explain later). Second, it means that I am increasingly finding myself relating to the world around me from what I perceive to be a maternal perspective. Maybe I'm getting broody; I'm thirty, I'm unfulfilled, my biological clock is ticking.... Or maybe, something else is at play. The notion of a man becoming Mother has its fair share of cultural stigma. Whether it be Norman Bates (*Psycho*) or Buster Bluth (*Arrested Development*), a man with too intimate a relationship with his mum is usually pathologized in popular culture as being disordered, perhaps psychotic, most likely gay. Maternal theorist Andrea O'Reilly points out that these prejudices stem from classic western mythology, namely Agamemnon and Oedipus Rex. These myths—the former which tells of a son who kills his mother and the latter which tells of a son who fucks his mother—have been "continually retold and reenacted in Western culture and fiction" ("In Black and White" 305). Robert Bly, champion of the mythopoetic men's movement and coiner of the term "father hunger," has argued that a man must "cut his soul away from his mother-bound soul" and move "from the mother's realm to the father's realm," lest he become too in touch with his feminine side (Bly ix). To this I would say that "becoming Mother" is as much of a political stance for me as it is a material transition.

In an era of uncertainty—namely the Anthropocene, as our epoch is coming to be called (a name that ominously gestures toward both what once initiated the temporal period as well as what will likely cause its forthcoming denouement)—there is an expanding sense of mothering, as well as what it does and might mean (Stromberg). Western society has long (and problematically) conceived of the environment as a great mother "Nature," and as this perceived female body is eroded by a male-dominated, frontier-seeking patriarchy, and its subsequent capitalist fantasies, mothers have been part of the force to kick back. This movement of mothers, which has included ecofeminists, has not been without its fair share of critical thorns. In suggesting that women may have a unique connection to the environment through maternal experience, ecofeminist discourse has been critiqued as essentializing care as a part of the feminine experience, universalizing women's maternalism and reinforcing women's place in the domestic sphere (MacGregor). Though the discourse of "care" may be problematic for feminism, what are the valences of a biological man honing his maternal capacity, particularly for a world in watershed?

Here is the groundwork that I want to lay before I move forward: it was my mother's approach to raising me, which I will label "maternal," that I attribute to my emotional and psychological growth. I associate my father's style of parenting with discipline, domination, and emotional unavailability—qualities which made me tense, aggressive, anxious, and in continuous need of approval. My father is not a bad guy—he is a generous man with a strong spirit—but in terms of his actual parenting style, like so many other fathers of his day, he led with a tight, patriarchal grip. While many women are quite happy not to foster a maternal persona and while many men do assume mother-work responsibilities, the vast majority of children are raised in households like mine, where parental roles operate along the lines of gender (see Ann Crittenden's *The Price of Motherhood*). There were clear and gendered differences between the way my mother and father raised me; my mother's maternal approach is more like what I see myself embodying today.

There were few men, with the exception of my mother's father, who exhibited softer, more "maternalistic" qualities with me when I was a kid. As a child, I experienced men as being dominant, volatile, and unable to process the intricacies of feelings. In contrast, there were three women, all of whom had a strong hand in raising me, who performed mother-work that was integral to my wellbeing and growth. My grandfather (my mother's father) blurred the lines of what one might traditionally think of as maternal and paternal styles of parenting and, perhaps, he is the reason that I am quite comfortable recognizing myself as maternal today.

The important piece missing in this preemptive defense of my chapter is a disclaimer about "maternal nature." Was it in my mother's "nature" to be more apt to mother me than my father? Was she inherently more of a warm, thoughtful, and sensitive caregiver? Was my father innately less emotionally available? Was an authoritarian approach to parenting part of his biological make-up? No, to all of these questions. For the record, the title of this essay is tongue-in-cheek: I don't believe that I am inheriting a genetic "nature" from my mother. Rather, I am actively developing one, modelling it after hers both consciously and subconsciously, much as she probably modelled her own after her mother (and, perhaps, her father as well).

So, the project of this paper is as follows: I am exploring my genesis into what I sense is a maternal queer being. I pursue this exploration with an eye on how feeling maternal interplays with nature—both my own and that of the "natural" world. Drawing on Maternal Theory and Queer Ecology, I narratively explore the experience of becoming a self-identifying maternal man in the absence of having children of my own and against a backdrop of ecological decline.

MOTHERS I HAVE KNOWN

Before I reflect on the relationship(s) with my mother(s), I should define "mothering" as a term to use more broadly throughout this paper. When I refer to "mothering," I refer to Sara Ruddick's conception of "[being] committed to meeting the demands that define maternal work.... The three demands—for preservation, growth, and social acceptance—[which] constitute maternal work ... [and which one accomplishes] by work of preservative love, nurturance and training" (Ruddick 17). I would add to this the qualities that I see as being inherent to a queer feminist style of mothering: an attention to difference and intrinsic value, emotional health, and openness, and the refusal to impose gender norms on natures that are inherently both rugged and soft, architectural and overflowing, feminine and masculine.

Here is what I do not want to idealize when I use the term "mothering," whether the mother subject is a woman or man. Fiona Joy Green describes how the mainstream media envisions the ideal mother: "She is a heterosexual woman who stays at home with her children while her husband ... support[s] them financially. Because of her 'innate' ability to parent and her 'unconditional love' for her husband and children, the idealized mother selflessly adopts their wants, needs and happiness as her own" (127).

Green's depiction of the idealized mother is what Andrea O'Reilly classifies as the institutionalized performance of "motherhood" and which she problematizes and distinguishes from the participation in "mothering." O'Reilly says, "The term 'motherhood' refers to the patriarchal institution of motherhood that is male-defined and controlled and is deeply oppressive to women, while the word 'mothering' refers to women's experiences of mothering that are female-defined and centered and potentially empowering to women" (*From Motherhood to Mothering* 2). Sara Ruddick defines a mother as "a person who takes responsibility for children's lives and for whom providing child care is a significant part of his or her working life" (40). Ruddick proposes that mothering can be a broader political or moral practice, "a revolutionary discourse," in fact (135). While I do not have children of my own, I consider my relationship to other children that I provide care for, as well as to my peers, my non-human animal companions, plants, places, and politics, to be highly maternally influenced.

From my perspective, three women each had integral roles in mothering me as a child and, to some extent, influenced the development of my own maternal capacity. At the foreground of this triad was my mother, Diane, who facilitated my relationships with my two other maternal figures: a long-term childcare provider, Maria, and my mother's mother, Della. I write this section of the essay as a personal exploration of my relationships with these women. I do not intend to speak for any of them but, rather, my imperative is to reflect on how I perceive their and my relationships to have influenced me. My mother and I have agreed that I should write this paper independently. I would like to acknowledge that at all points moving forward, my interpretations and memories of the relationships that I speak of are just that: my interpretations. The other individuals involved may, for all I know, recount these moments differently.

* * *

I was a sensitive boy. Starting from a young age, I was continually reminded about my "sensitive nature."

"You take after your Mother," my father would say soberly.

As an adult, I hate being reminded of my sensitivity. The proclamation of my sensitivity feels dismissive, reductive, and homophobic—would you prefer me to be an asshole? Two years into psychotherapy, I am still pondering the chicken-egg timeline of my sensitivity, wondering whether the constant defining of my "nature" as "sensitive" engineered me to be the emotionally exposed creature that I have become, or whether the adults in my life truly peered into my infantile soul and accurately proclaimed, Behold! Here lies a sensitive fellow—long before I knew it about myself. In any case, I was sensitive; I still am. I was also queer; I still am.

From five or six years of age, I fostered sexual attraction to other boys and acted on this attraction, enjoying an ongoing game of "doctor" with many of my close male friends. As doctor gave way to more blatant sexual exploration, I understood that my desire defined me as different from most boys, even the boys that I was experimenting with (perhaps because I knew that I liked the experimentation more than they did). Coupled with this were two other factors that made me feel like an outsider amongst boys. First, I had bad eczema on my feet, which meant that my feet were always sore. This condition made me less physically capable than the other boys in my gym class, which I interpreted as putting me in a feminized position. Second, and perhaps in connection with being less physically capable, I was chubbier than the other boys in class. My body was not taut and defined like theirs but rather soft, curvy and again—in my mind—feminine.

As a boy, I remember being obsessed with the idea of having breasts. Many little boys find the idea of having breasts alluring but to me it seemed like the ideal extension of my already feminized body. Beyond the sexualization of breasts—namely that which I learned about from the impossibly serpentine curves of Jessica Rabbit in *Who Framed Roger Rabbit?*—I had the sense that breasts were inherently maternal. When I envisioned myself with breasts, it was in part to imagine myself having maternal capacity, that is, a maternal presence that could take care of others in the way that I had been taken care of, but also in the ways that I had not been nurtured, particularly by men. As a creature that was beginning to sense his own queerness (queer in the sense of being strange), I fantasized about caring for other beings that were isolated by virtue of their strangeness. Animals were the most obvious example of this, given that society views the non-human as a tertiary form of life. There was also a boy at school who was widely disliked and bullied. I imagined holding this other boy and caring for him. There was a sexual element to the connection I felt with the boy, but also the desire to nurture and protect him.

When I was eight, my babysitter Maria caught my best (male) friend and me in a box-fort in my parent's basement, naked and simulating oral sex. I remember her peering through a crack in the fort, an area where the tape had peeled away. A genuine sense of alarm was visible on her face. Maria demanded that we come out of the fort and upstairs, exclaiming with palpable anxiety that what we were doing was "not right." I remember feeling both ashamed of her finding us in the middle of a dirty act—Maria being someone that I associated with purity, asexuality, and maternalism (I aligned those three traits in my brain as connected

… go figure!)—and also scared that she would tell my parents. I begged her not to tell on me and felt guilt as I recognized that I was putting her in an uncomfortable position. Hours after the dust had settled from the box-fort Stonewall raid, I remember Maria pulling me into her chest and rubbing my head, comforting me; her bosom was like a maternal chapel, where I might repent my homo-curiosity and make it go away. As an adult, I recognize the fault in this perception of Maria. Jacqui Gabb puts it this way: "Women transform from sexual object to nurturing subject as we enter into motherhood, being always defined by the reproductive (heterosexual) narrative" (8). Gabb makes the point that this perception of mothers perpetuates "the cultural myth that mothers are sexless, self-less others of their needy children" (8).

To her credit, I feel as though Maria knew that there was something different about me well before the incident in the box-fort. I do not believe that she was unaccepting of my difference but, rather, I imagine she was uncomfortable with the implications of it, being a dedicated childcare provider, a friend of my parents, and a devout Catholic. Whereas Maria may have had ideological reason to reject my sexuality, she treated it as secondary to my individuality; I was different and the specificity of my difference was not all that important, as long as I behaved appropriately. Although I had been upset to have my sexual act discovered by my caregiver, her impulse to stay with me—that is, to draw me close rather than push me away—was deeply comforting.

Throughout childhood, I was something of a "mama's boy." I was attached to my mum, which must have been of a burden for her, given that she worked fulltime in publishing. Nonetheless, she was extremely involved in my life and sheltered me from the macho culture that abounded around me, a culture that would insist I "toughened-up." I remember canoeing in Algonquin Park with my dad, two of his friends, and their kids. I was forced into a canoe with the eldest kid on the trip and his father, a notorious loose cannon. After six hours of canoeing, this man accused his son and I of "lily-dipping" our paddles; I giggled. Exasperated, the man yelled at me: "If ya don't start paddling harder, I'm gonna shove that fucking paddle up yer ass!" I knew two things for sure in that moment: one, men have problems and two, I was not going to let this incident go—ever. Upon relating the story to my parents, Mum did not really react. She never suggested that I should be more emotionally resilient, but she also resisted verbally eviscerating my father for putting me in a canoe with Jack Torrance (*The Shining*). She probably rolled her eyes and sighed and spoke privately with my dad—I don't remember exactly. What I sensed is that she understood that, in due time, I would learn to fend for myself. There was no need to school me in coping with this kind of hyper-masculine abuse—it was fucked-up and, frankly, more embarrassing for my father and his friend than for me.

Throughout my childhood, my homosexual explorations continued with a mix of shame and delight until, somewhere around my thirteenth birthday, the shame got the better of me. I remember being on a vacation with my parents at the nadir of a depression, instigated by guilt. I lay in bed in the hotel room in the middle of the afternoon, the curtains drawn, staring at the stucco ceiling, crying my eyes out. I was caught in between the desire to have my crimes discovered and the deeper fear that I would be dismissed as disgusting, perhaps even unlovable, if they were to be. I remember my mother checking up on me—knocking on the hotel room door, asking me if I was all right. I opened the door. She stood outside the room in her bathing suit and sunglasses; the breezy, tropical air contrasted with the cool, guilt-laden air of the hotel room. I wanted to tell her what was bothering me but it seemed too overwhelming, too disgusting, and too complicated to verbalize. So I said nothing. Nevertheless, her worried gaze told me that she knew something was wrong and knowing that she was onto me provided me with some level of solace. My depression continued on for many months, perhaps for even more than a year. The longer it went on, the more I was able to psychologically distance myself from my parents and in doing so I distanced myself from my shame as well. Nevertheless, Mother kept a close eye on me.

When I was fifteen, I met a boy on the streetcar during a class field trip, a boy whom my good friend Paula knew. Paula and I had dated briefly before we mutually came to understand that it was not to be. The boy on the streetcar was cute and despite wanting to have something to say to him, I could not really muster anything worthwhile and so I fidgeted with my lunchbox. When he got off the streetcar, Paula casually mentioned that he was gay. This blew my mind. How could he be gay? He seemed so normal. Within hours, I came out to my best friend. Four months later, that boy from the streetcar and I became boyfriends. The first time we had sex, I felt my guilt resurge and then, after sex was over, dissipate for good. I was now committed to this new identity and with that I could compartmentalize all of the "deviant" behaviour from my childhood into the box of my self-proclaimed queerness. Two years and two boyfriends later, I called my mother from a bar; I was drunk. She was in the bath when my dad handed her the phone.

"Mum, I have something I need to tell you," I said, as my best friend, Garth, sat opposite me, smoking.

I heard the tap of the bath squeaking as it was being turned off.

"What it is, Michael?" she asked me.

"I just want you to know that. . . . "

"What, Michael? Is everything Okay?"

"Oh, yeah. I just have something to tell you. Is Dad there?"

"No.... " I heard Mum walking on the bathroom tile, closing the door, probably ushering my dad out of the room. "He's not. Just tell me."

"Well, I'm bi," I said, feeling the pins and needles of anticipation set-in.

There was a pause. Mother's voice was very measured when she responded.

"I know, Michael. I think I've known that since you were a little boy."

Really? I thought to myself. Is that true or is that just the clichéd response that Mother feels she needs to give me?

"Really? That's weird," I said. "Okay. Well, that's all I had to say."

"Where are you, Michael?"

"I'm out with Garth. I'll be home later."

"You should tell your father this."

I felt a pit in my stomach. Couldn't she just tell him?

Telling my father about my sexuality was as unappealing as him telling me about his. The thought of the discussion with him made me feel totally exposed, like the dream where you go to work and forget your clothes, except in this version you're speaking to your father but forgot to take the penis out of your mouth from the night before.

"You can tell him if you want," I said.

There was another long pause.

"Well, let's talk about this more tomorrow. I really think you should sit down and speak to him, yourself."

"Okay. We'll talk about it tomorrow," I agreed.

We ended the conversation. Tomorrow came and my father visited me at the video store where I worked. He was jovial, friendly, and did what he does very well: convinced me that everything was okay without addressing the elephant emblazoned on my blushing face. It was a relief, but it was also the closest my father and I have come to discussing my sexuality. To be fair, I never did broach the topic with him; we don't have the tools, the intimacy. I felt justified in not talking to him about it, as my femininity had historically made him angry, even aggressive (or so I perceived). Why would I want to tell him? The idea of broaching the subject went against all my senses of self-preservation; to tell him would be to jump off a cliff hoping for water where I had always sensed stone. For a while, I hoped that my dad might find a way of raising the issue with me on his own, to prove to me that it was no big deal. He never did and I was quite happy to let it go.

On the other hand, my mum and I grew increasingly more comfortable with openly acknowledging my sexuality.

"Where are you, Michael?" Mother asked, as I sheltered my older friend's cellphone from the sounds of a rowdy bar.

"I'm in the gaybourhood," I said.

"Where?" Mother pressed on.

"Woody's," I related.

Pause.

"I hope you're not wearing that 'porn-star' T-shirt," she worried.

I had recently purchased a plain, blue T-shirt with the phrase "porn-star" written across the front of it.

"Why?" I asked.

"Are you wearing it?" she insisted.

"Maybe. Does it matter?" I asked, a rebellious insolence imbued in my tone.

"Think of the message it sends, Michael! Men will think you're some kind of poster-boy for the gay community. They'll think you're up for anything."

"I can handle it," I said, ending the conversation curtly.

Now as a thirty-year-old, I live with my partner of six years and my ninety-two-year-old grandmother—my mother's mother—in the house that she has occupied since she was in her twenties. My grandmother is a retired seamstress. She lost my grandfather sixteen years ago.

"Go ask the boss," Papa (my grandfather) would often tell me as a little boy if I asked him for something.

Whereas Papa would sit on the couch, playing guitar and singing Jewish war songs (he wasn't Jewish, so figure that one out), Nanny would be buzzing about the house, making life happen. In basic ways, my grandparents' parenting dynamic was gendered; Nanny looked after my physical care (scraped knees, baths, eating) and Papa led me on explorations (taking me into the basement to paint with him [he was an artist] or on fishing trips to the Nottawasaga River in Ontario). Papa was gentle, affectionate, interested in my thoughts, and sensitive to my emotional state. Nanny was as well, although she was tougher and more interested in the business of raising a grandchild than he was. Herein lies what I think is an important distinction: whereas Papa was very "maternal," Nanny was the one who performed the mother-work.

To this day, my grandmother is one of the toughest people I know. She is fiercely independent, self-assured, and always right (unless she is wrong and then there has been some cosmic mix-up that will remain unexplained). What surfaces as most significant to me when reflecting on my grandmother as a maternal figure is her balancing of compassion with responsibility.

Nanny's house always had cats. These were not cats that she had deliberately acquired but, rather, that had found her. If a mangy stray hung around her yard long enough, she would, with a roll of her eyes, let it inside. This was not a practice of being a sucker but rather of assuming responsibility for another being in need of care. Nanny never fussed over the cats much, but she certainly looked after them like her own.

She treated plants with a similar ethos; she was unafraid to prune them, pleased to shape them in the way that suited her, although she would never deny them their right to exist on some of their own terms—and she certainly never fussed over them (at least, not as much as I do). Nanny and I have been in an ongoing argument over an *Ailanthus* (aka a "Tree of Heaven") that grows in between her front porch and the neighbour's porch. According to the USDA Agricultural Library, the *Ailanthus* is a native species to northern China and has colonized urban areas in North America as an invasive. Whereas I argued to let the tree grow—it's doing so well!—Nanny insists that it be cut back each fall: "I'm not as gentle as you, Michael. Cut it back to just above that knot," she told me, pointing to the spot where the tree is to be cut to each October. "It grows quickly. It'll regrow next year. I just don't want it getting too out of hand."

Anyone else might just as soon have removed the tree altogether. But my grandmother knows this tree; she doesn't know what it's called but it has been in her yard for a long time. And so she tells me to cut it back to the spot she knows will allow it to flourish again next year but that will also keep it from taking up too much space. Pruning the *Ailanthus* exemplifies—at least, in my mind—my grandmother's maternal approach. She asserts her needs and locates ways that they can coexist with the needs of those she cares for. "I learned as a girl that Della has to take care of Della first," she will often remind me. Her motto reminds me of the airline safety announcement that goes something like, "Please put on your own oxygen mask before assisting a child or dependent with theirs." Good advice.

When I first imagined me and my partner moving in with Della, I envisioned us as a fiercely collaborative domestic trio: sipping tea together, gardening, redecorating, and going through old photo albums. But this was not to be. As I hauled in an oversized *Dracaena* (tropical houseplant) that I had previously saved from a cold, February sidewalk, Nanny looked at me in dread:

"Where the Hell's that going?"

"I was going to put it by the window," I responded tentatively. She shook her head.

"Oh, no. I don't like it."

"Huh?" I responded, confused.

I looked at the *Dracaena*; its snake-like branches twisted upwards to nine feet, its large plastic pot resembled something designed exclusively for car rental offices.

"Put it there for now but we're going to have to discuss this later," she announced, as she hobbled into the kitchen, shaking her head.

I put it where I had intended to put it, knowing that after a few days of circling the plant—privately surveying it—Della would come to appreciate it (although she will never admit to liking it). After months of ongoing arguments that tended to center around preemptive plant anxiety ("Too many plants"; "I am not going to water your plants for you"; invisible spots on her arms theorized to be caused by plants; a clogged toilet theorized to be clogged by a flushed plant...), Della surprised me and proved that the apple does not fall too far from the tree (although it may bounce and skip a generation).

"Give me that plant," my grandmother said, pointing outside to a sad looking *Pelargonium* cutting in a tipped-over pot. "I feel so sorry for that little plant. It keeps being knocked over. I thought it would have died by now but it's still alive."

"Yeah, I guess the squirrels got at it," I said defensively.

I went outside and brought it in, as she requested. Nanny pointed to a space on the ledge of her kitchen window, a coveted piece of foliar real estate. This is a peace offering, I thought to myself.

"Put it there," she told me. "I'm going to look after it."

I did. And so she has.

FATHER'S FOOTSTEPS

When I was seven or eight I had a dream that I was walking on the beach with my father. We left my mother to read under her umbrella; I wanted to join Dad on his walk. It was late in the afternoon and the beach was busy with sunbathers absorbing the fading rays. Beyond the rattle of beach talk, I could hear the sound of waves gently emptying their contents onto the sand as we walked along, dodging legs and towels.

"Keep up, Michael," my father told me.

The sand was wet and my feet were sinking into it. I felt anxiety build; the more I tried to keep pace with Father, the more my feet sank and the more I fell behind him. He didn't notice though. He looked peaceful and deep in thought; his feet carried him forward in confident strides.

The only faces around me were those of women smiling, talking, laughing, applying sunblock, and taking no notice of me. I watched Father's back move farther and farther away from me, mixing in with a mélange of moving skin ahead. I could try to go back and find my mum or I could try to keep up with Father. I looked down at his footprints stretched-out before me. I stepped into one; the feeling of compressed sand was a relief.

"Don't walk in his footprints," a voice said. I can't remember if it was a woman's or a man's voice.

I looked around to see who had spoken.

Nobody was looking at me and so I took a step into the next footprint. And then another into the next. And then another. And then there was the sound of rushing water. I started running, jumping between footprints. From the corner of my eye, I could see a titanic wave pouring up the beach toward me. I ditched the path of footprints and ran up the beach, away from the ocean. But within seconds the wave had caught up to me. It dissolved the sand from beneath my feet and pulled me down into its current.

As my body was dragged outward to sea, I could see Father walking along the beach, completely unaware that I was not behind him. As the wave mixed back into the ocean, I was thrown into a washing machine of saltwater bubbles. The next thing I remember, I could see myself from outside of myself; my body floated motionless just beneath the ocean's surface, Xs drawn over both of my eyes. I had drowned.

Even as a boy, I recognized that this dream was signalling a dysfunction in my relationship with my father; it almost seemed like a story the conscious mind, rather than the subconscious, would invent (apparently, I dream in clichés). When I reflect on the dream now, though, I sense that it was an experience of being unseen for who I was; I quite literally drown while trying to walk in my father's footsteps. And nobody took any notice.

As an adult, I have dealt with a moderate amount of depression. When I trace this depression backward through time, I realize that as a little boy I experienced a lot of anxiety as well. What was this anxiety about? Perhaps it was about a hidden part of myself, one that I felt I had to keep concealed in order to be accepted. This hidden part—connected to feeling feminine—was incongruous with my relationship with Father (a relationship that I was still attached to having). I sensed that I was expected to emulate Father's masculinity and I also sensed I was failing to do so.

Around the same time that I had the beach dream, I was taken to see a child psychotherapist to address a tick I had developed, connected to playing video games. In short, I would play video games obsessively and get furiously angry if I lost at them. I had a few violent spats of punching holes in the wall and an ongoing "tick" where I would turn my head to the side quickly to obtain a clicking sensation in my skull.

I barely remember the psychotherapy sessions, but I do remember the woman asking me questions about Father. I learned in my twenties that the therapist wrote an extensive report after the sessions, outlining how my tick was a product of anxiety caused by my inability to meet my father's expectations. Apparently, my father was quite hurt by these findings and, as a result, my mother dismissed them as unfair. Nonetheless, I have come to believe that the therapist was at least partly right. My inability (or perhaps unwillingness) as a boy to emulate Father—and my preference to hide under Mother's wing—created a lot of internalized anxiety. My father could be very intimidating. His temper was volatile. I spent a lot of time as a boy morphing myself to meet what I perceived to be his expectations, and yet I would still find myself falling short of them, making mistakes, getting him angry, or having him react dismissively to something I wanted to share with him (usually it was something emotionally-charged, connected to something I was passionate about).

To this day, Mother and Father battle within me like an ongoing board meeting, debating my every move:

"Your apartment looks too fussy; what's all this crap on the walls?" barks Father.

"Oh, let him be. He's expressing himself. Don't be such a fascist," Mother argues back.

"How do you have time to look after all these plants?" Father questions. "Have you applied to any new jobs?"

In reality, these arguments do not happen. My father has come a long way in being supportive. He comes to my living space and usually admires it; the last time he was over, I caught him taking a prolonged look at a framed print on my wall of two hunky men holding hands under a fruit tree. I sensed that his prolonged gaze at the print was a matter of him trying to find common ground with me; I appreciated it. Despite this, I still ferociously guard my identity around him. I cannot help but think he views my lifestyle and perhaps my personality as being a product of laziness, a failure to push myself hard enough to obtain my "natural," privileged status as a heteronormative man like him. To some extent, I sense that even my mum thinks that my life would be easier if I were more like my father. I could be wrong about that. What I know for sure is this: the voice in the beach dream telling me not to walk in his footsteps was my own; I am not sure why I chose to ignore it.

FAG MUM

A few years ago, my partner began babysitting for a single mother with twins. The woman expressed a particular interest in having a biological man around the house to help her sons get what she imagined they might not from her. The mother was quite happy for the boys to get to know me as well. After about a year, my partner and I offered to take the boys away to a cottage for the weekend. The mom complied, pleased to have a few days to herself.

The boys were five at the time. A lot of their interests had already been engendered to match their biology—sports cars, guns, action figures. To my surprise, though, the mum had tempered this by getting them used to wearing pink leggings and oversized women's sunglasses. Despite looking like little flamingos, one of the brothers was particularly stoic. That changed, however, when he met Darcy, our dog. Darcy ran toward him, tail-wagging, bounding with energy. The boy let out a guttural and prolonged shriek; his face contorted and turned bright red and he looked at me desperately. Totally impulsively, I ran over, picked him up, and held him. As the weekend went on, the kid would reach his arms up and ask me to carry him just about everywhere. And I would. We were on the steps, heading down to the lake when I reached down to pick him up. "Just let him walk for himself," my partner suggested. But I like carrying him, I realized. I liked picking him up and rubbing his head. I liked to find out how he was feeling.

The impulse to mother this kid was growing in me. The idea that men do not mother—or at best should re-imagine fatherhood—irks me (Doucet). Throughout my childhood, mothering has meant one thing and fathering another. In an era of queer and trans politics, I resist being denied the term that best describes to me the reproductive role that I have come to internalize as my own. Perhaps "queer parenting" or "feminist childrearing" are truer titles. Still, is it not more gender essentialist to argue against men looking at themselves through the maternal lens? As long as mothering is a recognized practice by mainstream culture, why shouldn't a man be able to opt into performing the tradition, if for no other reason than to take the radical stance of opting out of the traditional dad role? This is not to advocate for some crude imitation of the archetypal mother figure (like a drag performance of June Cleaver) but rather to embrace the tradition of mothering outside of the patriarchal framework. Anyway, semantics aside, the way I felt myself relating to this boy was what I know as maternal. It felt primordially so.

As a man without kids of his own—particularly a queer dude—interacting with children feels fraught; I never want to make parents uncomfortable by seeming too intimate with their kids. I am aware that, despite feeling maternal, I don't necessarily look maternal; I'm tall, I have a dark beard and a deep voice. I relate to mothers but they may not relate to me. I watch women pick-up crying children that they barely know. With ease, they put them over a shoulder and rub their backs. I worry that for me to do the same might raise eyebrows. But what message is being communicated to kids when men are afraid to reach down? What message is being reinforced amongst men? Sara Ruddick defines "preservation" that mothers perform as "to see vulnerability and to respond to it with care, rather than abuse, indifference, or flight" (19).

I'll take you camping is not the same thing as what are you feeling? Let's throw a ball is not the same thing as come here, it's okay.

While adventures and sports are valid activities, they cannot supplant a more immediate kind of intimacy, which mothering (be it via a woman or man) has historically aimed to perform.

Over the past ten years, I have taught arts and environmental education to kids in Canada, the United States, and Cambodia. More recently, I have taken over the administration and leadership of an after-school playgroup, a collection of children from a neighbourhood school, who have been looked after for a few hours each afternoon by young artists. The more I observe and interact with kids, the more I realize that many talents, ambitions, and feelings remain hidden in the foliage of complicated personas, mixed messages, and multi-faceted agendas—a thicket I am well acquainted with. In my experience, these nuanced parts of a child's personality are usually revealed to an adult only when the child is convinced that the adult is really with them. I am constantly amazed at how much intimacy kids require. I was teaching eight-year-olds in an inner-city area of the U.S. last summer and found that the kids constantly wanted to hold my hand, sit on my lap, play with my beard, and rub my hair. This seemed even truer for the boys in the group than the girls.

As a kid, I remember the moments where I began to grow self-conscious of my identity in front of discerning adults, of my sensitivity, of my attachment to my mum, of my interest in female icons. Being detached, broody, and "boyish" seemed more appropriate and so I learned to perform these traits, especially in front of men. In fact, when I was twelve or thirteen, I announced to my friend's parents:

"When I grow up, I'm going to be a psychopath."

"I'm not sure you mean that, Michael," the mother responded dryly.

"No. I do," I assured her.

For a brief moment, the idea of being a psychopath (as sensationalized in Hollywood teen thrillers) seemed like the ultimate form of male autonomy: no empathy, no fear, no limits. For a while, I fantasized about not having feelings. I pushed myself to be unaffected by the world around me. Eventually, probably around the time that I began to sense the inevitability of my queer sexuality, I broke and decided to let myself care again, publicly.

MICHAEL YOUNG

QUEER NATURES

As an environmentalist, I spend a lot of time dwelling on the state of the "natural" world. Humans are reproducing more than ever and we are doing so in tandem with the one of the greatest events of biodiversity loss in geologic history (Johnson). While the environment is terribly damaged, it is also strangely beautiful, depending on who is looking. If human culture is the antithesis of "nature," then our planet is already infected with artificiality. Planes streak through the troposphere, rigs hammer into the seabed, and many would prefer to live in manufactured climates rather than face the anthropogenically modified climes of the already warming outdoors. Some public thinkers accept that "nature" is a thing of the past. Bill McKibben, a popular environmental writer, argues that we have stepped beyond the tipping point in climate change—specifically, 340 parts per million of atmospheric carbon (according to CO2now.org, we are currently over 393 ppm)—where the earth is no longer the earth we have come to know but rather some runaway climatic experiment; McKibben calls it "Eaarth," the title of his 2011 release. If McKibben is right and our planet is in fact post-natural, then is environmentalism passé? Who cares about an environment that's already gone to the dogs?

If we look at the forests of North America, though, we can see that nature is relative. The romantic notion that before Europeans landed here, the forests were untouched is simply incorrect. Before Europeans colonized North America, Indigenous peoples occupied and utilized the forests of the continent. No North American national park may ever have been so devoid of human occupation as it is today. The forests themselves have always been kinetic; they have continuously evolved since they were first born of plant life, which emerged from the sea in the Cambrian era (Allen 66). Throughout a forest's life cycle the plant and animal species change and with these changes the very "nature" of the woods changes. Canadian writer Robert Thomas Allen puts it elegantly when he explains that rather than being a permanent structure, we might think of forests as "events" in time (71). In this sense, the concept of nature as a stable system that can be unhinged is problematic. Rather, nature is relative, reactive, and flexible; so is human nature.

When I came out, one of the recurring reactions to my announcement, specifically from straight friends but also from family members, went something like this: "Well.... What about AIDS?"

Rather than take offense to the correlation of my sexuality with disease, I tended to internalize the question. What about AIDS? On a subconscious level, I accepted that my choice to pursue an "unnatural" lifestyle meant that I deserved certain associated risks, in this case, disease. For a decade I was petrified of contracting HIV, not for fear of sickness, as much as for fear of it confirming I was living the wrong way. This internalization of feeling unnatural contributed to my having what my partner calls a "darkness" or something that I associate with my queerness (a kind of melancholic chip off my shoulder). This queer sensibility has informed both my ecological politics but also my reproductive ones.

Cate Sandilands has helmed the creation of "Queer Ecology," an academic discipline that explores how nature "organizes and is organized by complex power relations," which include sexuality ("Unnatural Passions" 6). In one of her first published forays into this territory, "Unnatural Passions? Notes Toward a Queer Ecology" (she has since co-edited an entire collection on the topic of Queer Ecologies [Sandilands and Erickson]), Sandilands discusses *North Enough: AIDS and Other Clear Cuts*, a memoir by Jan Zita Grover, who worked as a front-line healthcare worker in San Francisco at the height of the AIDS epidemic before moving to the north woods of Minnesota for a period of healing. Part of what Sandilands explores in this piece is the way in which Grover believed that she might find some "geographic cure" (Grover's words) for the horror she had internalized in San Francisco (Grover 5).

Instead of finding a place of natural wholeness, however, Grover found herself faced with a landscape that mirrored San Francisco: the north woods look riddled with disease; generations of clearcuts had left gaping pock marks on the landscape, often merely concealed by thin "idiot strips" of trees protecting highway drivers from the reality of barrenness beyond (Grover 142). Sandilands reflects on Grover's memoir:

> The idea that one might find natural wholeness in [the north woods] was shattered at the sight of its large, multiple

clear-cuts.... The post-contact history of the north woods reveals a region repeatedly marked by human greed and error.... No paradise found, here.... [But] in their ecological defilement ... these wounded landscapes ended up teaching. ("Unnatural Passions" 1-2)

Grover herself reflects, "[The north woods] offered me an unanticipated challenge, a spiritual discipline: to appreciate them, I needed to learn how to see their scars, defacement, and artificiality, and then beyond those to their strengths—their historicity, the difficult beauties that underlay their deformity" (6). Sandilands heralds this kind of thinking as a "queer ecological sensibility" or rather an ecological perspective that "focuses on dimensions of ... experience born in the specific history of a queer community, and [which] uses the resulting emotional resonances and conceptual links to live in nature in a way that reflects this queer experience. ("Unnatural Passions" 3).

So, as we move forward to face queer natures of the future (warmer climates, deformed landscapes, an unbalancing of species), how might we proliferate the queer ecological sensibility that Sandilands speaks of? The reproduction of this perspective—or as Grover calls it, a "spiritual discipline"—could help battle the dualistic thinking that envisions ecosystems as pure or infected, natural or unnatural, valuable or spent. Resisting these dualisms has to be important as we deepen in the muck of ecological crisis, a crisis that so many would like to imagine exists over a cliff, where on one side there is business as usual and on the other side—too late! The planet is on fire. In fact, we are in the middle right now, smoke all around us.

It is my contention that a patriarchal desire to conquer and control has created a world where natures have been tamed to the point of extinction and that this mirrors the traditionally patriarchal approach to fathering, which insists on "manhandling" children into heteronormative, capitalist citizens. In a world where consumerism has led to obsolescence, our entitlement to continue procreating is highly political. It seems paramount that if we are to move forward as a species, we do so in new ways, particularly with new values and new reproductive roles for men. Male mothering, which seems antithetical to patriarchy, might be one conceptual framework to begin with.

THE UGLY GARDEN

I go back to being a young boy where I imagined myself inhabiting a maternal body. I remember the desire to care for that which had been discarded, injured birds and bullied boys alike. As an adult, at any given time, I have two-dozen seedlings on the go. I germinate seeds the way some people chew tobacco or watch soap operas. With every bad news story in the media about a conservative government signing policy to further degrade the biosphere in the name of the economy, my hands tremble with the need to germinate. Honey-locust, burr oak, sweet persimmon, black cherry, red mulberry—these are some of the seedlings I am growing right now. As the cold winter sky looms over Toronto, the itching to make things green is uncontainable. Sometimes, I think about these plants when I'm in bed. I imagine where I might situate them outdoors. I imagine them growing slowly, in some cases, like the oaks, over hundreds of years, maturing long after I'm dead. I imagine how they might contribute to the landscape, feed the ecosystem, and provide shelter. This practice is maternal, despite the fact that I am no "natural" mum. I'm gay, I'm broke, I live with my grandmother—nobody is going to give me a child to raise. For the time being, I'm satisfying my reproductive impulse with a green thumb. And I'm just fine with that.

* * *

This February, after months of trying, my partner and I were granted an allotment garden in Toronto's High Park. Early one morning in March, I climbed the fence to get a look at the land. The air was cold and damp and the ground was just beginning to thaw. I stood in front of our six hundred square feet of green space. Stinging nettles predominated, with a few woody garlic necks still marking dormant beings below. The remnants of weeds were everywhere and many unidentifiable green tendrils poked through the dark soil promising more life to come. The garden looked ugly, unkempt. At the same time, it was perfect. I didn't want to touch anything until

I knew what each plant was. Part of me just wanted to let it grow on its own, come back in four months to see what had happened.

In a city stacked full of apartment dwellers and commuters whose main interaction with "nature" is a weekend in cottage country, the opportunity to nurture green space of one's own—particularly for the purpose of growing food—is coveted. I knew that I had to make something of this garden plot or risk losing it back into the pool of hungry applicants. I planned out how the plot might be organized and then I began cultivating the soil, trying to keep as many of the pre-existing perennials as possible. I grew seeds and bought seedlings and got to know what did well where. I decided that I was going to make this little piece of land more beautiful by preserving it, nurturing the life that dwelled up on it, and training the plants to grow on it in the most symbiotic ways possible. Though I am continually reminded by the media, literature, and the NGOs that I subscribe to that the world is in a state of "natural" decline, I am comforted by the idea that one can grow life anywhere. It is not necessarily in my biological nature to want to nurture life. But I have learned that the impetus to cultivate feels better than the impetus to dominate, accumulate, and extirpate and so, over time, I have come to follow suit.

WORKS CITED

"Ailanthus." USDA Agricultural Library. 2006. Web. 6 Nov. 2015.

Allen, Robert Thomas. *Illustrated Natural History of Canada, The Great Lakes*. Toronto: Jack McClelland, 1970. Print.

Arrested Development. Fox, 2003. Television.

Bly, Robert. *Iron John*. New York: Vintage, 1990. Print.

Crittenden, Ann. *The Price of Motherhood: Why the Most Important Job in the World Is Still the Least Valued*. New York: Picador, 2010. Print.

Doucet, Andrea. *Do Men Mother?: Fathering Care and Domestic Responsibility*. Toronto: University of Toronto Press, 2006. Print.

"Earth's C02 Homepage." *C02now.org*. 2015. Web. Web. 6 Nov. 2015.

Gabb, Jacqui. "Imagining the Queer Lesbian Family." *Mother*

Outlaws: Theories and Practices of Empowered Mothering. Ed. Andrea O'Reilly. Toronto: Women's Press, 2004. 8. Print.

Green, Fiona Joy. "Feminist Mothers: Successfully Negotiating the Tensions Between Motherhood and Mothering." *Mother Outlaws: Theories and Practices of Empowered Mothering.* Ed. Andrea O'Reilly. Toronto: Women's Press, 2004. 127. Print.

Grover, Jan Zita. *North Enough: AIDS and Other Clear-Cuts.* Saint Paul, MN: Graywolf Press, 1997. Web. 6 Nov. 2015.

Johnson, Kira. "The Sixth Great Extinction." *Voices for Biodiversity.* 2010. Web. 6 Nov. 2015.

MacGregor, Sherilyn. *Beyond Mothering Earth: Ecological Citizenship and the Politics of Care.* Vancouver: University of British Columbia Press, 2006. Print.

McKibben, Bill. *Eaarth.* New York: MacMillan, 2011. Print.

O'Reilly, Andrea. *From Motherhood to Mothering.* New York: SUNY Press, 2004. Print.

O'Reilly, Andrea. "In Black and White." *Mother Outlaws: Theories and Practices of Empowered Mothering.* Toronto: Women's Press, 2004. 305. Print.

Psycho. Dir. Alfred Hitchcock. Shamley Productions, 1960. Film.

Ruddick, Sara. *Maternal Thinking: Toward a Politics of Peace.* Boston: Beacon Press, 1989. Print.

Sandilands, Catriona. "Unnatural Passions? Notes Toward a Queer Ecology." *Invisible Culture: An Electronic Journal for Visual Culture.* 2005. Web. 6 Nov. 2015.

Sandilands, Catriona and Bruce Erickson, eds. *Queer Ecologies.* Bloomington: Indiana University Press, 2010. Print.

Stromberg, Joseph. "What Is the Anthropocene and Are We in It?" *Smithsonian.* 2013. Web. 6 Nov. 2015.

The Shining. Dir. Stanley Kubrick. Warner Brothers, 1980. Film.

Who Framed Roger Rabbit? Dir. Robert Zemeckis. Touchstone, 1988. Film.

Contributor Biographies

Dwayne Avery is currently conducting postdoctoral research at York University's Department of Film. His research explores representations of contemporary parenting in post-network television. He received his PhD from McGill University in 2011.

C. Wesley Buerkle is Associate Professor of Communication and Performance at East Tennessee State University. He has written about women's bodies and agency in early birth-control rhetoric as well as mediated images of masculinity. His current research agenda includes this manuscript as well as a study of pregnancy manuals written for men.

Justin Butler is a social worker in New York City. He also writes, plays music, and walks a lot. He received his BA from Sarah Lawrence College in Bronxville, NY, and his MSW from Smith College, Northampton, MA.

Andrea Doucet is the Canada Research Chair in Gender, Work, and Care and Professor of Sociology and Women's & Gender Studies at Brock University. Her book *Do Men Mother?* (2006) was awarded the John Porter Tradition of Excellence Book Award from the Canadian Sociology Association; she is currently completing a second edition of the book.

Alys Einion, PhD, is a feminist, lesbian, midwife, lecturer, researcher, pagan, author, mother, and novelist with a passion for reading and writing. She lives and works by the sea with her son and two cats and researches lesbian and queer families, creativity in education, and narratives and narrative representations of women and childbearing. Her first novel, *Inshallah*, was published by Honno Press in 2014.

Joanne S. Frye is Professor Emerita of English and Women's Studies at The College of Wooster. She is author of *Living Stories, Telling Lives: Women and the Novel in Contemporary Experience* and *Tillie Olsen: A Study of the Short Fiction*, as well as articles on Virginia Woolf, Gail Godwin, Maxine Hong Kingston, Tillie Olsen, and issues in feminist literary criticism and maternal memoir. Her most recent book is *Biting the Moon: A Memoir of Feminism and Motherhood* (Syracuse University Press, 2012).

Fiona Joy Green, PhD, is a feminist mother who believes in the power of feminism in contributing to the agency of children and parents and to revolutionizing mothering. She holds the positions of Professor of Women's and Gender Studies and Associate Dean of Arts at the University of Winnipeg and is the author of *Practicing Feminist Mothering* and a co-editor of *Chasing Rainbows: Exploring Gender-Fluid Parenting Practices*.

Jack Hixson-Vulpe is a PhD candidate at York University and works with the 519 Education and Training Department. His research focuses on gay-straight alliances and inclusive policy in primary schools. He has been invested in community activism and education for over a decade and is a qualified primary school teacher.

David A. King has an array of experience in the arts. He was a company member with the international touring company *Imago Theatre* from Portland, Oregon. He worked in New York City at the Harlem School of the Arts and now resides in Winnipeg, Manitoba, where he provides arts programming to the city's Centennial, Point Douglas, and North End neighbourhoods.

A.J. Lowik is a PhD student with the Institute for Gender, Race, Sexuality, and Social Justice at the University of British Columbia and is the recipient of the Joseph-Armand Bombardier CGS Doctoral Scholarship. A.J.'s work focuses on the reproductive experiences of trans people, theories of gender corporeality, community-based participatory research, engaged scholarship, queer liberation theory, and transfeminisms.

Nick J. Mulé, PhD, is associate professor in the School of Social Work at York University. A queer activist for many years, Nick is the founder, past chairperson, and current member-at-large of Queer Ontario. In addition, he is a psychotherapist in private practice serving LGBTQ populations in Toronto.

Jeffrey Nall, PhD, is a visiting lecturer in philosophy at the University of Central Florida where he teaches courses in humanities and philosophy. Nall is also an adjunct instructor in Women, Gender, and Sexuality Studies at Florida Atlantic University (FAU). Nall holds a Master of Liberal Studies from Rollins College and a PhD in Comparative Studies from FAU. He is the author of *Feminism and the Mastery of Women and Childbirth: An Ecofeminist Examination of the Cultural Maiming and Reclaiming of Maternal Agency During Childbirt*h (2014). He resides in Vero Beach with his best friend, April, and their four amazing children.

Gary Lee Pelletier is a PhD candidate in the Gender, Feminist, and Women's Studies Graduate Program at York University. His current research focuses on the intersection of queer negative affects, feminisms, and the burgeoning North American Men's Rights Movement. He lives in Toronto with his partner, many cats, many plants, a dog, and his hip ninety-two-year-old grandmother.

Ruth Trinidad Galván is associate professor in the Language, Literacy, and Sociocultural Studies Department at the University of New Mexico. Her research focuses on gendered transmigration and communities left behind. She is associate editor of the *Journal of Latinos and Education* and co-editor of the *Handbook of Latinos and Education.*

Michael Young is a writer, actor, arts educator, and environmentalist. He holds an MES in Environmental Studies and a BFA in Music from York University, as well as a post-graduate diploma in Theatre Acting from LAMDA in the UK. As a writer, Michael has published two graphic novels—*The iDance* and *Unbelievable Philip*—with Oxford University Press, articles in *GUTS Magazine*, *A/J Alternatives Journal* and *Undercurrents: A Journal of Critical Environmental Studies*. As an actor, Michael has worked on stage and screen, including TV spots on Global and Showcase and a leading role at The Centaur Theatre in Montreal. At present, Michael is developing screenwriting projects for TV and the web and runs an alternative after-school program for kids in Toronto's West End.